CATS

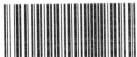

CATS

DR. BRUCE FOGLE

FIREFLY BOOKS

A FIREFLY BOOK

Published by Firefly Books Ltd., 2000

First printing

First published in Canada in 2000 by
Firefly Books Ltd.
3680 Victoria Park Avenue
Willowdale, Ontario M2H 3K1

Canadian Cataloguing in Publication Data

Fogle, Bruce
Cats

Includes index.
ISBN 1-55209-554-1

1. Cat breeds. 2.Cat breeds – Pictorial works. I. Title

SF442.F73 2000 636.8 C00-931261-7

Produced for Dorling Kindersley by
PAGE*One*

PROJECT DIRECTORS Bob Gordon and Helen Parker
EDITOR Michael Spilling
DESIGNERS Melanie McDowell, Tim Stansfield, Suzanne Tuhrim

Reproduced by Colourscan, Singapore

Printed and bound in Italy
by L.E.G.O., Italy

INTRODUCTION

LONGHAIRS

CONTENTS

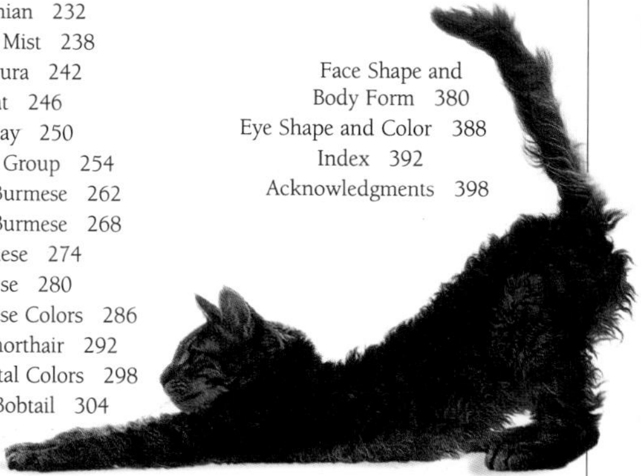

HISTORY OF SELECTIVE BREEDING

Cats have been kept in human homes for millennia, but only in the last century or so has selective breeding been actively pursued. At the end of the 19th century, the first cat shows stimulated the creation of breed clubs throughout Europe and North America. The first breeds were those that had developed naturally, but soon breeders were using their newly acquired knowledge of inheritance patterns to create a palette of coat colors and patterns. This recent human intervention in feline evolution has produced some remarkable results.

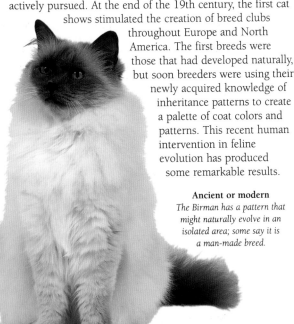

Ancient or modern
The Birman has a pattern that might naturally evolve in an isolated area; some say it is a man-made breed.

The Start of Breed Registries

Possibly the first cat show was held in the time of Shakespeare, at St. Giles' Fair in Winchester, England, in 1598. Shakespeare called the cat a "harmless, necessary creature," and this show was probably about mousing abilities as much as personality and looks. On the other side of the world, in Thailand, the *Cat Book Poems* recorded cats of varying colors and types. The first formal cat show was held in 1871 in London. It was organized by Harrison Weir, who wrote the standards for all the breeds shown and acted as one of the three judges. The first cat show to attract wide attention in North America was organized by James T. Hyde in 1895 at Madison Square Garden, New York; a Maine Coon was judged champion. Associations formed to create rules for shows: in 1887 the National Cat Club was started in Britain, with Harrison Weir as its president, and in 1896 the American Cat Club became North America's first registry.

Modern Registries

The world's largest registry of pedigree cats is the Cat Fanciers' Association (CFA), founded in 1906, which has clubs in the United States and Canada, South America, Europe, and Japan. The CFA's registering philosophy is purist, allowing, for example, only four Burmese colors. Perhaps the most liberal or experimental of registries is The International Cat Association (TICA), founded in 1979 and based in North America. This registry accepts new breeds more rapidly than any other association, and encourages experimentation. Britain's Governing Council of the Cat Fancy (GCCF) was formed in 1910. Its policies are staid, but less so than CFA's, and it has registering bodies in South Africa, New Zealand, and Australia. Throughout Europe, many registries belong to the Fédération Internationale Féline (FIFé), established in 1949. FIFé claims to be the largest feline organization in the world.

Old and New Breeds

Cat breeds can be broken down into two groups, which emerged chronologically. The first are the breeds that appeared naturally in free-breeding, although possibly isolated, feline populations. Many of these are characterized by coat color or pattern, and genetically these are almost always "recessives" that breed true. For example, the Abyssinian's ticked pattern is a recessive trait, emphasized through selective breeding. Some other breeds are characterized by distinctive mutations: the Japanese Bobtail (*see page 150*) and tailless Manx (*see page 176*) are examples. Some breeds developed naturally into types that were then formally recognized as breeds; the British, American, and European Shorthairs (*see pages 164, 190, and 212*), Norwegian Forest Cats and Siberians (*see pages 58 and 64*), and Maine Coons (*see page 46*) are in this category. A final major feature defining these early breeds is coat length.

Character cats
There is a new tendency to breed for temperament: the famously placid Ragdoll is the most obvious example.

Island breed
Bobbed tails are found throughout Asia, but the inevitably limited gene pool of an island was needed to develop the Japanese Bobtail.

More recently, breeds have been developed actively and some times very scientifically. Oriental Shorthairs (*see page 292*), Ocicats (*see page 338*), Angoras (*see page 132*), and Asians (*see page 254*) in Britain, have been newly created. This is the "growth" area in the cat world, with more new breeds appearing in the 20th century than in the entire history of domestic cats before this time. Breeders argue that if they select for outward good health, they can produce healthy cats with even a small gene pool. However, genetic health problems and lowered resistance to disease can take time to show.

BREED PROFILES EXPLAINED

A few decades ago, there were just a handful of recognized breeds. Today, there are dozens. New mutations have been adopted by some registries, new breeds have been created from existing breeds through the introduction of new colors and coat lengths, and breeds from one country have been recognized in others.

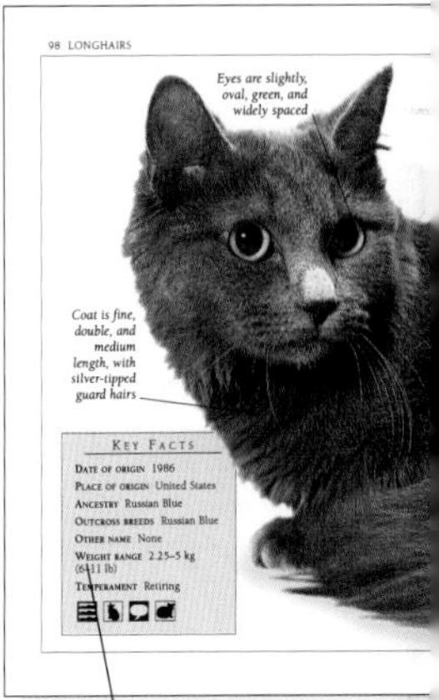

98 LONGHAIRS
Eyes are slightly, oval, green, and widely spaced
Coat is fine, double, and medium length, with silver-tipped guard hairs
KEY FACTS
DATE OF ORIGIN 1986
PLACE OF ORIGIN United States
ANCESTRY Russian Blue
OUTCROSS BREEDS Russian Blue
OTHER NAME None
WEIGHT RANGE 2.25–5 kg (6–11 lb)
TEMPERAMENT Retiring

Key facts
Summarizes information on history, names, breeds allowed as outcrosses, personality traits, and level of grooming required

UNDERSTANDING THE PROFILES

Essential information about a breed, such as the history, names, outcross breeds, and traits can be easily summed up in a list of brief points: this information has been placed in a Key Facts box for instant reference. However, such a list of points can never give a full and fair impression of a whole breed, so greater detail is given in the breed description and history. Any additional information about build or particular colors is contained in the captions and labels to the main and secondary photographs.

Annotations
Detail requirements of breed standards for showing

Main picture
Illustrates physical characteristics, wherever possible in the breed's most notable or popular colors

Introductory text
Outlines physical and psychological traits of breeds

NEBELUNG 99

Body is lithe and slender, but not tubular

Blue
The Nebelung standard is very similar to that of the Russian Blue, calling for the same lithe appearance, the same silver tipping, and a semi-long version of the characteristic double coat.

78 LONGHAIRS

SCOTTISH FOLD 79

SCOTTISH FOLD

With the same distinctive ears as its shorthaired cousins (*see page 186*), the longhaired Scottish Fold's coat gives it a lush, warm look. Like all longhairs, the breed is best seen in winter, when it sports an imposing ruff, elegant breeches, and a huge, fluffy tail. All kittens are born with straight ears, which begin to fold at about three weeks of age. The joint problems that result from breeding Fold-to-Fold appear at four to six months: a short, thickened tail is a sign that might be missed in a longhaired kitten, so tails should be checked carefully – and always gently.

BREED HISTORY Cats with folded or pendulous ears have been recorded for over two centuries. All Scottish Folds, however, can be traced back to Susie, a white farm cat born in 1961 in Scotland. Two geneticists, Pat Turner and Peter Dyte, oversaw the early development of the breed, and found that Susie carried the longhair gene, which could be carried in shorthaired offspring and appear in later generations. The Fold is still rare: the absence of any longhaired outcross breed makes the longhaired version even rarer.

BREED COLOURS
All colours and patterns, including pointed, sepia, and mink occur

BROWN TABBY · RED TABBY · LILAC · WHITE

Blue Smoke and White
This cat falls short of the show standards: the ears are not pressed tightly to the head, and the face shows tabby markings rather than the even blue required.

Head is well-rounded with prominent cheeks and whisker pads

Coat is medium to long, soft, and standing away from body

Breed history
Traces breed from origins to acceptance by registries

Breed colors
Gives accepted colors for registries in roman type, and other colors in italics

Breed Descriptions

Each breed profile includes a description of the breed's appearance and character. While the appearance of pedigree cats is highly consistent, the personality traits can vary: much depends on the individual cat's experiences. Breed histories outline the breed's ancestry and its route to acceptance by the registries. Some histories are easy to trace, but others are less distinct: older breeds may be wrapped in romantic myths, and even the exact origins of some of the newer breeds have been a matter of debate. Details of the standards expected of show-quality cats are contained in the annotations.

The Breed Symbols

The details of personality in these profiles were gathered through questionnaires sent to breeders and breed clubs. They provide a guide to typical tendencies, but an individual cat may not match some of these traits: one may even find some silent Siamese.

LITTLE GROOMING | MODERATE GROOMING | DAILY GROOMING

QUIET | VOCAL

SEDATE | SOCIABLE | ACTIVE | SELF-CONTAINED

Questionable status.
In most associations, the pointed kittens born in this Oriental Shorthair litter would be registered as Siamese. Some, such as the CFA, refuse to grant these kittens status as anything but "any other variety" Orientals.

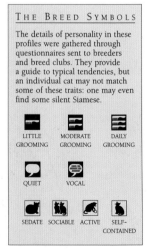

INTERNATIONAL DIFFERENCES

Not all registries recognize the same breeds, or the same colors and patterns in each breed. The same breed may even develop different looks in different countries: for example, the Siamese colors recognized in Britain and Europe are listed as a separate breed by CFA in North America. Information on the colors accepted by the main registries – GCCF for British cats, FIFé for Europe, CFA for North America and Japan – has been listed in roman text, while additional colors that occur but are either not accepted, or may be accepted in other major registries, are listed in italics.

INTRODUCTION TO LONGHAIRS

Genetically, all longhaired cats share the recessive allele that causes their coats to grow longer than those of their wildcat ancestors (*see page 362*). Some sources still state that the gene for long hair was introduced into these domestic cats from the wild Pallas' cat of Tibet, but there is no evidence that this is true: a simple genetic mutation is almost

Norwegian Forest Cat
Breeds that developed in harsh climates, such as the Norwegian Forest Cat, or the Maine Coon, show their origins in their coats. They tend to have water-repellent topcoats and thick, insulating undercoats.

certainly the cause. Although their exact origins are unknown, longhairs occurred naturally centuries ago in Central Asia. Some of these cats reached Europe: The French authority Dr. Fernand Mery reported that specimens were brought to Italy around 1550. Early longhairs in Europe were called Russian, French, or Chinese; three centuries passed before these cats acquired official classifications. After the Crystal Palace Cat Show in London in 1871, standards were published for Persians, also called Longhairs (*see page 16*), and Angoras. Some longhaired breeds – such as Tiffanie (see page 116) and Nebelung (*see page 96*) are the result of introducing the longhair gene into shorthaired breeds.

Somali

Longhaired kittens occurred in Abyssinian litters for many years before an attempt was made to develop them into a separate breed. The resulting Somali is now one of the more popular cats in North America.

PERSIAN

This breed, usually an indoor dweller, is a lounge lizard. The Persian, also known as the Longhair, is a relaxed observer. In statistical surveys of veterinarians, the Persian is cited as the quietest and least active of cat breeds, and the one most likely to accept other cats into its home. This does not mean that the breed is entirely passive: In Britain and mainland Europe, pedigreed cats have more access to the outdoors than they do elsewhere, and the Persian will guard its territory and catch and dispatch prey with surprising ease, given its shortened face. The coat needs daily care; veterinarians are frequently called on to clip densely matted coats. Breed problems include polycystic kidney disease and a higher than average incidence of retained testicles.

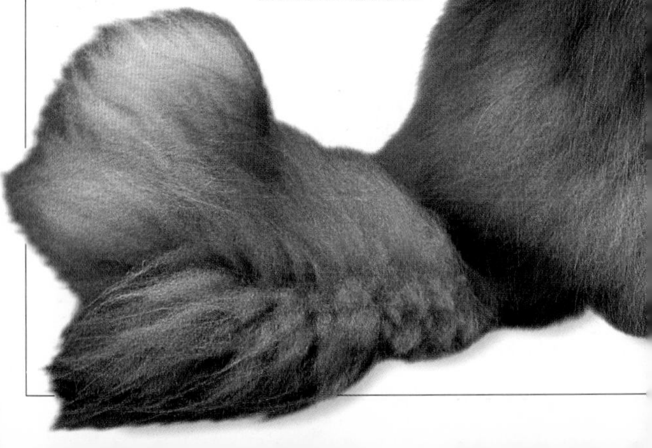

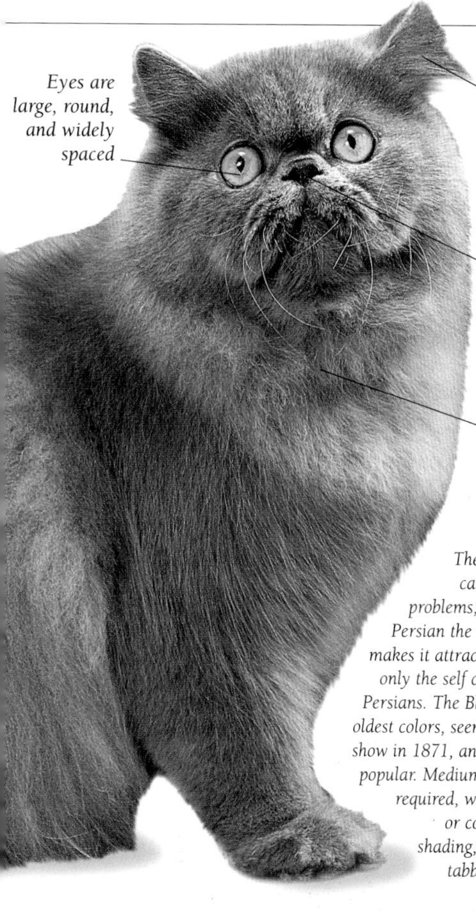

Eyes are large, round, and widely spaced
Ears are small, round-tipped, and set low on the head
Nose is short and broad with a definite stop
Neck is short, thick, and sturdy

Blue Self

The shortened face can lead to health problems, but it gives the Persian the infant look that makes it attractive. In Britain, only the self colors are called Persians. The Blue is one of the oldest colors, seen at the first cat show in 1871, and has remained popular. Medium to pale blue is required, with deep orange or copper eyes. Any shading, white hairs, or tabby markings are penalized.

Breed Colors

SELF AND TORTIE COLORS
Black, Chocolate, Red Self, Blue, Lilac, Cream, Tortoiseshell, Chocolate Tortie, Blue-Cream, Lilac-Cream, White (Blue-, Orange-, Odd-Eyed)

SMOKE COLORS
Colors are as for self and tortie, except White

SHADED
Shaded Silver (green-eyed), Pewter (orange-eyed), Red Shaded Cameo, Golden Persian, Cream Shaded Cameo, Tortie Cameo, Blue-Cream Cameo
Other self and tortie colors

TIPPED
Chinchilla, Red Shell Cameo, Cream Shell Cameo, Tortie Cameo, Blue-Cream Cameo
Other self and tortie colors

TABBY (CLASSIC ONLY)
Brown, Chocolate, Red, Blue, Lilac, Tortie, Chocolate Tortie, Blue Tortie, Lilac Tortie
Cream, other tabby patterns

SILVER TABBY (CLASSIC ONLY)
Silver
Any other tabby colors, other tabby patterns

BICOLOR (STANDARD AND VAN)
All allowed self, tortie, and tabby colors with white
All self and tortie colors, smoke, shaded, and tipped colors, and silver tabbies with white

Red and White

Originally, only Black, Blue, Red, and Cream bicolors were allowed. This Red and White has symmetrical markings, which the standard no longer requires.

Tail is full and short, but not disproportionate to body

Silver Shaded

Once classified with the tipped Chinchilla, the darker Silver Shaded is now judged separately. Like almost all silvered Persians, it has green eyes.

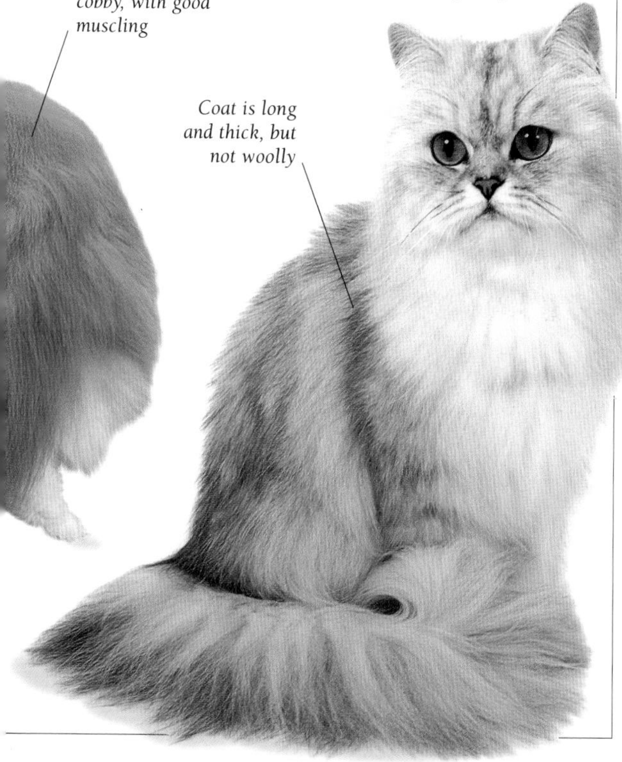
Body is large and cobby, with good muscling
Coat is long and thick, but not woolly

Breed History The first documented ancestors of the Persian were imported from Persia into Italy in 1620 by Pietro della Valle, and from Turkey into France by Nicholas-Claude Fabri de Peiresc at about the same time. For the next two centuries, their longhaired descendants, known by a variety of names, were status symbol pets. In the late 19th century, the Persian was developed within the guidelines of Harrison Weir's first written breed standards. The original stocky build is still an essential mark of today's Persians, although other characteristics have been dramatically altered. The breed was recognized by all registries by the turn of the century.

Coat is soft

Key Facts

Date of origin 1800s

Place of origin Great Britain

Ancestry Middle-Eastern Persians

Outcross breeds None

Other name Called Longhairs in Great Britain

Weight range 8–15 lb (3.5–7 kg)

Temperament Interested observer

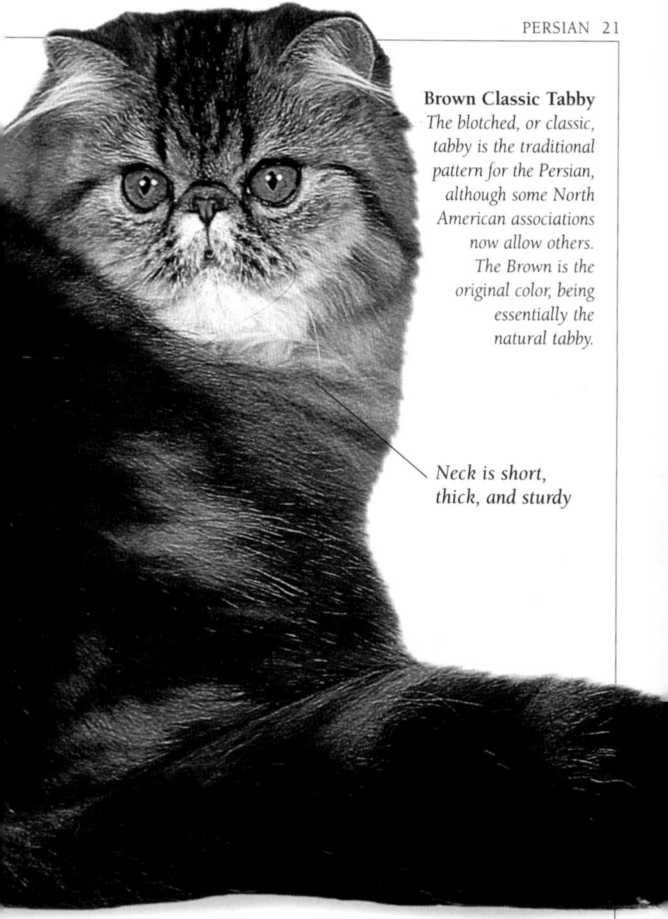

Brown Classic Tabby
The blotched, or classic, tabby is the traditional pattern for the Persian, although some North American associations now allow others. The Brown is the original color, being essentially the natural tabby.

Neck is short, thick, and sturdy

NEWER PERSIAN COLORS

Originally recognized only in a limited range of colors, the Persian is now bred in an abundance of new shades. However, a new color range is not the only development: the coat, build, and, most dramatically, the face have all changed this century. Early Persians were less compact, with short, but not flat, faces. While breeders in Europe still select for moderate noses, American breeders and show judges have tended to prefer a flatter, or "ultra-type" face. This reached its most extreme in the "Peke-faced" Persian. Due to its narrowed nostrils and tear ducts, the look is no longer desirable.

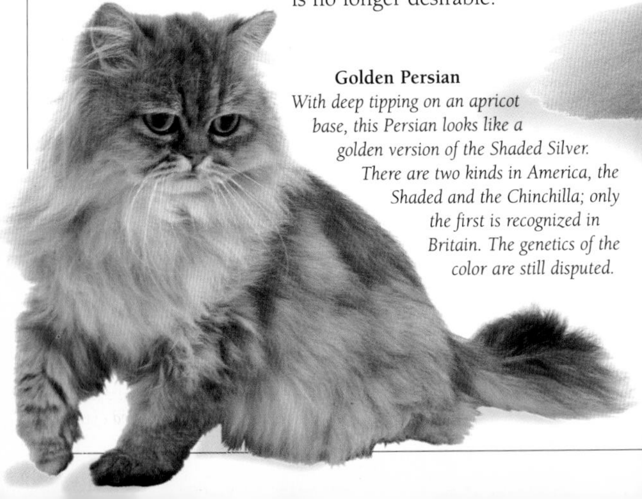

Golden Persian

With deep tipping on an apricot base, this Persian looks like a golden version of the Shaded Silver. There are two kinds in America, the Shaded and the Chinchilla; only the first is recognized in Britain. The genetics of the color are still disputed.

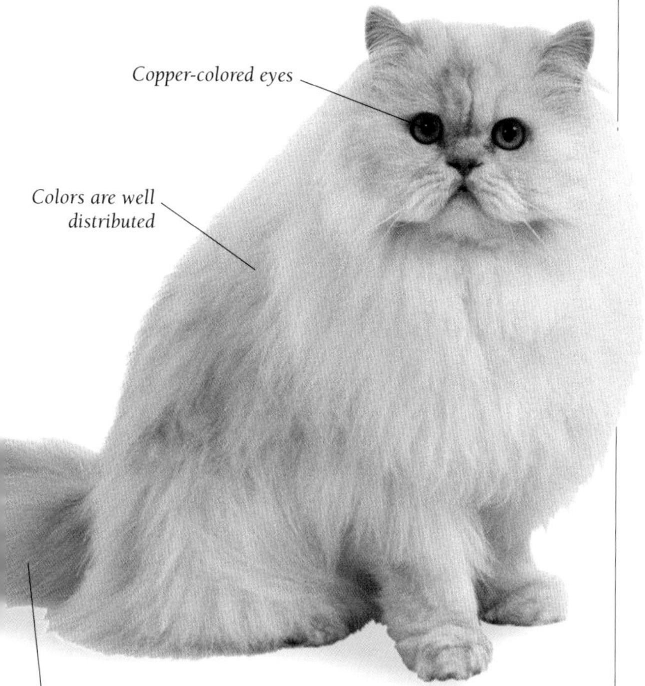
Copper-colored eyes
Colors are well distributed
Tail has long, bushy hair

Cream Shell Cameo

Chinchillas and Shaded Silvers were recognized early in the Persian's history, but other tipped Persians were not developed until after World War II. This Cream Shell Cameo is essentially a Cream Chinchilla, with warm-toned tipping to the hairs and deep, brilliant, copper-colored eyes.

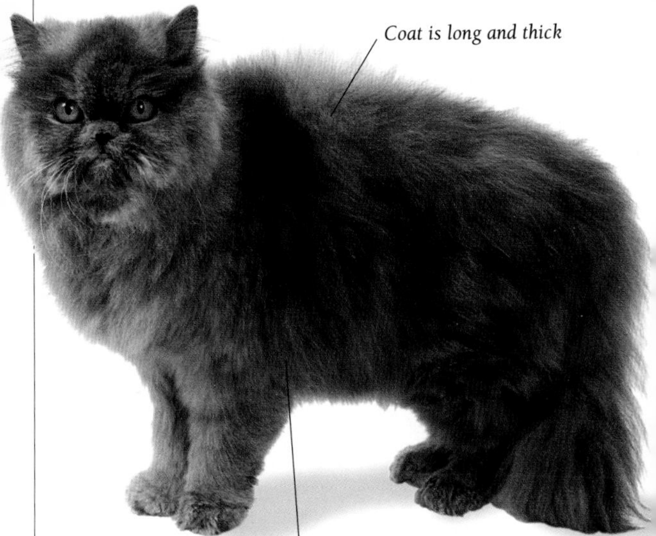
Coat is long and thick
Pastel-toned coat

Blue-Cream

Although this color has existed from the early days of the breed, it was not recognized until 1930; this was chiefly because the genetics of coat colors were not understood, and Blue-Creams were produced only by accident.

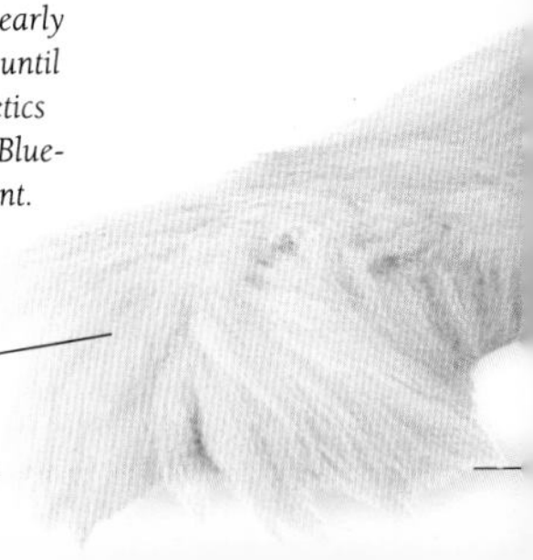
Tail is cream-colored

Cream Shaded Cameo

This dilute version of the Red Shaded Cameo is a cooler, lighter color. Only Red, Cream, Tortie, and Blue-Cream Shaded Cameos are accepted in Britain, because the original breeding was done with Tortoiseshells. The Shaded Silvers and Pewters have different origins.

Chocolate and White

Tortie-and-whites were recognized in the 1950s, and other colors in the 1960s. In 1971, markings one-third to half white were permitted by the standard, a change that greatly boosted its popularity. All colors and patterns are now accepted in both standard and Van distribution.

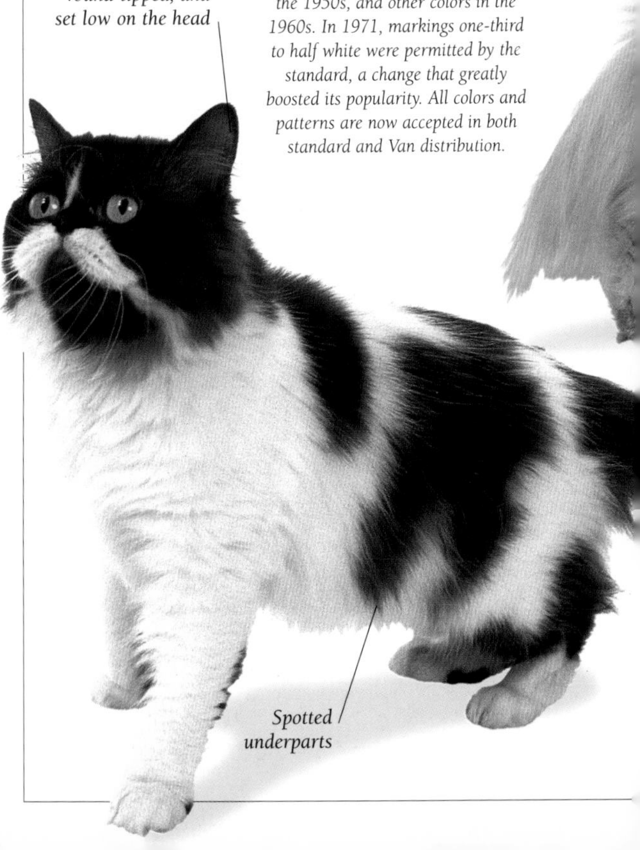
Ears are small, round-tipped, and set low on the head
Spotted underparts

Paws are large and rounded, preferably tufted
Tail is mostly colored

Red Shaded Cameo

The inhibitor gene was present in Persians from the start, but Cameos came to the scene relatively late. They were developed in a breeding program in the United States during the 1950s and were accepted by CFA in 1960. They were subsequently established worldwide, and breeding began in Europe in 1962.

HIMALAYAN PERSIAN

Possibly the first deliberate hybridization of two breeds, this version of the Persian was also the first recognized "export" to another breed of the Siamese pointed pattern (*see page 280*). The resulting cat has the luxurious coat of the Persian, and the exotic color pattern of the Siamese. Eye color is less intense than in the Siamese.

Seal Point

The mask of a mature Himalayan Persian will cover the face, but should not extend over the rest of the head. Males should have more extensive masks than females.

Body is large to medium-sized, set low on legs
Shading develops on older cats

BREED COLORS

SELF AND TORTIE POINTS
Blue, Chocolate, Cream, Lilac, Red, Seal, Blue-Cream, Chocolate Tortie, Lilac-Cream, Seal Tortie

TABBY POINTS
Colors are as for self and tortie points

CREAM TABBY POINT

RED POINT

BLUE POINT

SEAL TABBY POINT

Key Facts

Date of origin 1950s

Place of origin Britain and the United States

Ancestry Persian, Siamese

Outcross breeds Persian

Other name Called a Colorpoint Longhair in Britain

Weight range 8–15 lb (3.5–7 kg)

Temperament Calm and friendly

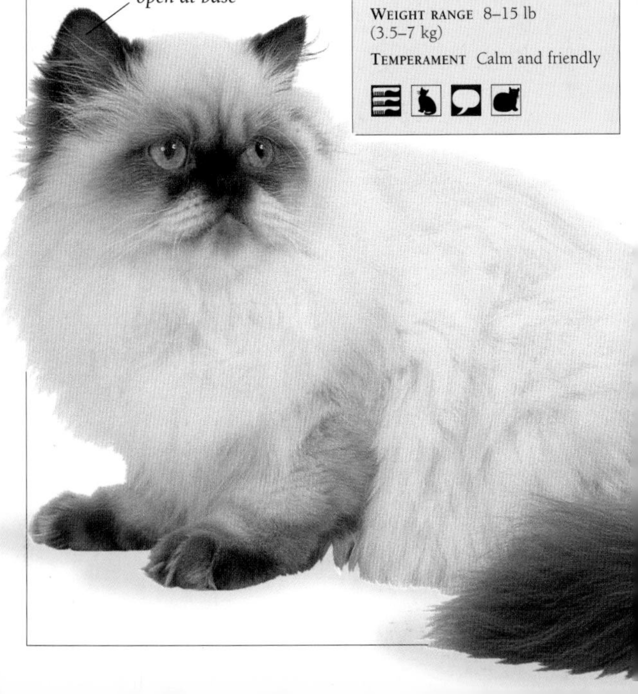
Ears are small and round tipped, and not unduly open at base

Chocolate Point
This color combines an ivory-white body with brown points, providing an even tone and depth.

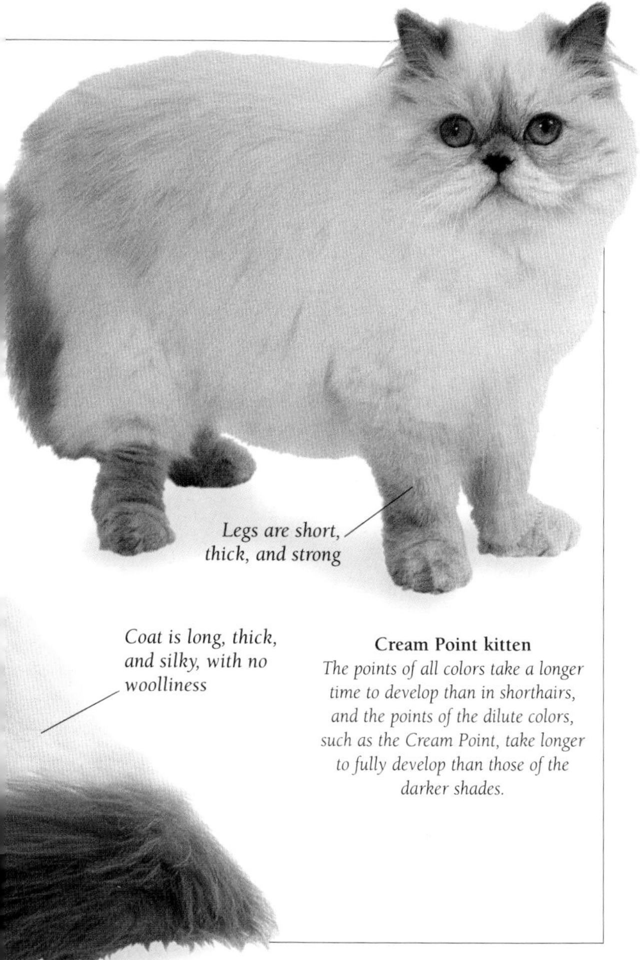
Legs are short,
thick, and strong
Coat is long, thick,
and silky, with no
woolliness

Cream Point kitten

The points of all colors take a longer time to develop than in shorthairs, and the points of the dilute colors, such as the Cream Point, take longer to fully develop than those of the darker shades.

Pattern has evenly colored points and minimal shading on body
Frill on shoulders and chest

Lilac Point

This color has warm-toned lilac points and a magnolia-white body. Himalayans are interbred with other types of Persian. Because the pointing gene is recessive, offspring from these matings carry the potential for producing Colorpoint kittens, which will be noted in their pedigrees. Carriers of the pointing gene will not differ in type from other Persians.

Tail is short, but not in proportion to body, and bushy

Breed History The first experiments in cross-breeding Siamese and Persians were made in the 1920s in Europe: A breed known as the Khmer existed in mainland Europe until the 1950s, and some say that the Birman (*see page 34*) is also a result of these experiments. In the 1930s, American geneticists investigating inherited traits bred a black longhair with a Siamese. The first generation were all black longhaired cats, but produced a pointed longhair cat when backcrossed. This was later called the Himalayan Persian, after the pointed pattern seen in Himalayan rabbits. In Britain, the breed was accepted as the Colorpoint Longhair in 1955; in mainland Europe, the name Khmer was changed to match. Interest in Himalayan Persians during the 1950s in North America led to recognition by all major registries by 1961.

BIRMAN

This strikingly marked breed, with its mysterious history, is a well-built cat with highlighted paws and large, blue eyes. Its silky hair is not as thick as that of the Persian (*see page 16*), and is less prone to matting, but daily grooming is still necessary. The breed was almost extinct in the 1940s, when only two individuals remained in France. These were outcrossed with other cats to perpetuate the breed, increasing the genetic base and introducing a variety of point colors. As with all breeds with a small genetic base, inbreeding may increase hereditary problems; fortunately, only rare skin and nerve disorders are hereditary in this breed.

Profile
The Birman profile, illustrated here on a Red Point, is strong, with a slight dip, but no defined nose stop or break. The chin tapers slightly from the nose, but it should not be receding.

Face
The Blue Point shows a full mask from nose to forehead, connected to the ears by "tracings." In self colors, the mask should be even and dense, and the nose leather should match the coat.

Breed Colors

SELF AND TORTIE POINTS
Seal, Chocolate, Red, Blue, Lilac, Cream, Seal Tortie, Chocolate Tortie, Blue Tortie, Lilac Tortie

TABBY POINTS
Colors are as for self and tortie points

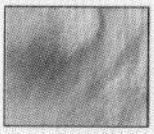
SEAL TORTIE TABBY

CHOCOLATE

Seal Point

The "classic" Birman, these colors exemplify those described in the legendary version of the breed's origins: white mittens and gauntlets on the paws, dark brown points, a golden body, and blue eyes. For a long time, only the Seal and its dilute form, the Blue, were accepted.

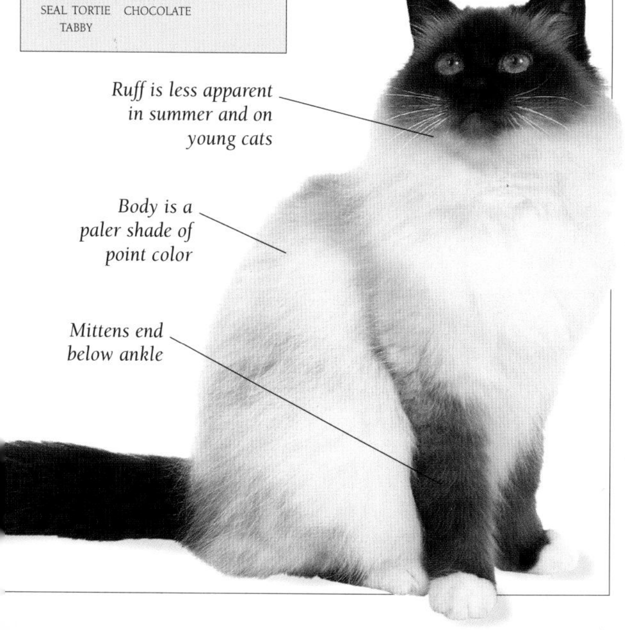
Ruff is less apparent in summer and on young cats
Body is a paler shade of point color
Mittens end below ankle

Lilac Point

Together with the Chocolate, this was one of the first "new" colors to be accepted. The points must be pinkish-grey, with the nose leather to match, and the body a warm magnolia color.

Body is long and strongly built

Breed History According to tradition, the Birman descends from the temple cats of Burma (Myanmar), specifically from Sita, a pregnant female brought to France in 1919 by August Pavie. Legend links Birmans to a white cat called Sinh who lived in a temple dedicated to Tsun-Kyan-Kse, a golden goddess with sapphire eyes. When the temple was attacked, Sinh took on the goddess's colors and inspired the monks to fight the attackers. The breed may be a distant relation of the similarly patterned Siamese (*see page 280*) and originate from Burma, but a less romantic version holds that Birmans were created by French breeders at the same time as the Himalayan Persian (*see page 28*) was developed.

Blue Tabby Point

The tabby pattern was one of the earlier additions to the range of Birman points, and now comes in a full range of colors. Tabby Points should show clear frown marks and lighter "spectacles," spotted cheek pads, striped legs, and a ringed tail.

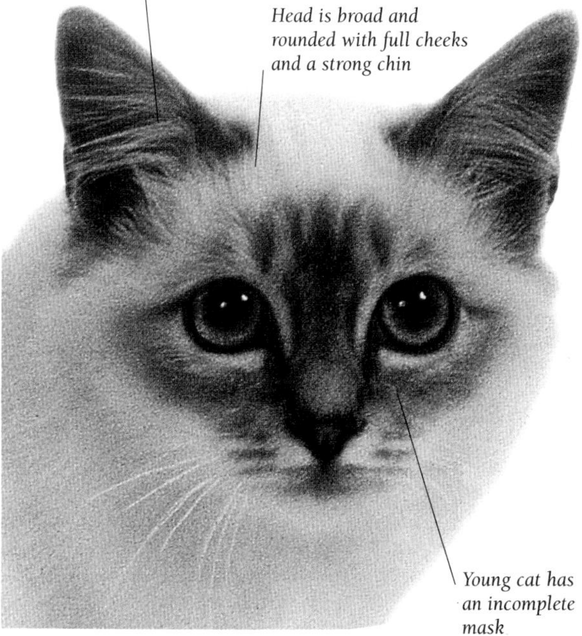

Ears are medium-sized and well spaced
Head is broad and rounded with full cheeks and a strong chin
Young cat has an incomplete mask

Eyes are a deep blue color and almost rounded

Key Facts

Date of origin Unknown

Place of origin Burma or France

Ancestry Disputed

Outcross breeds None

Other name Sacred Cat of Burma

Weight range 10–18 lb (4.5–8 kg)

Temperament Friendly and reserved

Seal Tortie Point

A good Tortie Point can be difficult to produce because although the patterning need not be entirely even, and a facial blaze is not necessary, each of the points must show an intermingling of the colors. The lighter shading over the body must also be slightly uneven.

Cream Point

Together with the Red Point, this is one of the most recent additions to the Birman range. This is a young cat; with maturity the mask extends to cover all of the face, and tabby markings are not a serious fault in these two colors.

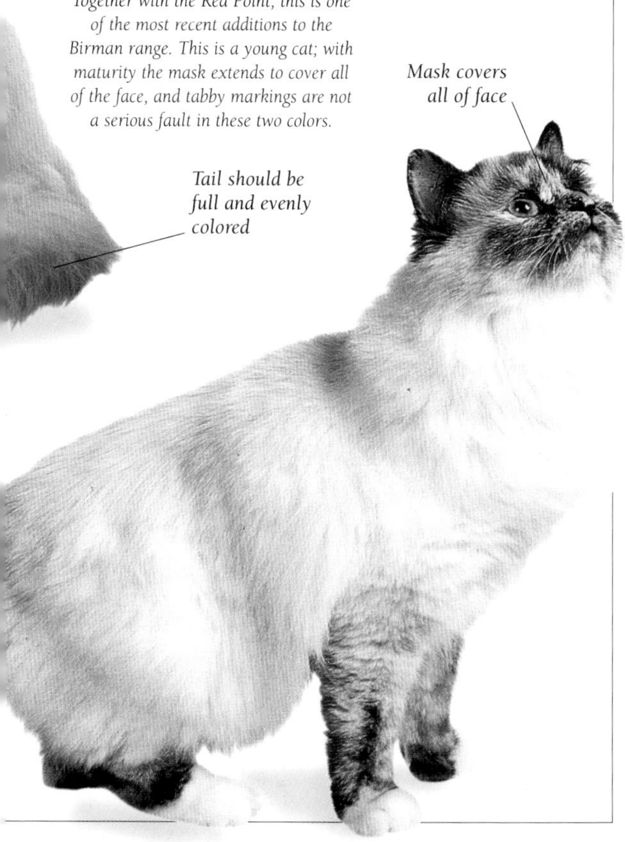
Mask covers all of face
Tail should be full and evenly colored

RAGDOLL

Mostly known for its famously placid disposition, the Ragdoll is a large and surprisingly heavy cat. Its medium-long coat has a soft texture and does not mat as readily as that of the Persian (*see page 16*). Ragdolls are essentially pointed cats, born white and slowly developing color and pattern over two years. Although well-muscled and with a weight advantage over many other cats, this breed has a gentle disposition. The Ragdoll is open to training with rewards and can easily be induced to use a scratching post.

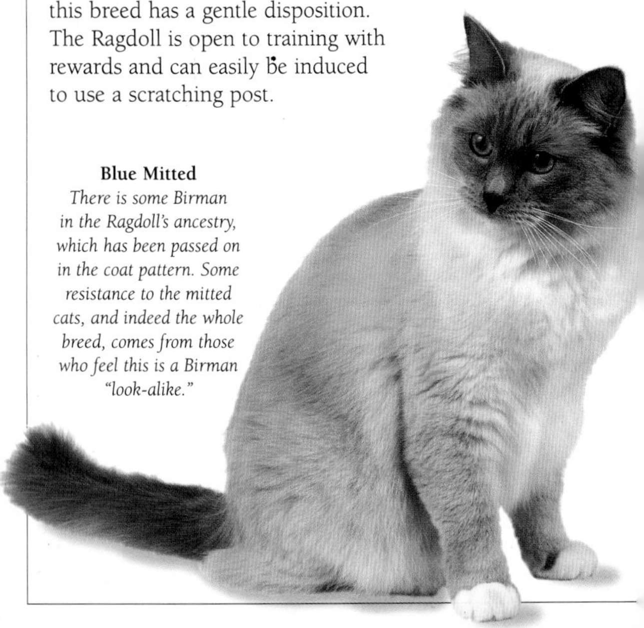

Blue Mitted

There is some Birman in the Ragdoll's ancestry, which has been passed on in the coat pattern. Some resistance to the mitted cats, and indeed the whole breed, comes from those who feel this is a Birman "look-alike."

Head is medium to large, with full cheeks and a rounded muzzle

Ragdoll head

In profile, the face should have a very gentle break for the nose, which is of medium length. This Seal Mitted has a narrow white blaze on the nose, which is allowed in this coat pattern.

Breed Colors

POINTED
Seal, Chocolate, Blue, Lilac

MITTED
Colors are as for pointed

BICOLOR
Colors are as for pointed

CHOCOLATE BICOLOR

LILAC POINT

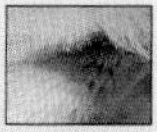

CHOCOLATE POINT

Seal Bicolor

The standard requires the white area to begin in an inverted "V" on the face and cover the entirety of the underparts from the chin to the base of the tail. The forelegs should be entirely white, the hindlegs white on the lower part.

Breed History

Although the Ragdoll is a new breed, its history is confused. In the 1960s, Californian breeder Ann Baker bred the first Ragdolls from Josephine, a white, probably non-pedigree, longhair, and Daddy Warbucks, a Birman or a Birman-type tom. She claimed that Ragdolls went limp when handled. She formed a breed association, but its Ragdolls were not accepted by other associations. Other individuals later bred her Ragdolls to produce the breed accepted by the major registries today. The Ragdoll's success resulted from the demand for placid, indoor-dwelling cats. Similar breeds are now being developed, all with equally cozy names.

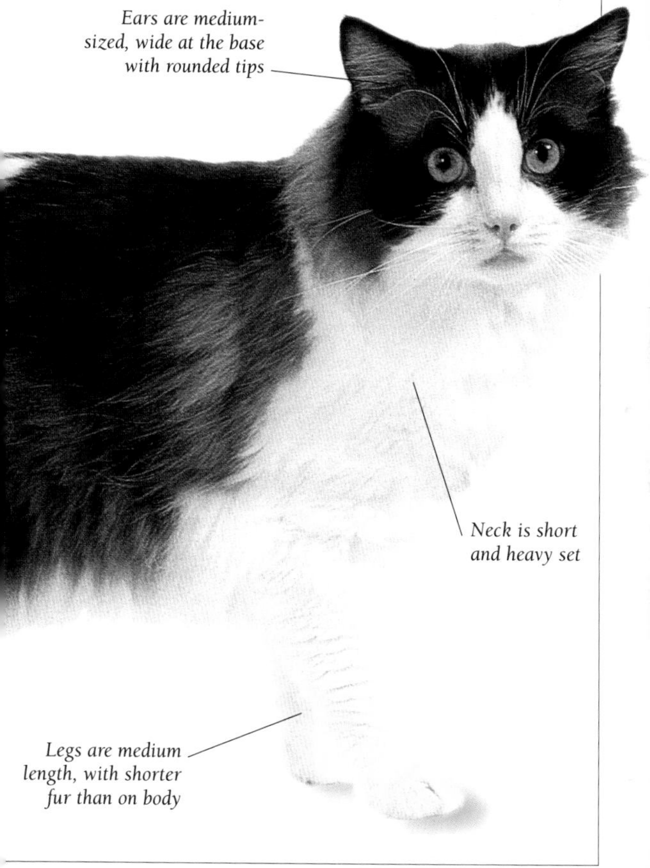
Ears are medium-sized, wide at the base with rounded tips
Neck is short and heavy set
Legs are medium length, with shorter fur than on body

KEY FACTS

DATE OF ORIGIN 1960s

PLACE OF ORIGIN United States

ANCESTRY Unclear

OUTCROSS BREEDS None

OTHER NAME None

WEIGHT RANGE 10–20lb (4.5–9 kg)

TEMPERAMENT Genial and relaxed

Body is long and muscular, with a broad chest
Coat flows on body
Paws are large, round, and tufted
Coat is of medium length, dense and silky

Seal Point

This color and its dilute, blue, are the most common colors found in Ragdolls: It has proved difficult to produce chocolate and lilac colors, and some breeders believe there are other colors in the gene pool. The body color on Ragdolls can be deeper than on other pointed breeds.

MAINE COON

Strong, tranquil, and luxurious to both look at and touch, the Maine Coon has recently become an outstandingly popular companion. Maines look their best in winter when the heavy, glossy coat is at its most luxurious. A distinctive characteristic that sets this breed apart from others is its frequent and enchantingly happy chirping trill, which it uses as a greeting to its human or feline family. While the Maine enjoys the company of people, it is not a dependent breed, but is content to pursue its own activities; some owners report that these include swimming. Females retain their dignity more than males, who tend to be slightly goofy, but no Maines are lap cats; these are friends, not babies.

Maine face
The preferred look of the Maine Coon, in particular the size and set of the ears, varies among different breed associations. Generally, the eyes should be green, gold, or copper, with blue or odd eyes allowed in whites.

Breed Colors

SELF AND TORTIE
Black, Blue, Cream, Red, Tortoiseshell, Blue Tortie, White (Blue-, Green-, Odd-, Orange-Eyed)

SMOKED AND SHADED
Colors are as for self and tortie with the exception of White

TABBY (CLASSIC, MACKEREL)
Brown, Red, Blue, Cream, Tortie, Blue Tortie

SILVER TABBY
Colors are as for standard tabbies

BICOLORS
All self, tortie, and tabby colors with white

CREAM SHADED

BLACK SMOKE

BROWN CLASSIC TABBY

BLUE SILVER TABBY

Black

The Maine Coon is traditionally associated with tabby colors, but selfs are widely bred. Dark colors show the glossy quality of the coat.

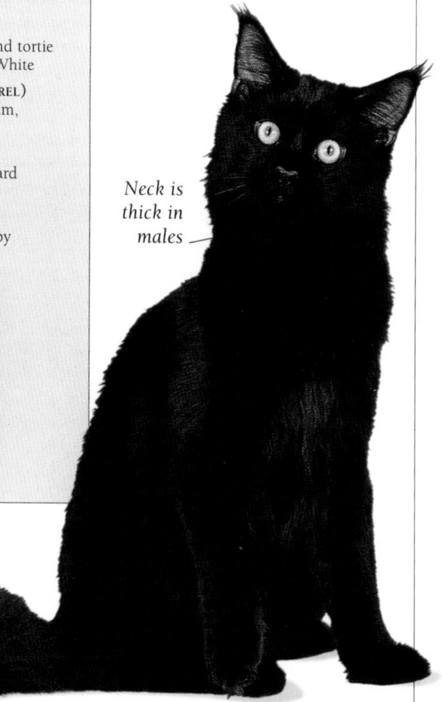

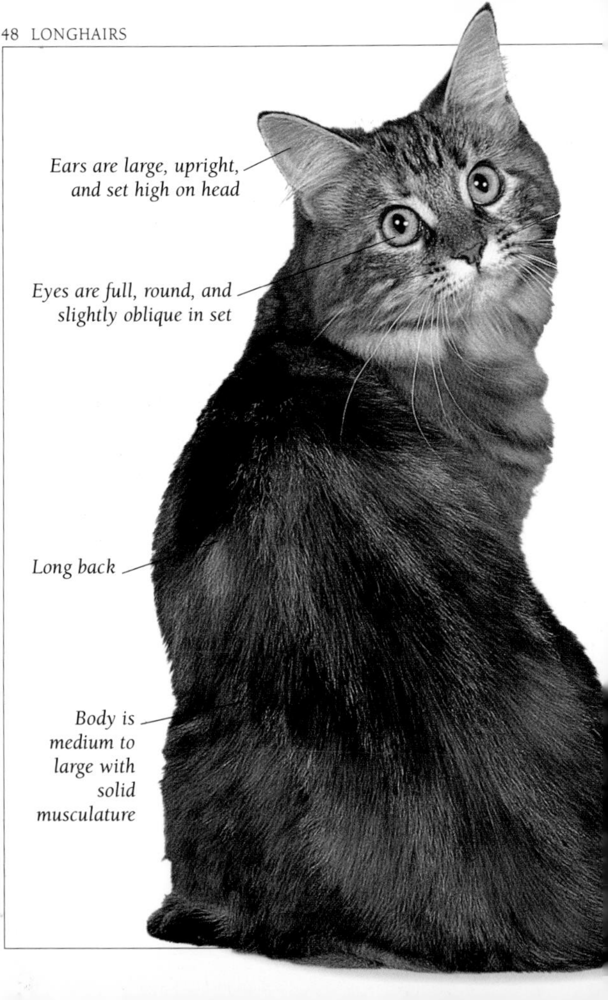
Ears are large, upright, and set high on head
Eyes are full, round, and slightly oblique in set
Long back
Body is medium to large with solid musculature

Tortie Tabby

The image of the Maine Coon as a big, shaggy, tabby cat is so ingrained into public consciousness that any cat answering to this description is liable to be tagged as a Maine by the unscrupulous. True Maines comply to a rigorous standard, and careful breeding is needed to produce rich colors consistently. The size of the Maine Coon has also become a matter of some controversy: Claims of breeding lines that tip the scales at weights of 33 lb (15 kg) remain unsubstantiated.

Breed History The distant history of the Maine is unknown. Its probable ancestors include British cats that came with early settlers, and longhaired Russian or Scandinavian cats from ships in the ports of Maine. The harsh New England winter suits cats with dense coats and of a size sufficient for hunting hares. The black-and-white Captain Jenks of the Horse Marines was the "first" Maine, noted at Boston and New York shows in 1861, when the breed first became popular. At the turn of the 20th century, the Maine lost ground to the luxuriously coated Persians. It survived as a breed because farmers recognized its excellent hunting ability. Interest rekindled in the 1950s, and became extensive by the 1980s; it is now one of the most popular breeds in the world.

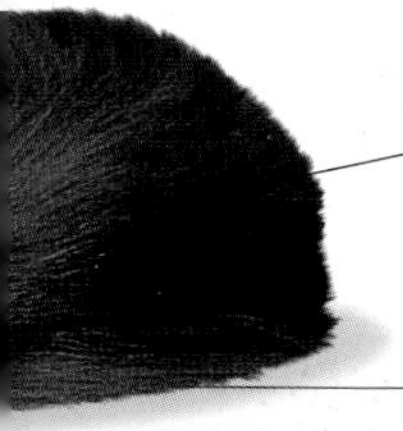

Tail is long, with flowing fur

Head is slightly longer than it is wide

Red Classic Tabby

Only the striped and blotched tabbies are recognized in Maines, in keeping with their traditional image. Reds should show good rufousing, setting them apart from the usual ginger coloring seen on random-bred cats.

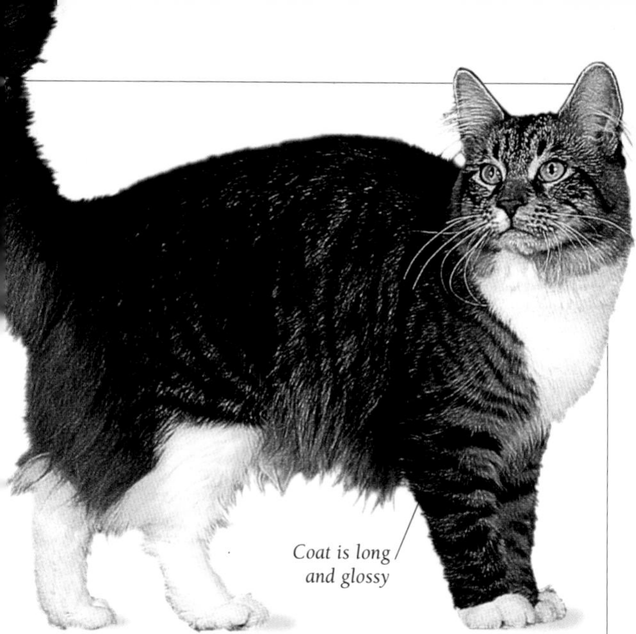

Brown Mackerel Tabby and White

Originally, only brown tabbies were given the name Maine Coons: The coat, together with the massive build and huge tail, made these cats resemble raccoons. Other colors and patterns were generally called Maine Shags in the early years of the breed.

Key Facts

Date of origin 1860s

Place of origin United States

Ancestry Farm cats

Outcross breeds None

Other name Maine Shag

Weight range 9–22 lb (4.10 kg)

Temperament Gentle giant

MAINE COON VARIATIONS

The structure of the Maine Coon's coat is undoubtedly that of a farm cat. Despite being long and thick, it requires surprisingly little maintenance, and it is water-repellent, so washing is rarely necessary. Some of the colors, however, have raised questions among breeders: It has been suggested that Persians were used to introduce the smoke and silver colors. This seems unlikely, because many cats in the random-bred cat population of North America, which had nothing to do with Persians, carry the inhibitor gene that causes these colors. In Britain, the same color range is allowed in self, smoke, shaded, tabby, and silver tabby coats. In North America, the situation is more complex.

Blue and White kitten
The sturdy build of this breed is apparent from an early age. The Maine Coon can be unpredictable in its maturing, with some excellent breed examples only emerging as such in full adulthood.

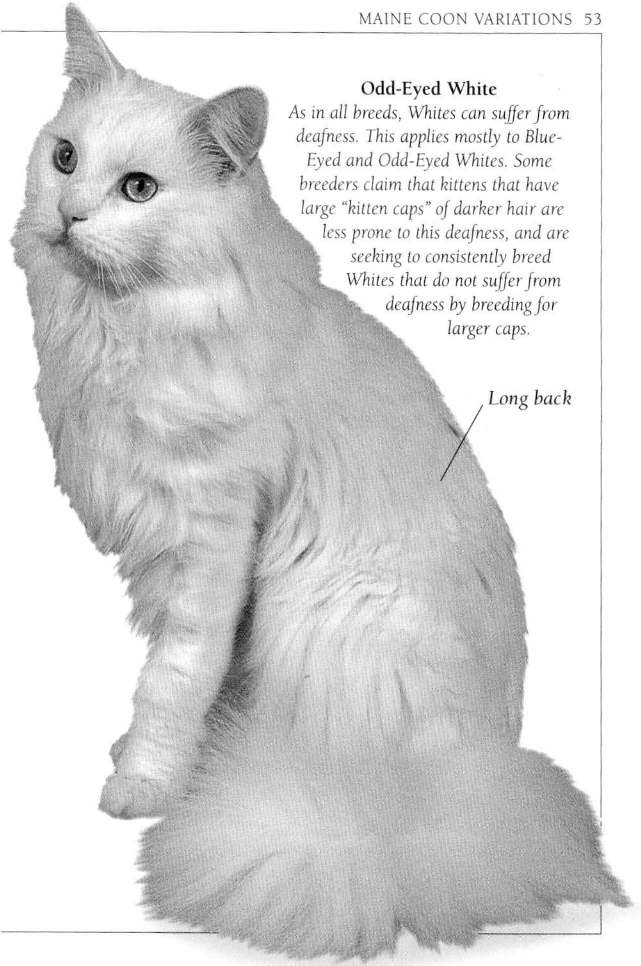

Odd-Eyed White

As in all breeds, Whites can suffer from deafness. This applies mostly to Blue-Eyed and Odd-Eyed Whites. Some breeders claim that kittens that have large "kitten caps" of darker hair are less prone to this deafness, and are seeking to consistently breed Whites that do not suffer from deafness by breeding for larger caps.

British look

This Silver Tabby is an example of the look that is preferred by the GCCF for the Maine Coon. A broad face with oval eyes is topped by moderately sized ears, angled out from the corners of the head. The body and legs are correspondingly stocky, giving an impresssion of a cat that could hold its own anywhere.

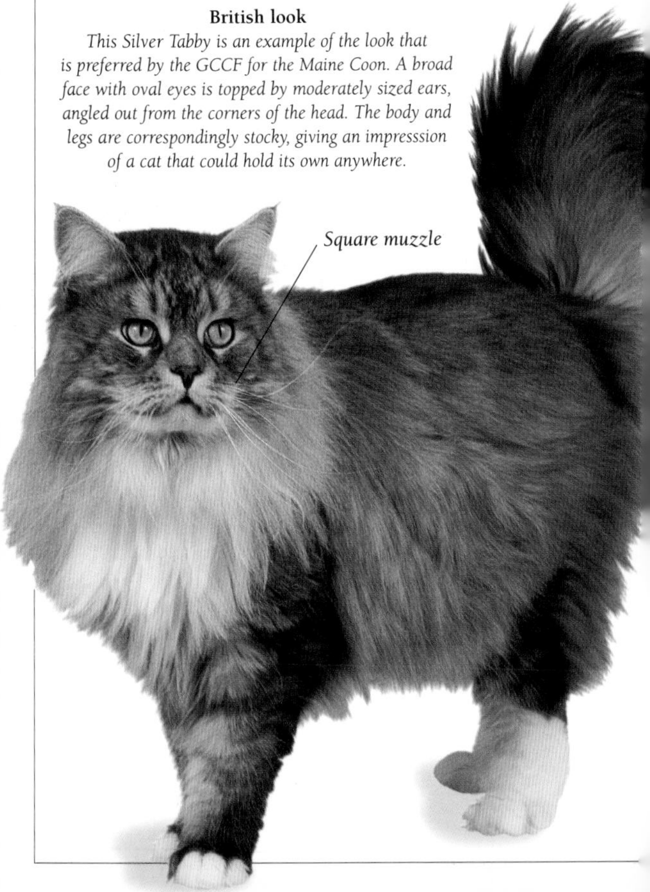

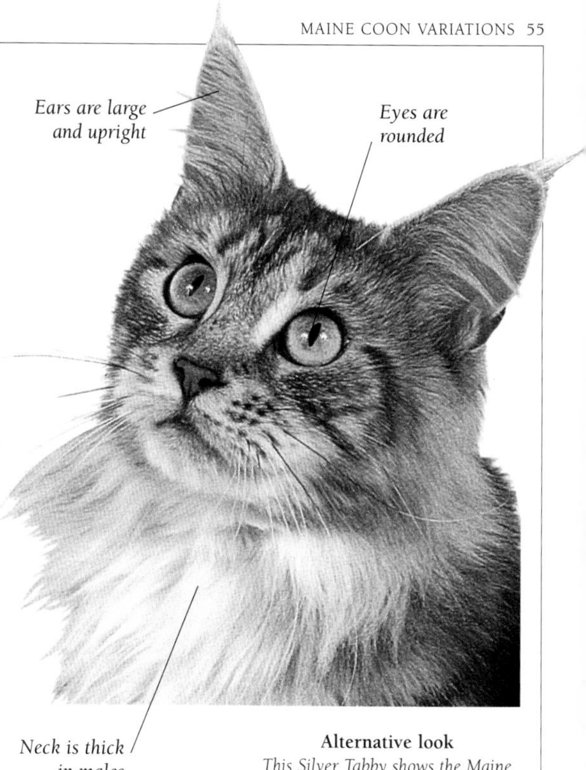
Ears are large
and upright
Eyes are
rounded
Neck is thick
in males

Alternative look

This Silver Tabby shows the Maine Coon style preferred by TICA, a primarily North American registry. The face is slightly more angular than the preferred British look, with larger ears set higher on the head, and rounder eyes.

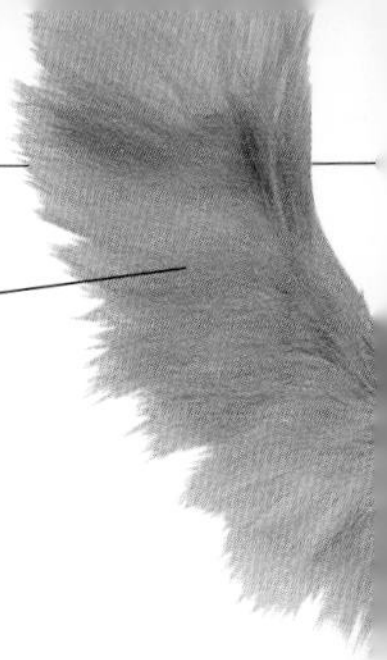
Long tail with flowing fur

Maine Wave

These controversial cats are full-pedigree Maine Coons, with a rex mutation. This mutation was once thought to be lethal, but different lines now seem to be breeding healthily. The coat lacks guard hairs, and so is completely unlike the typical Maine coat; consequently, these cats are unlikely ever to be accepted as part of the breed. As the mutation is recessive, they are also unlikely to disappear.

Coat is long and glossy
Eyes are round and slightly oblique in set

Paws are rounded and tufted

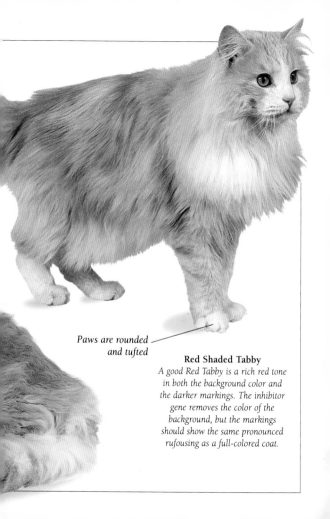

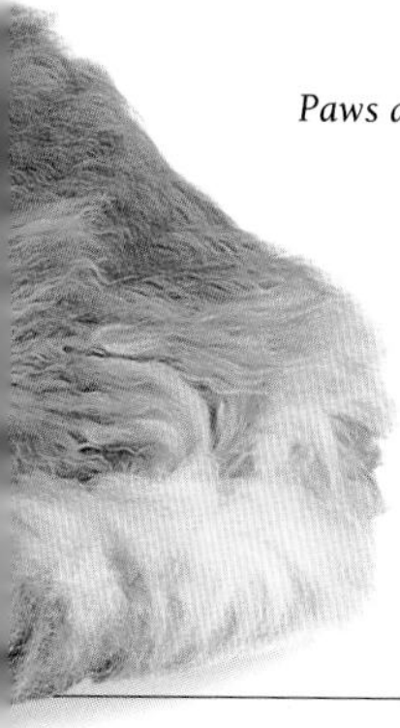

Red Shaded Tabby

A good Red Tabby is a rich red tone in both the background color and the darker markings. The inhibitor gene removes the color of the background, but the markings should show the same pronounced rufousing as a full-colored coat.

NORWEGIAN FOREST CAT

Reserved with strangers but calmly confident with people it knows, the Norwegian Forest Cat shares attributes with the Maine Coon (*see page* 46) and Siberian Forest Cat (*see page* 64). Large size and long hindlegs give the "Wegie" a commanding presence. Norwegian breeders like to think of this "natural cat" as their little lynx. While it makes a gentle household cat, it defends its territory vigorously. It is a superb climber and hunter, and owners who live near streams report that their Wegies fish.

BREED COLORS

SELF AND TORTIE COLORS
Black, Red, Blue, Cream, White (Blue-, Green-, Odd-, Orange-Eyed), Tortoiseshell, Blue-Cream

SMOKE COLORS
Colors are as for self and tortie colors, except White

SHADED AND TIPPED COLORS
Colors are as for self and tortie colors, except White

TABBY COLORS (CLASSIC, MACKEREL, SPOTTED)
Brown, Red, Blue, Cream, Tortie, Blue Tortie

SILVER TABBY COLORS
Colors and patterns are as for standard tabbies

BROWN TABBY

BLUE AND WHITE

RED TABBY

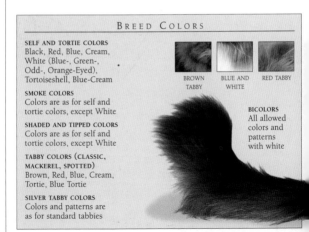

BICOLORS
All allowed colors and patterns with white

Silver Tabby

The breed standard for the Norwegian Forest requires that its appearance reflect its heritage as a farm cat. The most important features are type and coat quality; there are no points specifically allocated to coat color in the scoring system.

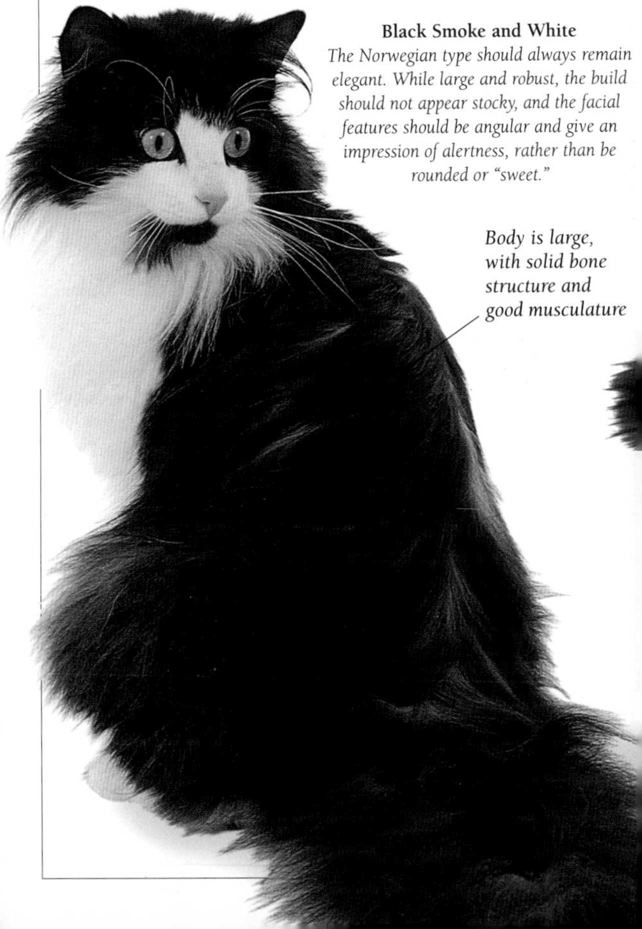

Black Smoke and White

The Norwegian type should always remain elegant. While large and robust, the build should not appear stocky, and the facial features should be angular and give an impression of alertness, rather than be rounded or "sweet."

Body is large, with solid bone structure and good musculature

Breed History Cats arrived in Norway around AD 1000, via the Viking trade routes with the Byzantine East. Proof that cats were traded directly from Byzantium to Norway is suggested by Norwegian cat populations with coat colors common in Turkey but rare across Europe. The harsh Scandinavian winter favored large, longhaired cats, which became popular with farmers. Planned breeding did not begin until the 1970s, and the breed did not arrive in the United States until 1979 and Britain in the 1980s.

Silver Tabby and White
In almost all cats, coats will sometimes appear slightly yellowed or "tarnished" due to rufous genes; the effect is most obvious in silver tabbies. Although regarded as a flaw in many breeds, it is not a fault in Wegies.

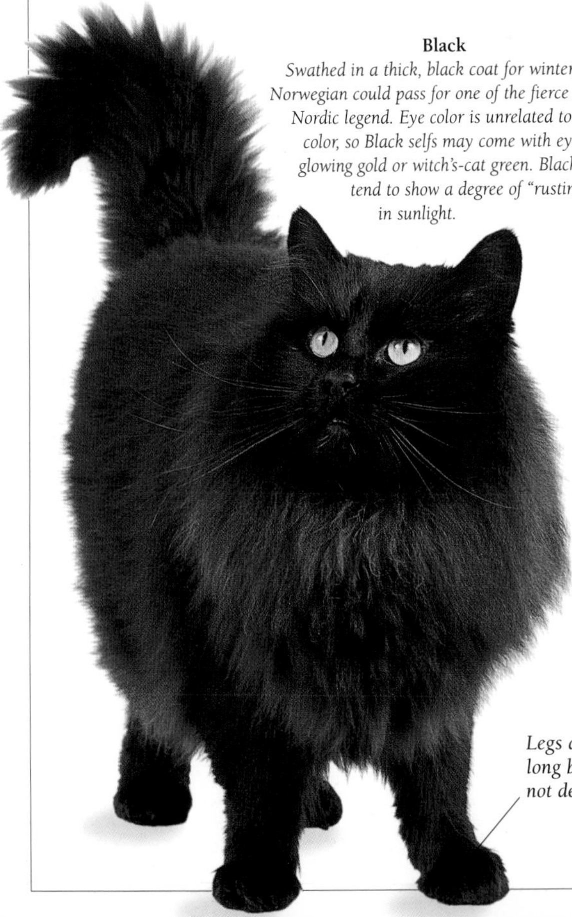
Legs are long but not delicate

Black

Swathed in a thick, black coat for winter, the Norwegian could pass for one of the fierce cats of Nordic legend. Eye color is unrelated to coat color, so Black selfs may come with eyes of glowing gold or witch's-cat green. Black coats tend to show a degree of "rusting" in sunlight.

Key Facts

Date of origin 1930s

Place of origin Norway

Ancestry Farm cats

Outcross breeds None

Other name Skogkatt or Skaukatt, Wegie

Weight range 7–20 lb (3–9 kg)

Temperament Reserved and contained

Blue Tabby and White

Tabbies and bicolors are both common in the random-breeding cat populations from which the Norwegian derives. The predominance of tabbies and bicolors reflects the population from which the breed is descended.

Head is triangular, with a long straight profile and strong chin
Tail is long and bushy, equal in length to body

SIBERIAN

Famed for its harsh winter, the homeland of this breed favored large, sturdily built cats with thick, protective coats. It is impossible to be sure of this cat's ancient ancestry, but what is certain is that the Siberian has been perfected by its environment, just like the Norwegian Forest Cat (*see page 58*). Every aspect of this cat is honed for survival in tough conditions: Its topcoat is strong, plentiful, and oily, and its undercoat is dense enough to keep out the keenest winds.

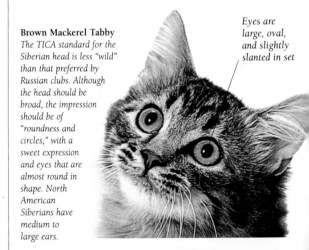

Brown Mackerel Tabby
The TICA standard for the Siberian head is less "wild" than that preferred by Russian clubs. Although the head should be broad, the impression should be of "roundness and circles," with a sweet expression and eyes that are almost round in shape. North American Siberians have medium to large ears.

Eyes are large, oval, and slightly slanted in set

BREED COLORS

SELF AND TORTIE
Black, Red, Blue, Cream, Tortoiseshell, Blue Tortie
All other self and tortie colors

SMOKED AND SHADED, AND TIPPED COLORS
Colors are as for self and tortie

TABBIES, SILVER TABBIES (CLASSIC, MACKEREL, SPOTTED)
Brown, Red, Blue, Cream, Tortie, Blue Tortie
Ticked pattern, all other self and tortie colors

BICOLORS
All allowed self, tortie, and tabby colors with white
All self, tortie, and tabby colors with white

CREAM AND WHITE

TORTIE AND WHITE

BLUE

SILVER TABBY

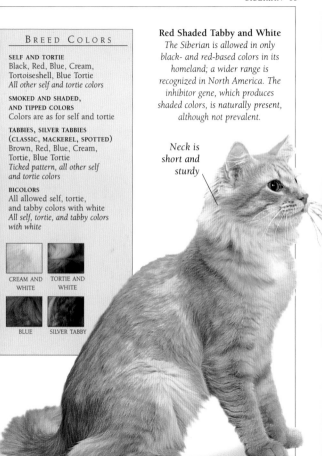

Neck is short and sturdy

Red Shaded Tabby and White
The Siberian is allowed in only black- and red-based colors in its homeland; a wider range is recognized in North America. The inhibitor gene, which produces shaded colors, is naturally present, although not prevalent.

Breed History Longhaired cats are found across the northern wastes of Russia. Like many natural breeds, the Siberian was not regarded as noteworthy until fairly recently. Serious breeding to standardize the type began in the 1980s, and the breed is recognized by a wide range of registries in its homeland, including the All-Russian Cat Club. Siberians were imported into the United States in 1990, through the efforts of Elizabeth Terrell. Her cattery name, Starpoint, can be found in the pedigrees of most of the top Siberians in America. Among major registries, only TICA recognizes the Siberian. Some Russian clubs fear that the cats exported to the West are not always the best. The "TICA face" is different from that in Russia, and the Siberian may develop two distinct looks internationally.

Tortie Tabby and White
Siberian females are, as in many breeds, slightly smaller and lighter than the males. In both sexes, the hindlegs are slightly longer than the forelegs when straight, and the body is carried with a slightly arched spine.

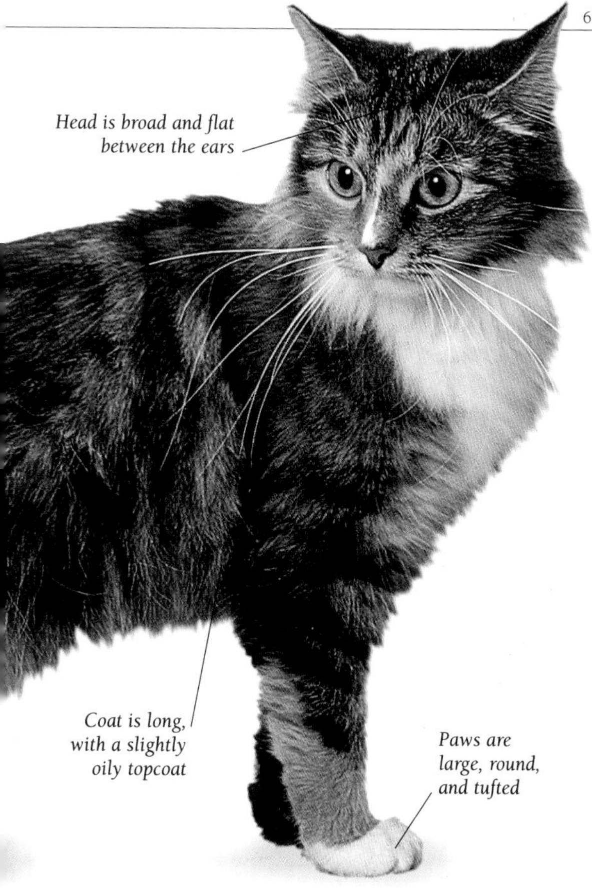
Head is broad and flat between the ears
Coat is long, with a slightly oily topcoat
Paws are large, round, and tufted

Key Facts

Date of origin 1980s

Place of origin Eastern Russia

Ancestry Household and farm cat

Outcross breeds None

Other name None

Weight range 10–20 lb (4.5–9 kg)

Temperament Sensible and resourceful

Ears are medium in size, with rounded tips, and angled out
Tail is medium length and thick, with a rounded tip

Brown Spotted Tabby and White

Originally, there was a great predominance of tabby coats in the Siberian, as is to be expected of a breed that developed where natural enemies abound. Breeders are almost certain to wish to develop a wider range of self and shaded colors, but tabbies of all patterns still make up a fairly high proportion of the breed.

Brown Classic Tabby

The appearance of the Siberian is more reminiscent of a wildcat than any other breed. The face is also unique: Great breadth, and oval, slightly tilted eyes, give a distinctly wild and decidedly Asiatic cast. Russian cat clubs wish to see this wild appearance preserved.

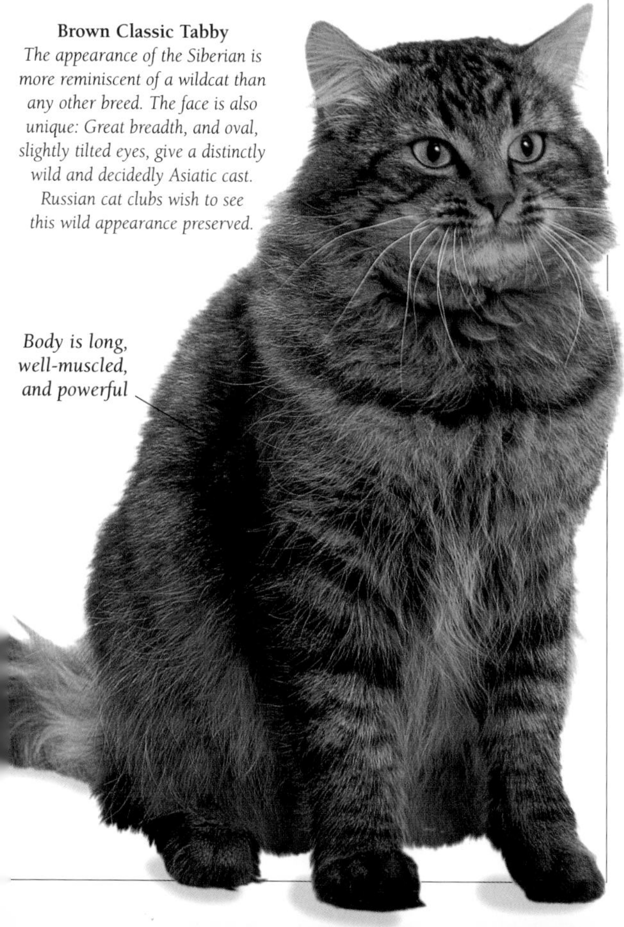

Body is long, well-muscled, and powerful

AMERICAN CURL

This quiet and gentle breed is simply the household cat of the United States with a single, striking mutation: Its ears curl back away from the face toward the back and center of the head. This distinctive feature gives the Curl a dramatic, pixie-like face, full of astonishment. The trait is dominant, so a Curl bred to any cat should give at least 50 percent Curls. The rest, called American Curl Straight Ears, are used for breeding programs or sold as pets.

BREED COLORS

SELF AND TORTIE
Black, Chocolate, Red, Blue, Lilac, Cream, White, Tortoiseshell, Blue-Cream
All other self and tortie colors

SMOKE
Colors as for self and tortie, except White and with the addition of Chocolate Tortie
All other self and tortie colors

SHADED AND TIPPED
Shaded Silver, Shaded Golden, Shaded Cameo, Shaded Tortoiseshell, Chinchilla Silver, Chinchilla Golden, Shell Cameo, Shell Tortoiseshell
All other self and tortie colors

TABBIES (ALL PATTERNS)
Brown, Red, Blue, Cream, Brown Patched, Blue Patched
All other self and tortie colors

SILVER TABBIES
Silver, Chocolate Silver, Cameo, Blue Silver, Lavender Silver, Cream Silver, Silver Patched
All other self and tortie colors

BICOLORS (CLASSIC AND VAN)
Black, Red, Blue, Cream, Tortoiseshell, Blue-Cream, and all tabby colors with white
All other self and tortie colors

SELF AND TORTIE POINTS
Seal, Chocolate, Flame, Blue, Lilac, Cream, Tortie, Chocolate Tortie, Blue-Cream, Lilac-Cream
All other colors, sepia, and mink patterns

LYNX (TABBY) POINTS
As for self and tortie points, except Red
All other colors, sepia, and mink patterns

Ears point at back of head
Coat is silky and flowing, with minimal undercoat

Tortoiseshell and White
This pattern, also called Calico in North America, is almost exclusively female. The Curl's moderate breed standard favors females; in heavier breeds they can lose awards to sturdier males.

Breed History People most often acquire cats by adopting strays; this is the origin of the Curl. In 1981, a stray kitten appeared at Grace and Joe Ruga's home in Lakeland, California. Cats are adept at targeting nurturing individuals: Grace Ruga left food on her porch for the stray kitten, who ate it, liked the ambience of the household, and made it her new home. An affectionate black female, she had a long, silky coat and unusual ears. Joe Ruga named her Shulamith, meaning "peaceful one," after the shepherdess in the *Song of Songs*. All Curls trace their origins to Shulamith. In December that year, Shulamith had a litter of four kittens, two of which had the same curly ears. These cats were shown in California in 1983, and the breed is fully recognized in North America. The first Curls to reach Europe arrived in Britain in 1995; they are unlikely to be accepted by the GCCF or FIFé.

Body is moderately muscled and semi-foreign in build

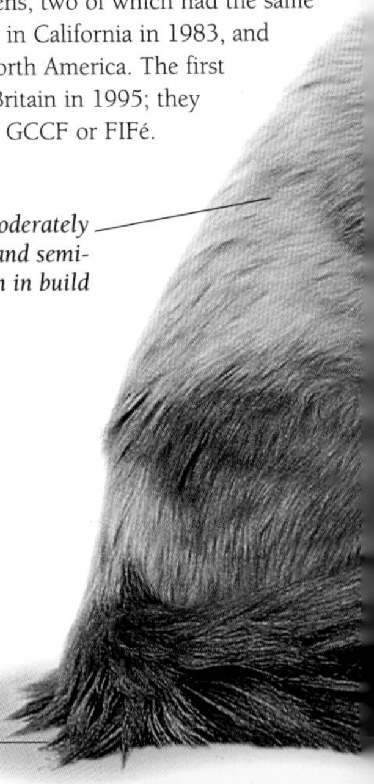

Seal Point

The pointed pattern, once confined to a single breed, is now found in a vast range of cats. Newer breeds, such as the Curl, usually have this pattern. Longer coats generally soften and lighten the pointing.

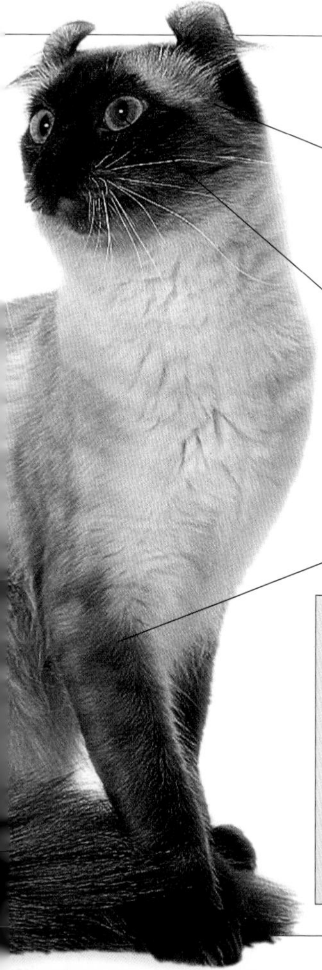
Head is a rounded, modified wedge shape
Eyes are walnut-shaped and slightly tilted
Legs are medium length and bowing

KEY FACTS

DATE OF ORIGIN 1981

PLACE OF ORIGIN United States

ANCESTRY American household cat

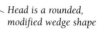

OUTCROSS BREEDS Nonpedigreed domestic cat

OTHER NAME None

WEIGHT RANGE 7–11 lb (3–5 kg)

TEMPERAMENT Quietly affable

MUNCHKIN

Without doubt the most controversial and extraordinary breed to emerge in years, the Munchkin is defined by a single, dominant factor: Its leg bones are short. There is no direct effect on other bones, and breeders claim that the short legs have no detrimental side effects; only time will tell. The flexible feline spine may save the breed from the back and hip problems of dwarfed dog breeds, but in all other species, dwarfs are prone to arthritis. Where cats often live indoors, short legs may not seem a disadvantage.

Ears are triangular and moderately large in size

Head is medium-sized, neither round nor wedge-shaped
Eye and coat color are not related to each other

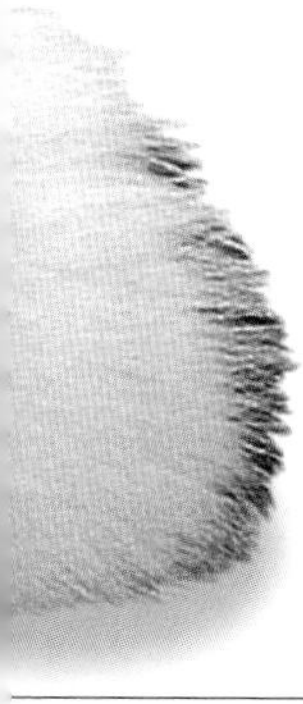

Munchkin head

The shape is between an almost equilateral triangle and a modified wedge: "Medium" and "moderate" are the words most used in the standard. This is likely to be reassessed as the breed is developed.

Black and White kitten

It is apparent at birth which kittens in a litter are Munchkins and which are not. Proponents of the breed claim that one of the breed's most attractive traits is not in its physique, but its personality; Munchkins are said to retain their kittenish curiosity and comical behavior into adulthood.

Red and White

The Munchkin is recognized in all possible colors and patterns; it would also be almost impossible to limit the range in a breed that is outcrossed to random-bred cats. Tabbies and bicolors are more common than Oriental shades and patterns.

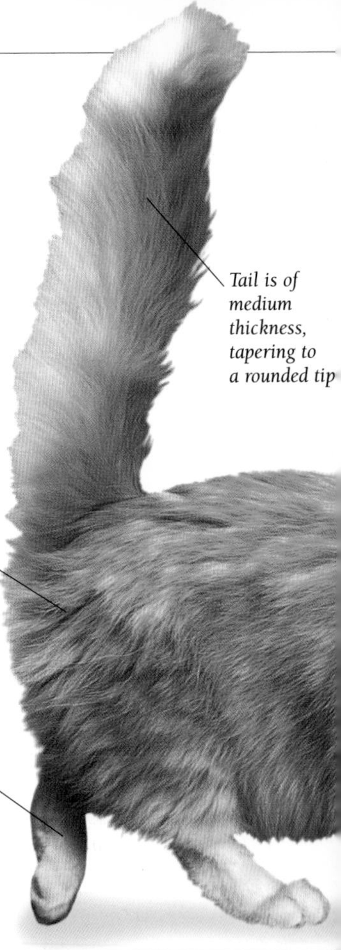
Tail is of medium thickness, tapering to a rounded tip
Body is medium-sized, with level spine or slight rise from shoulder to rump
Legs are short and straight with paws turned out slightly

Breed History Dwarfed individuals occur in many species, and the cat is no exception. The Munchkin originated in a mutation in Louisiana, in 1983. As breeders began to work with the mutation, outcrossing to nonpedigreed cats, controversy grew along with popularity. TICA granted the Munchkin "new breed" status in 1995; as yet, it is the only major registry to recognize the breed, and the standard is still very broad. Breeders of other pedigree breeds have expressed fears that dwarfed "editions" of their breeds will emerge. Although the lure of novelty cannot be denied, and some breeders may choose to pursue such a course, the TICA standard specifically bars any other pedigree breeds as outcrosses, and no registry would be likely to look favorably on dwarfed versions of established breeds.

Eyes are large and walnut-shaped, with an open expression

Key Facts

Date of origin 1980s

Place of origin United States

Ancestry Household cats

Outcross breeds Nonpedigreed cats

Other name None

Weight range 5–9 lb (2.25–4 kg)

Temperament Appealing and inquisitive

SCOTTISH FOLD

With the same distinctive ears as its shorthaired cousins (*see page 186*), the longhaired Scottish Fold's coat gives it a lush, warm look. Like all longhairs, the breed is best seen in winter, when it sports an imposing ruff, elegant breeches, and a huge, fluffy tail. All kittens are born with straight ears, which begin to fold at about three weeks of age. The joint problems that result from breeding Fold-to-Fold appear at four to six months: A short, thickened tail is a sign that might be missed in a longhaired kitten, so tails should be checked carefully – and always gently.

BREED HISTORY Cats with folded or pendulous ears have been recorded for over two centuries. All Scottish Folds, however, can be traced back to Susie, a white farm cat born in 1961 in Scotland. Two geneticists, Pat Turner and Peter Dyte, oversaw the early development of the breed, and found that Susie carried the longhair gene, which could be carried in shorthaired offspring and appear in later generations. The Fold is still rare: The absence of any longhaired outcross breed makes the longhaired version even rarer.

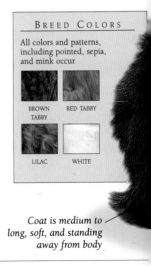

BREED COLORS

All colors and patterns, including pointed, sepia, and mink occur

BROWN TABBY

RED TABBY

LILAC

WHITE

Coat is medium to long, soft, and standing away from body

Blue Smoke and White

This cat falls short of the show standards : The ears are not pressed tightly to the head, and the face shows tabby markings rather than the even blue required.

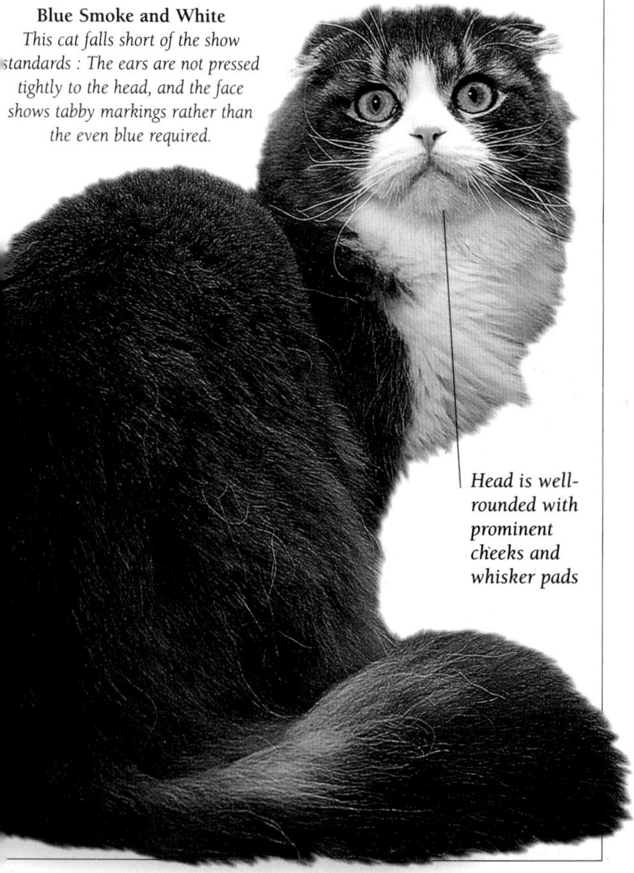
Head is well-rounded with prominent cheeks and whisker pads

Tortie Tabby and White

This combination of tortoiseshell and tabby is also called "patched tabby" in CFA or "torbie" in TICA. The tabby pattern should show clearly in both brown and red patches, which are larger and more defined in bicolors such as this one. The required eye color, which should be as brilliant as possible, is gold.

Coat is soft, and standing away from the body

Key Facts

Date of origin 1961

Place of origin Scotland

Ancestry Farm cats, British and American Shorthairs

Outcross breeds British and American Shorthairs

Other name Highland Fold

Weight range 6–13 lb (2.4–6 kg)

Temperament Quietly confident

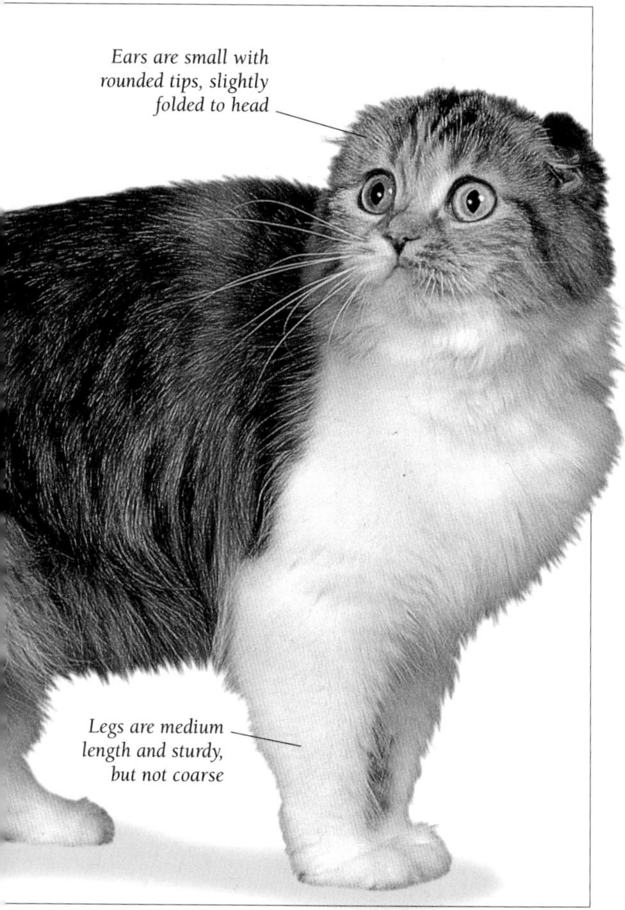
Ears are small with rounded tips, slightly folded to head
Legs are medium length and sturdy, but not coarse

SELKIRK REX

This is possibly the most striking of all of the rexed breeds. It shares the distinction of being longhaired with the La Perm (*see page 142*), but its appearance is quite unique. The long, thick coat is at its best in heterozygous cats, with one rexing and one straight-haired gene: This combination gives a loose, ringleted effect. All three hair types are present in the coat, and a longhaired Selkirk in molt may shed as much hair as a Persian (*see page 16*).

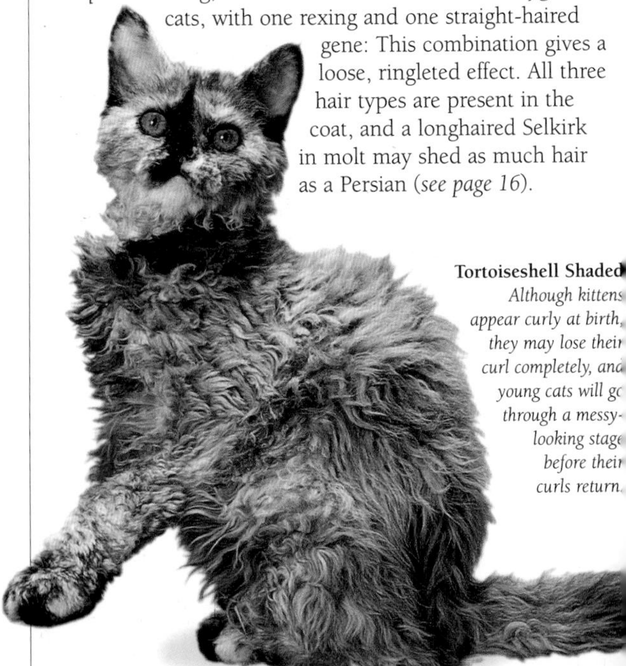

Tortoiseshell Shaded
Although kittens appear curly at birth, they may lose their curl completely, and young cats will go through a messy-looking stage before their curls return.

Head is rounded with a short, squared-off muzzle
Eyes are rounded and widely spaced

Selkirk head

Unlike the other rexed breeds, the Selkirk Rex has a sturdy, rounded look. The muzzle is short and broad, with a distinct nose stop, and both the cheeks and the whisker pads are full. The color of the eyes is not related to that of the coat.

Breed Colors

All colors and patterns, including pointed, sepia, and mink

CREAM

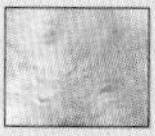
WHITE

BLUE

Breed History The Selkirk is the latest breed of Rex, appearing in 1987. The very first Selkirk Rex, Miss DePesto of NoFace, or Pest, was a shorthaired kitten born at a pet rescue center in Montana. She came into the household of Jeri Newman, who was a breeder of Persians. Jeri mated the new arrival to her black Persian champion, Photo Finish of Deekay. The resulting litter included longhaired and shorthaired kittens, with a mixture of straight and curly coats. This variety showed not only that Pest's rexing mutation was a simple dominant, but that she, like many random-bred cats, was carrying the recessive longhair gene. Consequently, from the start, the Selkirk Rex has had both longhaired and shorthaired classes: The two are not formally separated, and the allowed outcrosses for the breed continue to include the Persian.

Key Facts

Date of origin 1987

Place of origin United States

Ancestry Rescued cat, Persian, Exotic, British and American Shorthairs

Outcross breeds Pedigree parent breeds

Other name None

Weight range 7–11 lb (3–5 kg)

Temperament Patiently tolerant

Red Shaded Tabby

The ringlets of the coat reveal the white undercoat, making this pattern far less dramatic than it is in a longhair with a straight coat. Tabby markings on the body are softened by the curl; the less obscured they are, the better. Frown lines and spectacles remain clearly visible on the face.

Tail is thick, tapering slightly to a rounded tip

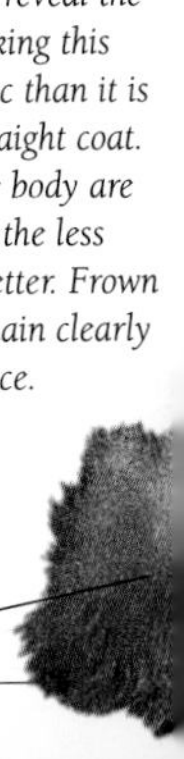

Ears are medium-sized, pointed, and set well apart
Body is muscular and rectangular, with slight rise to hindquarters

TURKISH VAN

With its soft coat, and large, rounded eyes, this breed might seem the ideal lap-cat. Turkish Vans descended, however, from rural cats in an area where life was hard, and retain minds of their own. The breed is distinguished for two reasons: the restricted color of its coat, so distinctive that the pattern is called Van even in other breeds, and its reputation for enjoying a dip in hot weather, which has earned it the name of "Swimming Cat" in its homeland.

Ears are large and set high on the head
Eyes are large and oval

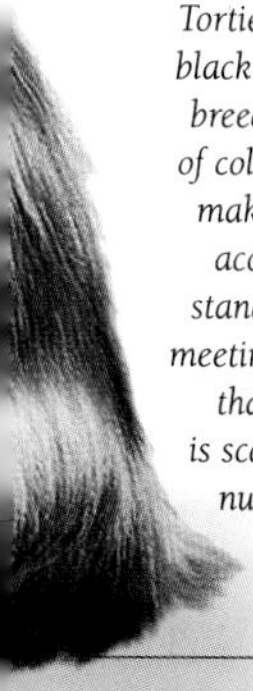

Tortie and White

Tortie Vans appeared when black was introduced to the breed. The "thumbprints" of color above this cat's tail make it less than perfect according to the breed standard; the difficulty of meeting the standard means that although the Van is scarce, there are a high number of pet kittens available.

Van face

The color markings on a Van's head should not extend below the level of the eyes, or beyond the base of the ears. Ideally, there should be a white blaze on the forehead.

BREED COLORS

BICOLORS (AMBER-, BLUE-, ODD-EYED)
Auburn, Cream, with White
Black, Blue, Tortoiseshell, Blue-Cream, with White

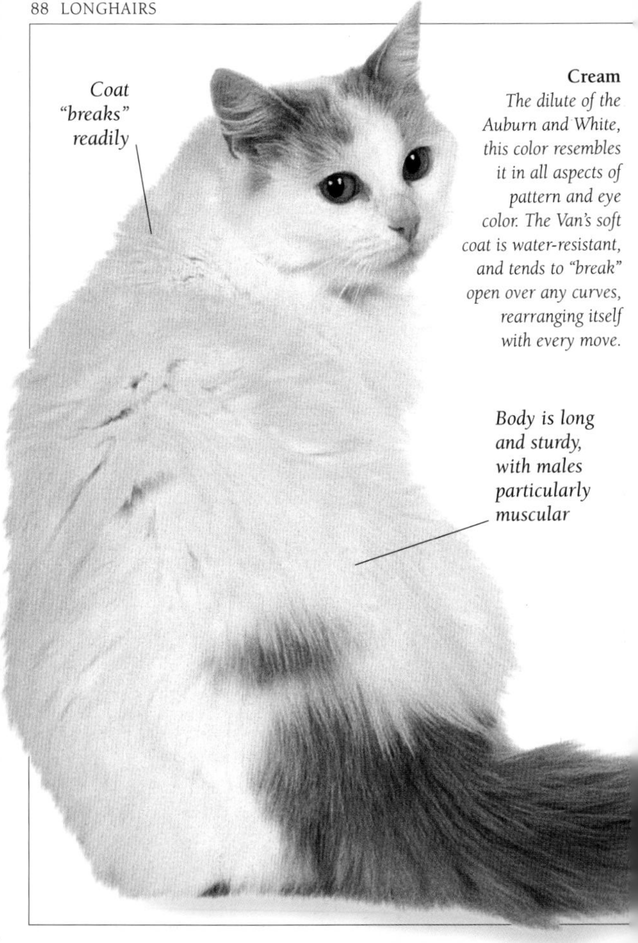
Coat "breaks" readily
Body is long and sturdy, with males particularly muscular

Cream
The dilute of the Auburn and White, this color resembles it in all aspects of pattern and eye color. The Van's soft coat is water-resistant, and tends to "break" open over any curves, rearranging itself with every move.

BREED HISTORY The modern history of this breed began when two cats were brought to Britain in 1955. The breed spread across Europe, but was not quickly accepted by registries. In 1982, Turkish Vans reached the United States, where they are accepted by CFA and TICA. In GCCF, only the auburn and the cream are allowed. Other registries allow black-based colors.

Auburn
This color is known as red in most other breeds; only in the Van does it have this more poetic name. This coat pattern, accompanied by amber eyes, was the original appearance of the Van when it arrived in the West. The coat should be chalk-white, the markings ideally confined to the top of the head and the tail.

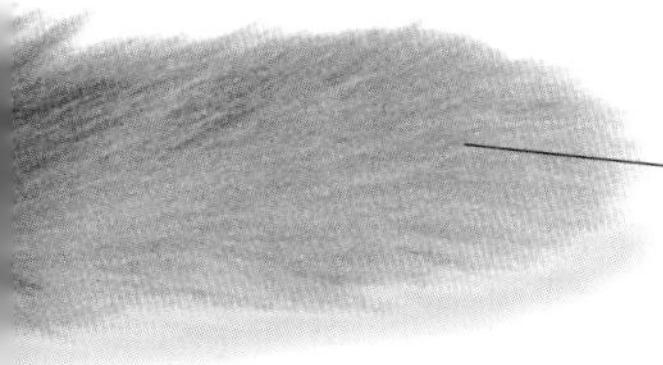

Tail is full brush, and as long as the body

Blue

Blue coloring can vary widely in depth, and this cat, an early Blue, is darker than most breed standards allow. Introducing new colors into the Van inevitably brought in some undesirable traits. The rich, golden eye color is a difficult quality to fix, and some green eyes have appeared.

KEY FACTS

DATE OF ORIGIN Pre-18th century

PLACE OF ORIGIN Lake Van region, Turkey

ANCESTRY Household cats

OUTCROSS BREEDS None

OTHER NAME Turkish swimming cats

WEIGHT RANGE 7–19 lb (3–8.5 kg)

TEMPERAMENT Self-possessed

Legs are medium length, with neat, rounded paws

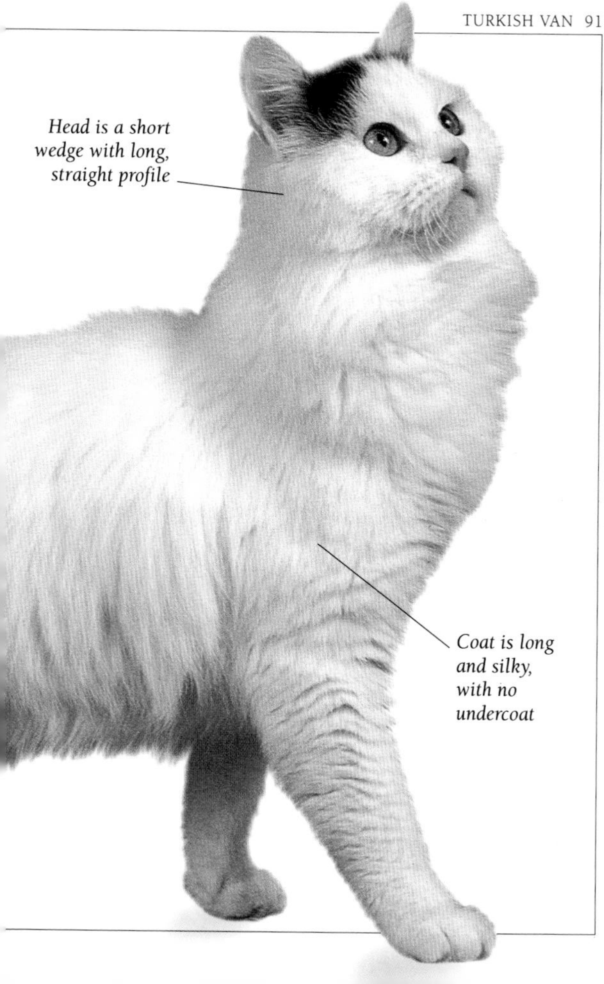
Head is a short wedge with long, straight profile
Coat is long and silky, with no undercoat

CYMRIC

Solid, and with a bunny-hop gait, this breed matches the original shorthaired Manx (*see page 176*) in all but coat, which is semi-long and double. Although the Cymric originated in North America, the name comes from "Cymru," the Welsh name for Wales, which is believed to have had its own strain of tailless cats. The breed is also known as the Longhaired Manx, but it is the more poetic name that has become established.

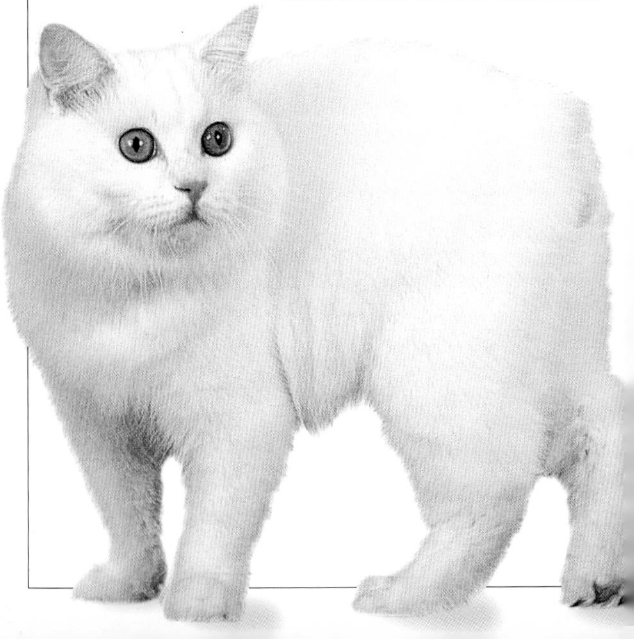

Breed History Although its name suggests a Welsh ancestry, this is an exclusively North American breed. Manx cats have always produced the occasional longhaired kittens: In the 1960s, breeders, including Blair Wright in Canada and Leslie Falteisek in the United States, worked to gain recognition for these longhaired variants. By the 1980s, CFA and TICA both recognized the cats as a separate breed with the name Cymric, but CFA has now reclassified them as Longhaired Manx. The breed is not recognized in Britain.

Orange-Eyed White

White Cymrics' eyes may be deep blue, brilliant copper, or one of each color. The coat should be pure white, with no hint of any yellowing, and no stray colored hairs should be present.

Breed Colors

SELF AND TORTIE
Black, Red, Blue, Cream, White, Tortoiseshell, Blue-Cream
All other self and tortie colors

SMOKE
Black, Blue
All other self and tortie colors

SHADED AND TIPPED
Shaded Silver, Chinchilla Silver
All other self and tortie colors

POINTED
All colors and patterns in pointed, sepia, and mink

TABBIES (CLASSIC, MACKEREL)
Brown, Red, Blue, Cream, Brown Patched, Blue Patched
Spotted and ticked patterns, all self and tortie colors

SILVER TABBIES
Silver, Patched Silver
All other standard tabby colors

BICOLORS (STANDARD AND VAN)
All self and tortie colors with white
All colors and patterns with white pointed

BLACK AND WHITE

CHOCOLATE (NOT CFA)

RED TABBY

BLUE

Brown Mackerel Tabby and White

The coat color and markings are relatively unimportant in the Cymric's points system. Most importantly, the Cymric should not have a tail, while it should be of a cobby appearance, and have a rounded head with prominent cheeks and whisker pads. Cymrics can take two years to develop the required deep flanks and rounded body.

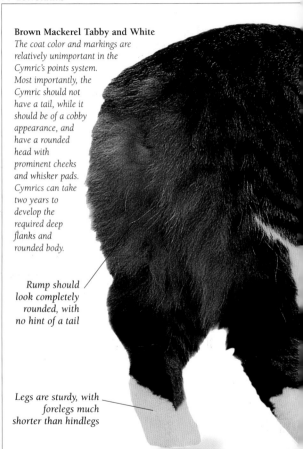

Rump should look completely rounded, with no hint of a tail
Legs are sturdy, with forelegs much shorter than hindlegs

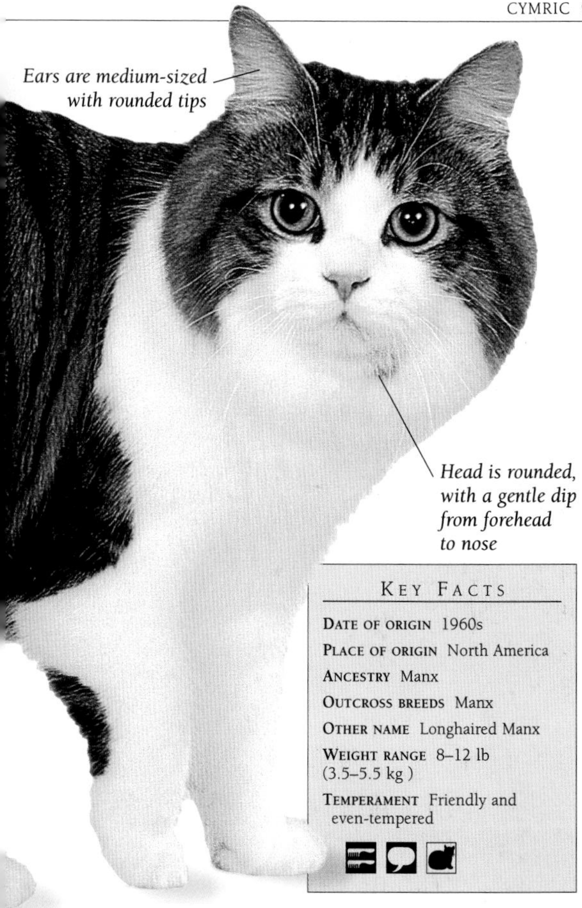
Ears are medium-sized with rounded tips
Head is rounded, with a gentle dip from forehead to nose

KEY FACTS

DATE OF ORIGIN 1960s

PLACE OF ORIGIN North America

ANCESTRY Manx

OUTCROSS BREEDS Manx

OTHER NAME Longhaired Manx

WEIGHT RANGE 8–12 lb (3.5–5.5 kg)

TEMPERAMENT Friendly and even-tempered

NEBELUNG

The silver-tipped, blue hair gives this breed a luminous elegance. Light reflects off the Nebelung's guard hairs, creating a misty incandescence. Only when you stroke the hair against the grain do you notice the solid blue ground color to the shafts of the guard hair and the down. This new breed, meaning German for "mist-creature," is based upon a "lost" strain of the Russian Blue (*see page 224*).

BREED COLORS
SELF COLORS Blue

Head is a modified wedge, with flat forehead and straight profile

Nebelung head

The face has a slight smile. The green eyes take time to develop, beginning as yellow in kittens. A green ring should appear around the pupil by four months, and the eyes should turn green with maturity.

BREED HISTORY Blue shorthairs and longhairs from Russia were exhibited over 100 years ago. Shorthairs became known as the Russian Blue, but the longhairs lost their separate identity. In 1986, Siegfried, the founding father of this revived breed, was mated to his longhaired sister, who produced blue kittens. The Nebelung was recognized as a breed by the TICA in 1987, and the CFA in 1993.

Ears are wide at the base, with slightly rounded tips

Eyes are widely spaced
Coat is fine, double, and medium length, with silver-tipped guard hairs

KEY FACTS

DATE OF ORIGIN 1986

PLACE OF ORIGIN United States

ANCESTRY Russian Blue

OUTCROSS BREEDS Russian Blue

OTHER NAME None

WEIGHT RANGE 6–11 lb (2.25–5 kg)

TEMPERAMENT Retiring

Body is lithe and slender, but not tubular

Blue

The Nebelung standard is very similar to that of the Russian Blue, calling for the same lithe appearance, the same silver tipping, and a semi-long version of the characteristic double coat.

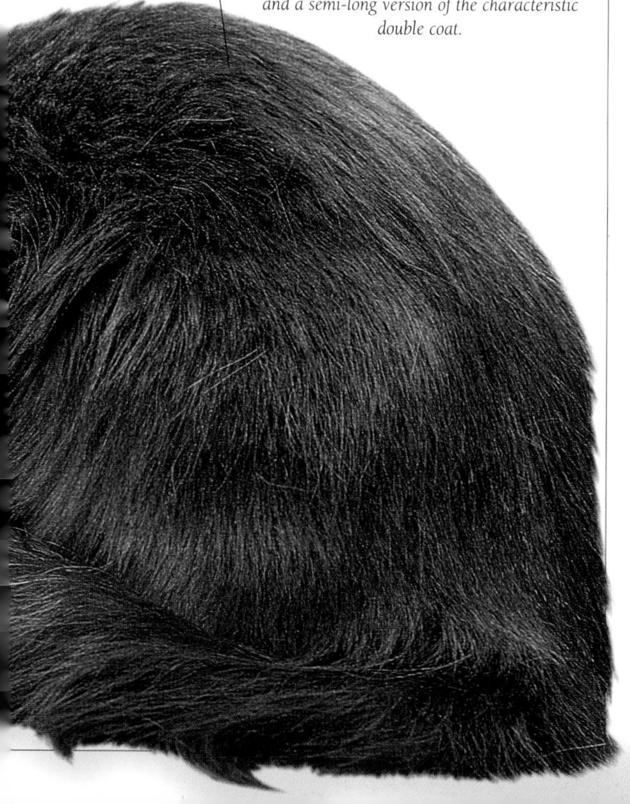

TURKISH ANGORA

Graceful and athletic, with fine bones and a silky coat, this is a breed that fits the fashions of today. It is a small to medium-sized cat with a muscular body, covered by a single coat that shimmers when it moves. Turkish Angoras come in all colors other than the Oriental shades. These cats are vivacious, quick-witted, and quick-moving. Some breeders still believe that they are descended from the wild Pallas' cat of central Asia. The story goes that Tartars domesticated the Pallas' cat and took it to Turkey, but this is very unlikely. The Turkish Angora's medium-long coat is probably the result of a mutation that occurred over centuries among isolated domestic cats in central Asia.

Tortoiseshell Smoke

Smoke Angoras were first documented in Britain in the latter part of the 19th century. Smoke Turkish Angoras should appear to be full-colored cats in repose, the undercoat only apparent with movement. The loss of the long coat in summer decreases the effect.

Turkish Angora head
The head is a smooth wedge, with the narrow muzzle continuing the lines without a pronounced pinch at the whisker pads. The eyes may be any color from copper through gold and green to blue.

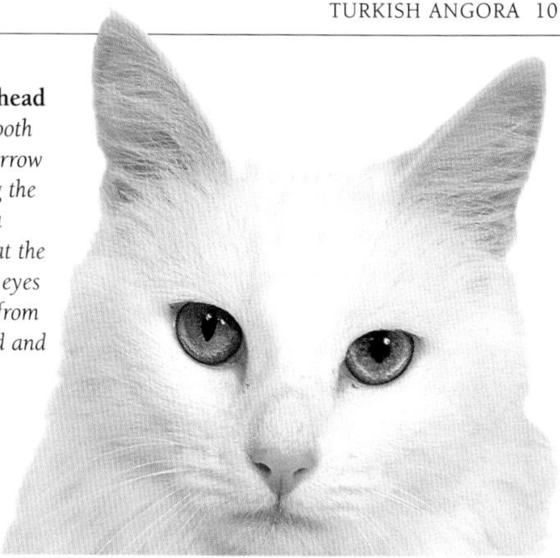

Breed Colors

SELF AND TORTIE COLORS
Black, Red, Blue, Cream, Tortie, Blue-Cream, White
All other self and tortie colors

SMOKE COLORS
As for self and tortie colors, except White

TABBY COLORS (CLASSIC, MACKEREL)
Brown, Red, Blue, Cream
Spotted and ticked patterns, all other self and tortie colors

SHADED COLORS
As for self and tortie colors, except White

SILVER TABBY COLORS (CLASSIC MACKEREL)
Silver
Spotted and ticked patterns, all other self and tortie colors

BICOLORS
All self and tortie colors with white
All other colors and patterns with white

RED

BLUE TABBY

BLUE-CREAM

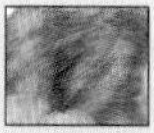

SHADED SILVER

Breed History Angoras from Turkey first reached France and Britain in the 17th century. By the beginning of this century, crossbreeding with other longhaired cats had led to the virtual extinction of the breed outside Turkey. The breed is said to have been saved through a breeding program at Ankara Zoo, although this may be a rather romanticized tale. Certainly, breeders in Sweden, Britain, and the United States imported Angoras after World War II from Turkey, where the breed is now protected.

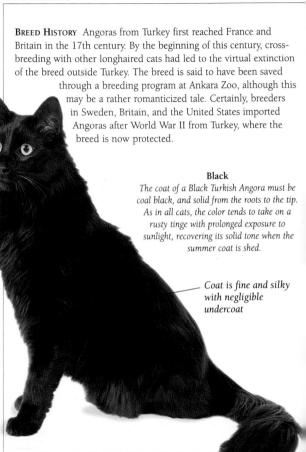

Black

The coat of a Black Turkish Angora must be coal black, and solid from the roots to the tip. As in all cats, the color tends to take on a rusty tinge with prolonged exposure to sunlight, recovering its solid tone when the summer coat is shed.

Coat is fine and silky with negligible undercoat

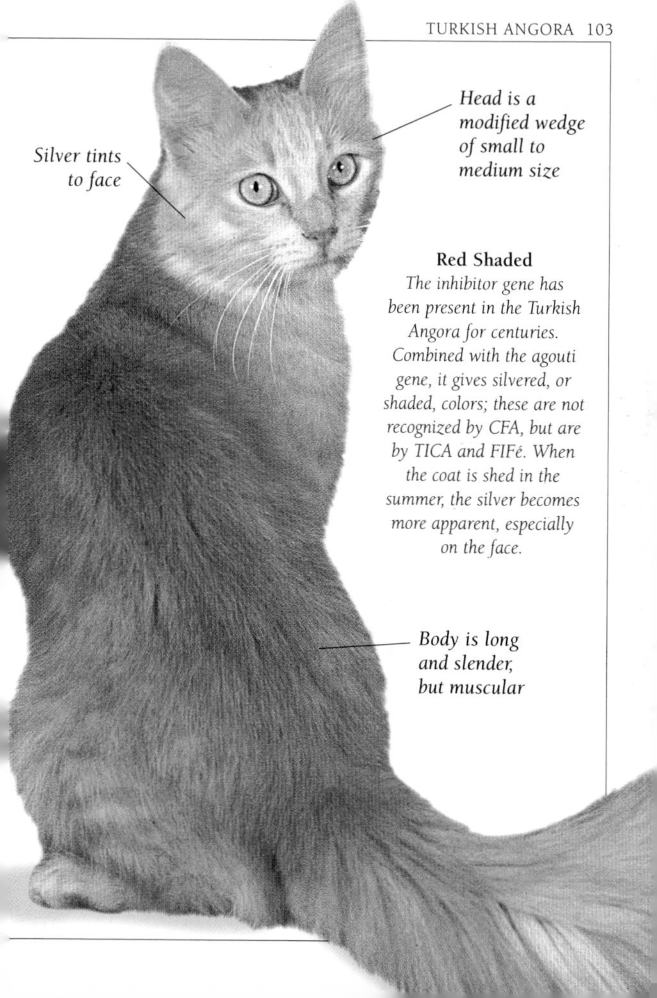
Silver tints to face
Head is a modified wedge of small to medium size
Body is long and slender, but muscular

Red Shaded

The inhibitor gene has been present in the Turkish Angora for centuries. Combined with the agouti gene, it gives silvered, or shaded, colors; these are not recognized by CFA, but are by TICA and FIFé. When the coat is shed in the summer, the silver becomes more apparent, especially on the face.

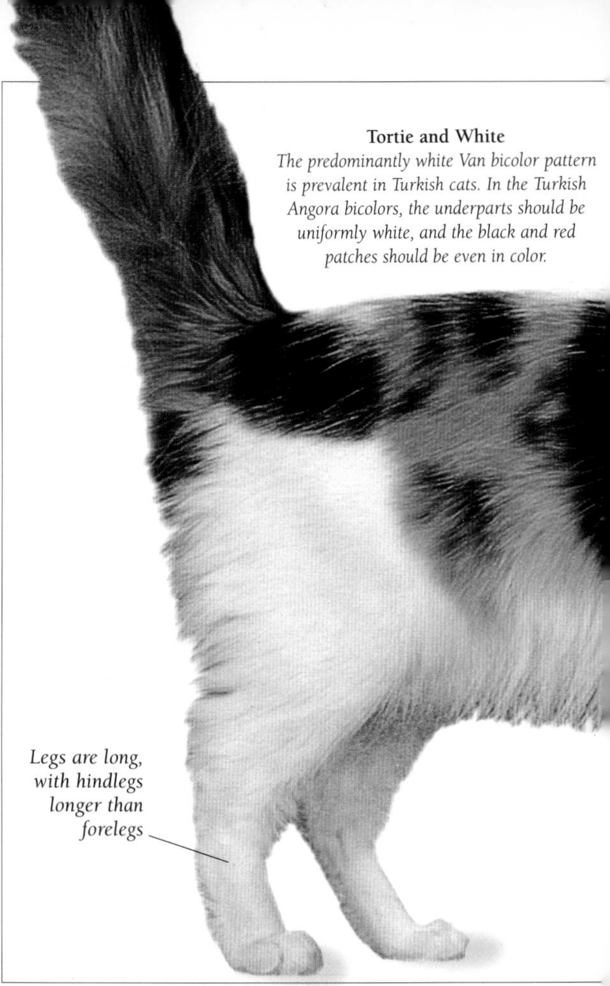

Tortie and White

The predominantly white Van bicolor pattern is prevalent in Turkish cats. In the Turkish Angora bicolors, the underparts should be uniformly white, and the black and red patches should be even in color.

Legs are long, with hindlegs longer than forelegs

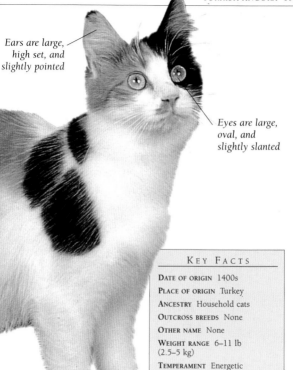

Ears are large, high set, and slightly pointed
Eyes are large, oval, and slightly slanted

Key Facts

Date of origin 1400s

Place of origin Turkey

Ancestry Household cats

Outcross breeds None

Other name None

Weight range 6–11 lb (2.5–5 kg)

Temperament Energetic exhibitionist

SOMALI

With its bushy tail and arched back, this cat is one of the world's most popular new breeds. Like its shorthaired Abyssinian forebear (*see page 232*), the Somali has a ticked coat: Each hair on its body has three to twelve bands of color. The bands are darker than the ground color and produce a vibrant shimmer when the cat is in full coat. The facial markings are striking, resembling theatrical eyeliner. Somalis are natural hunters and thrive in the outdoors.

Lilac

The Lilac's warm-toned coat has an oatmeal base with lilac-toned ticking; the paw pads and nose leather should be a matching mauvish pink.

Somali face
All Somalis have dark-rimmed eyes surrounded by "spectacles" of lighter hair, and show clear tabby markings on cheeks and forehead. This young Black Silver shows slight tarnishing, which should fade. Silver Somalis have white chests and underparts.

Full ruff is typical

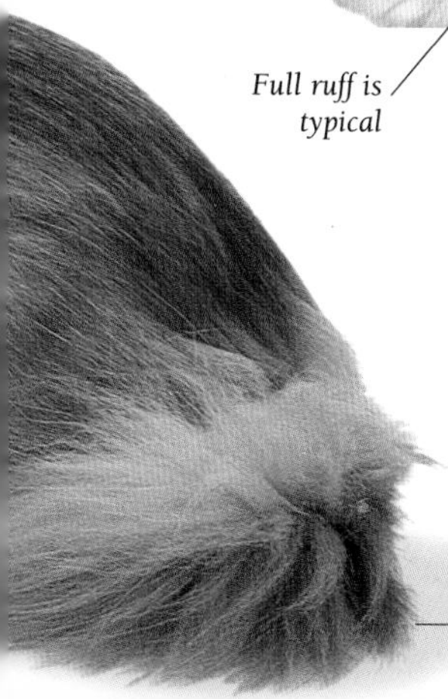

Breed Colors

TABBIES (TICKED)
Usual, Chocolate, Sorrel, Red, Blue, Lilac, Fawn, Cream, Usual Tortie, Chocolate Tortie, Sorrel Tortie, Blue Tortie, Lilac Tortie, Fawn Tortie

SILVER TABBIES (TICKED)
Colors are as for self and tortie

BLUE

SORREL

CREAM

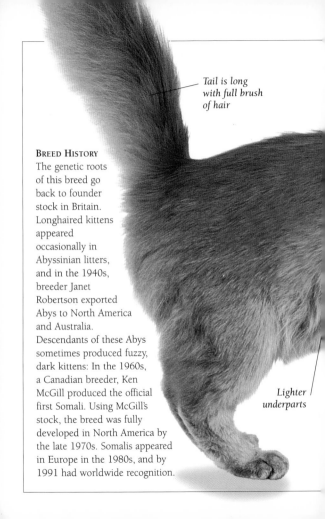

Tail is long with full brush of hair
Lighter underparts

Breed History

The genetic roots of this breed go back to founder stock in Britain. Longhaired kittens appeared occasionally in Abyssinian litters, and in the 1940s, breeder Janet Robertson exported Abys to North America and Australia. Descendants of these Abys sometimes produced fuzzy, dark kittens: In the 1960s, a Canadian breeder, Ken McGill produced the official first Somali. Using McGill's stock, the breed was fully developed in North America by the late 1970s. Somalis appeared in Europe in the 1980s, and by 1991 had worldwide recognition.

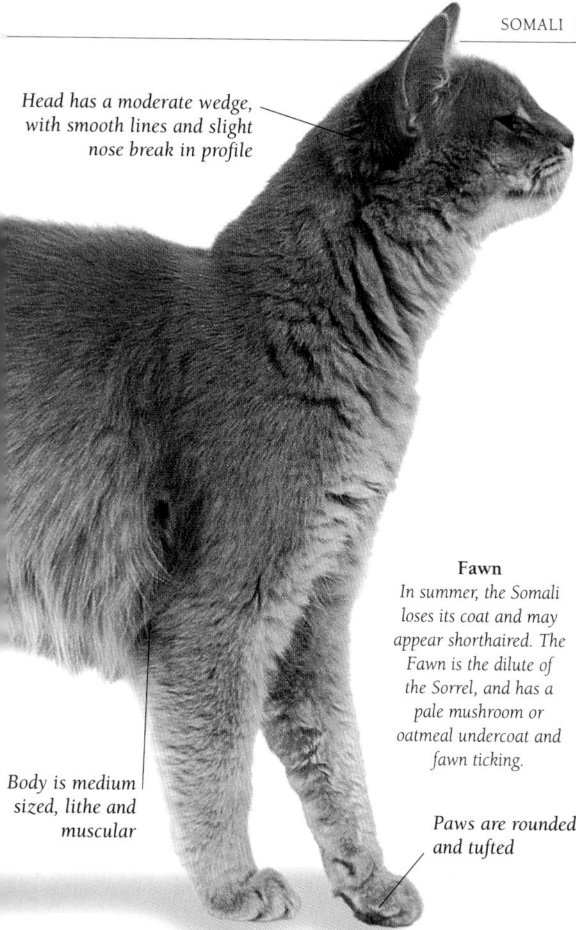

Head has a moderate wedge, with smooth lines and slight nose break in profile
Body is medium sized, lithe and muscular
Paws are rounded and tufted

Fawn

In summer, the Somali loses its coat and may appear shorthaired. The Fawn is the dilute of the Sorrel, and has a pale mushroom or oatmeal undercoat and fawn ticking.

Key Facts

Date of origin 1963

Place of origin Canada and the United States

Ancestry Abyssinian

Outcross breeds None

Other name Longhaired Abyssinian

Weight range 8–12 lb (3.5–5.5 kg)

Temperament Quiet but extroverted

Ticking has at least three dark bands on each hair

Usual or Ruddy

Called Ruddy in North America, this was one of the first colors to be accepted for showing. The base coat is a red-brown shade of apricot, while the ticking is black. The body type, together with the full coat, have earned the breed the nickname of "fox cat."

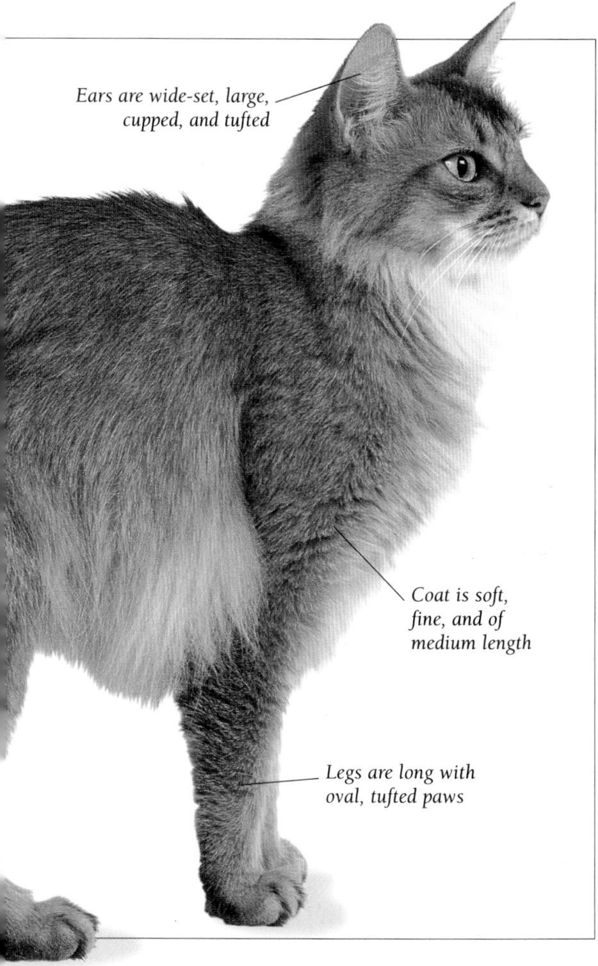
Ears are wide-set, large, cupped, and tufted
Coat is soft, fine, and of medium length
Legs are long with oval, tufted paws

CHANTILLY/TIFFANY

Still extremely rare, the Chantilly has a moderate disposition, neither as quiet as a Persian nor as active as Oriental-type longhairs. The Chantilly will communicate happiness with an endearing "chirp," that sounds like a pigeon cooing; once you have been chirped at, you become addicted to this pleasurable sound. Although the first examples of the breed were deep chocolate in color, the Chantilly comes in the whole range of colors, as well as tabby patterns. This is a late bloomer: The medium length, single coat is not fully mature until two to three years of age.

BREED COLORS

SELF AND COLORS
Chocolate, Cinnamon, Blue, Lilac, Fawn

TABBY COLORS (MACKEREL, SPOTTED, AND TICKED)
Colors are as for self colors

Chocolate Tabby kitten
Although this breed is usually described in terms of self colors, tabbies are also bred. Kittens can take some time to show their potential; eye color in particular can take years to reach its full intensity.

BREED HISTORY This companionable and undemanding breed is not as new as its recent fame suggests, but its history is beset by confusion. In 1967, in New York, Jennie Robinson purchased a pair of longhaired cats of unknown background, although the color implied a Birman parentage. Signe Lund, a Florida breeder, bought the cats, and coined the name Tiffany. As she also bred Burmese, the association with that breed was inadvertently perpetuated. In 1988, in Alberta, Canada, Tracy Oraas reestablished the breed, concluding that they were probably an offshoot of the Angora (*see page 132*).

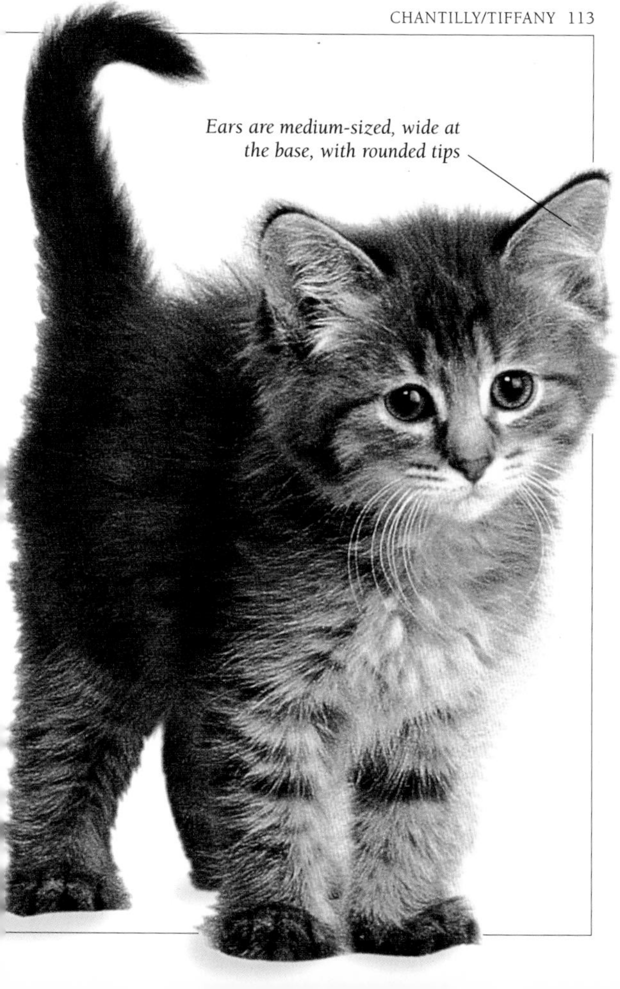
Ears are medium-sized, wide at the base, with rounded tips

KEY FACTS

DATE OF ORIGIN 1970s

PLACE OF ORIGIN Canada and the United States

ANCESTRY Uncertain

OUTCROSS BREEDS Angora, Havana Brown, Nebelung, Somali

OTHER NAME Tiffany, Foreign Longhair

WEIGHT RANGE 6–12 lb (2.5–5.5 kg)

TEMPERAMENT Gentle and conservative

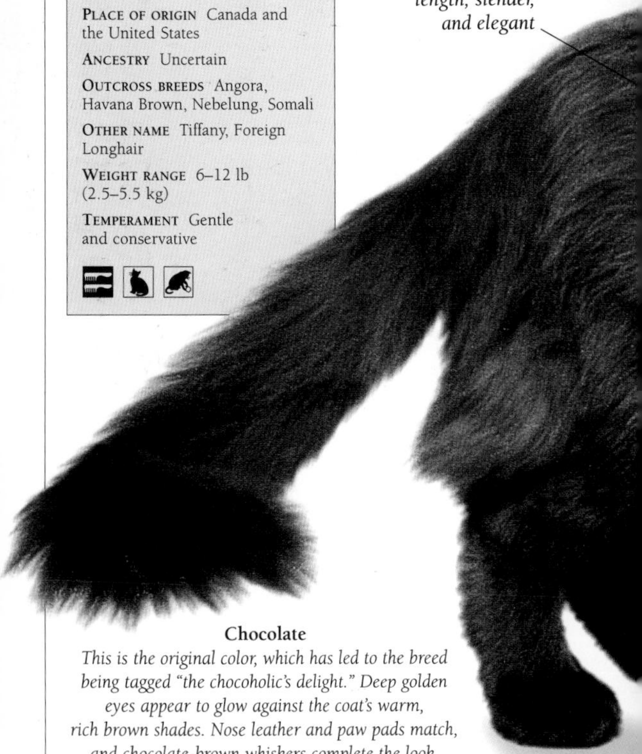
Body is medium length, slender, and elegant

Chocolate

This is the original color, which has led to the breed being tagged "the chocoholic's delight." Deep golden eyes appear to glow against the coat's warm, rich brown shades. Nose leather and paw pads match, and chocolate-brown whiskers complete the look.

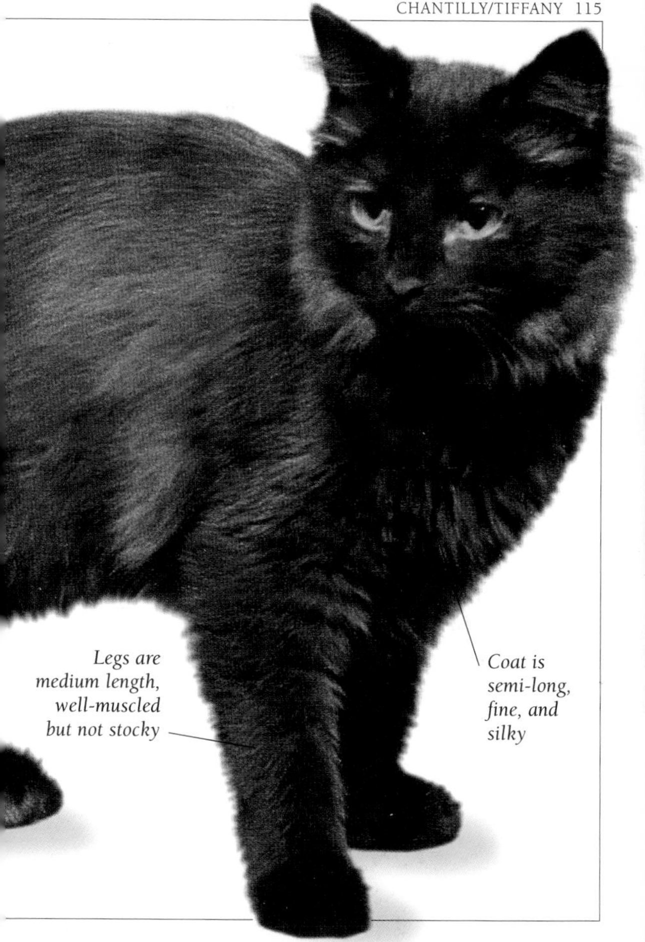

Legs are medium length, well-muscled but not stocky
Coat is semi-long, fine, and silky

TIFFANIE

Although sometimes confused with their namesakes from North America (*see page 112*), Tiffanies have nothing to do with that breed. Essentially longhaired Asians (*see page 254*), they are descended, in well-recorded breeding programs, from Chinchilla Persians (*see page 16*) and Burmese (*see page 262*). Tiffanies take after their longhaired forbears only in coat; the conformation is Burmese. In temperament, they combine the traits of their parent breeds to great advantage, with more liveliness than the average Persian and more restraint than the Burmese: The breed standard lays stress on good temperament. An easygoing, easy-to-care for longhair, the Tiffanie deserves wider popularity.

BREED COLORS

SELF COLORS (SOLID, SEPIA)
Black, Chocolate, Red, Blue, Lilac, Cream, Caramel, Apricot, Black Tortie, Chocolate Tortie, Blue Tortie, Lilac Tortie, Caramel Tortie

SHADED COLORS (SOLID, SEPIA)
Colors are as for self colors

TABBIES (SOLID, SEPIA, ALL PATTERNS)
Brown, Chocolate, Red, Blue, Lilac, Cream, Caramel, Apricot, Black Tortie, Chocolate Tortie, Blue Tortie, Lilac Tortie, Caramel Tortie

Coat is semi-long, fine, and silky

Brown

This color is one of those often confused with the Chantilly/Tiffany. Although it looks like a very dark chocolate, the color is in fact black, slightly degraded by the sepia pointing pattern; it is called Sable in the Burmese. Sepia pointing is allowed in self Tiffanies; the long coat prevents their being mistaken for Burmese.

Head is a short wedge with a distinct nose-break in profile

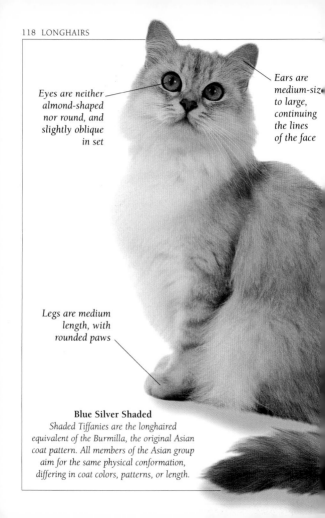

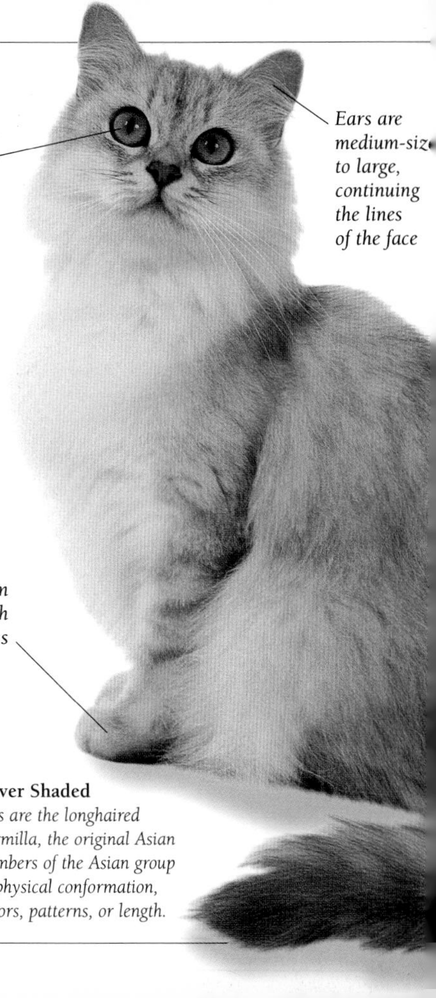

Eyes are neither almond-shaped nor round, and slightly oblique in set
Ears are medium-siz
to large, continuing the lines of the face
Legs are medium length, with rounded paws

Blue Silver Shaded

Shaded Tiffanies are the longhaired equivalent of the Burmilla, the original Asian coat pattern. All members of the Asian group aim for the same physical conformation, differing in coat colors, patterns, or length.

Breed History The Tiffanie, essentially a longhaired Burmese, is the only longhaired member of the Asian breed group. This group's origins can be traced back to an accidental mating, in London in 1981, of a Chinchilla Persian and a Lilac Burmese belonging to Baroness Miranda von Kirchberg. The first-generation offspring were shorthaired, shaded Burmillas, but subsequent breedings inevitably brought the recessive longhair and sepia pointing genes back to the surface. The breed group was developed with the help and support of Burmese breeders, and remains quite distinct from this breed. There are two distinct threads in the Asian group, however: FIFé cats come from some of the same lines as GCCF cats, but more diverse lines are now used in Britain.

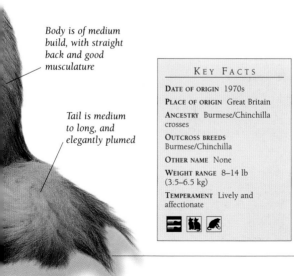

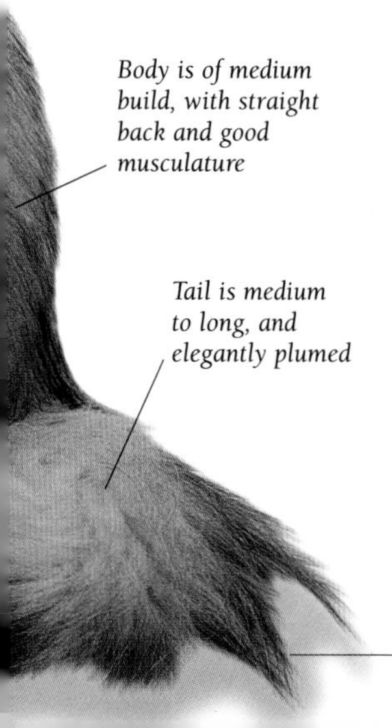
Body is of medium build, with straight back and good musculature
Tail is medium to long, and elegantly plumed

Key Facts

Date of origin 1970s

Place of origin Great Britain

Ancestry Burmese/Chinchilla crosses

Outcross breeds Burmese/Chinchilla

Other name None

Weight range 8–14 lb (3.5–6.5 kg)

Temperament Lively and affectionate

BALINESE

Slender, fine-boned, and refined as royalty in appearance, the Balinese is in fact an intensely social breed, happiest when it is underfoot or at the center of activity. Highly inquisitive, it is indefatigable in its investigation of vacuum cleaners, cupboards, and shopping bags. Its tubular body permits it to accomplish Houdini-like acts of contortion: Veterinarians know that, like the Siamese (*see page 280*), this is a superb escape artist, seemingly able to pick locks. The Balinese is an energy burner, and needs both mental and physical stimulation. A typical pointed cat, it does not have dramatically long hair, and from a distance some might be mistaken for a Siamese, except for the graceful plume of the tail.

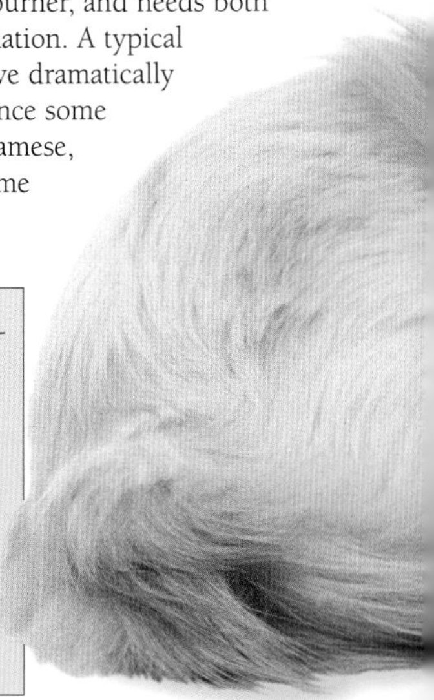

BREED COLORS

BALINESE POINT COLORS
Seal, Chocolate, Blue, Lilac

JAVANESE POINT COLORS (IN CFA)
Red, Cream, tortie and tabby versions in all colors
Cinnamon, Fawn, Smoke, Silver and particolor versions

RED TABBY

BLUE TORTIE

Lilac Point

The dilute version of the Chocolate, the Lilac Point is a study in delicacy. The warm, magnolia coat may bear soft lilac shading, while the nose leather and paw pads are pinkish or faded lilac to tone with the points. As in all the colors, the eyes should be a clear, vivid, and brilliant blue. This color is also generally called Lilac Point in the various North American associations, although it has also been called Lavender Point and even Frost Point.

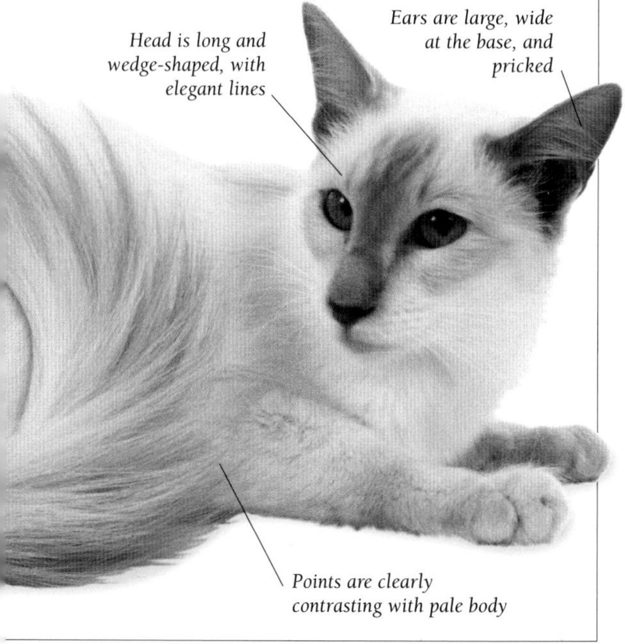

Head is long and wedge-shaped, with elegant lines
Ears are large, wide at the base, and pricked
Points are clearly contrasting with pale body

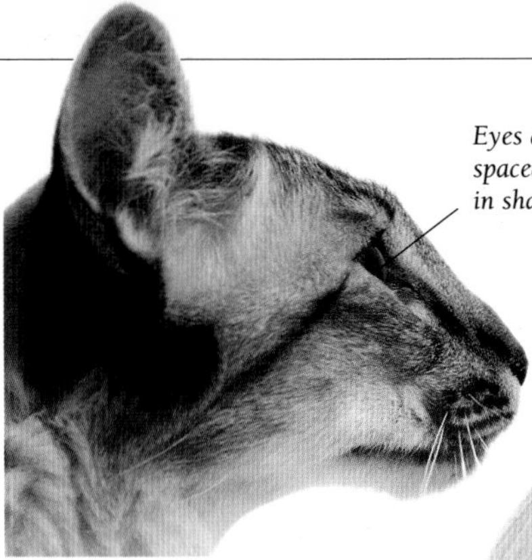
Eyes are widely spaced, and Oriental in shape and set

Balinese head
From the front, the Balinese face is wide between the ears, narrowing in straight lines to a fine muzzle. Seen in profile, the nose should be straight and the chin strong. This Seal Tortie Point has a fully developed mask.

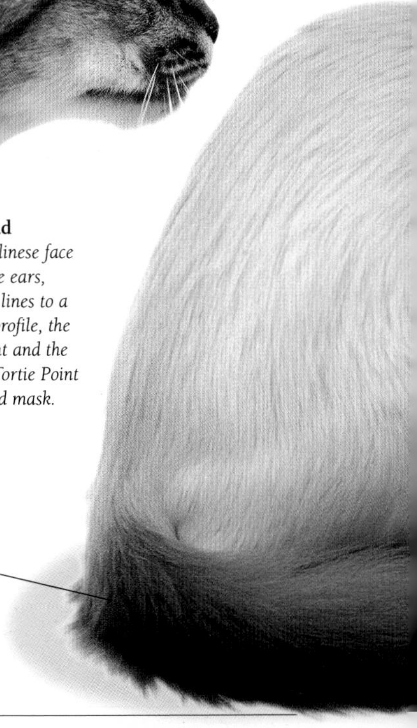
Tail is long and plumed

Blue Point

The standard for the Blue calls for a body of glacial white, with points and any shading on the back to be a cold blue. The nose leather must also be blue. It should not be possible to mistake a Blue Point for a Lilac Point in any respect.

This Blue Tabby Point shows clear facial markings in the mask
Coat is medium-long, fine, and silky, lying flat
Paws are small and oval, with pads to match points

Seal Point

Points of an even, deep brown and a soft shading of fawn on the body characterize the Seal Point. The Seal is less warm than the Chocolate.

KEY FACTS

DATE OF ORIGIN 1950s

PLACE OF ORIGIN United States

ANCESTRY Longhaired Siamese

OUTCROSS BREEDS Siamese in the United States, Angora in Britain

OTHER NAME Some colors called Javanese in the United States

WEIGHT RANGE 2.5–5 kg (6–11 lb)

TEMPERAMENT Energetic and exhibitionist

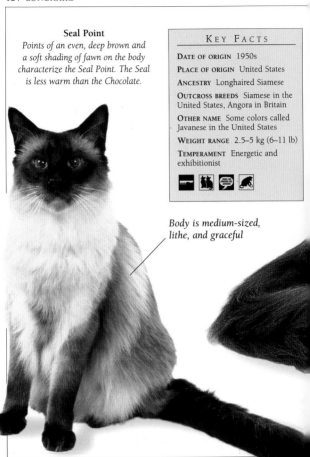

Body is medium-sized, lithe, and graceful

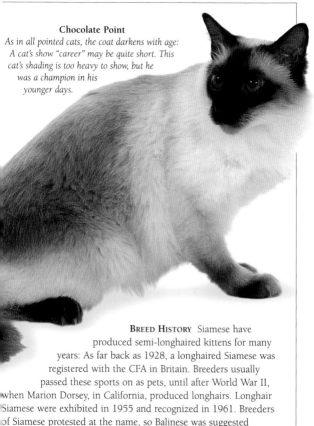

Chocolate Point

As in all pointed cats, the coat darkens with age: A cat's show "career" may be quite short. This cat's shading is too heavy to show, but he was a champion in his younger days.

Breed History Siamese have produced semi-longhaired kittens for many years: As far back as 1928, a longhaired Siamese was registered with the CFA in Britain. Breeders usually passed these sports on as pets, until after World War II, when Marion Dorsey, in California, produced longhairs. Longhair Siamese were exhibited in 1955 and recognized in 1961. Breeders of Siamese protested at the name, so Balinese was suggested because the cats reminded a breeder of Balinese dancers.

NEWER BALINESE

Originally, only seal, blue, chocolate, and lilac points were recognized in the Balinese and Siamese: Breeders have worked to create the other colors and patterned points we know today. In Britain and Australia, the name Balinese encompasses all colors and patterns. However, the CFA in North America still recognizes only the four "traditional" colors in these breeds. Other colors, such as red and cream, and the tabby and tortie patterns, are classed as separate breeds. The longhairs are called Javanese in North America, while the shorthairs are known as Colorpoint Shorthairs.

Chocolate Tortie Point

Chocolate Tortie Point patches are a mixture of light chocolate and varying shades of red; larger red areas may show faint tabby marks.

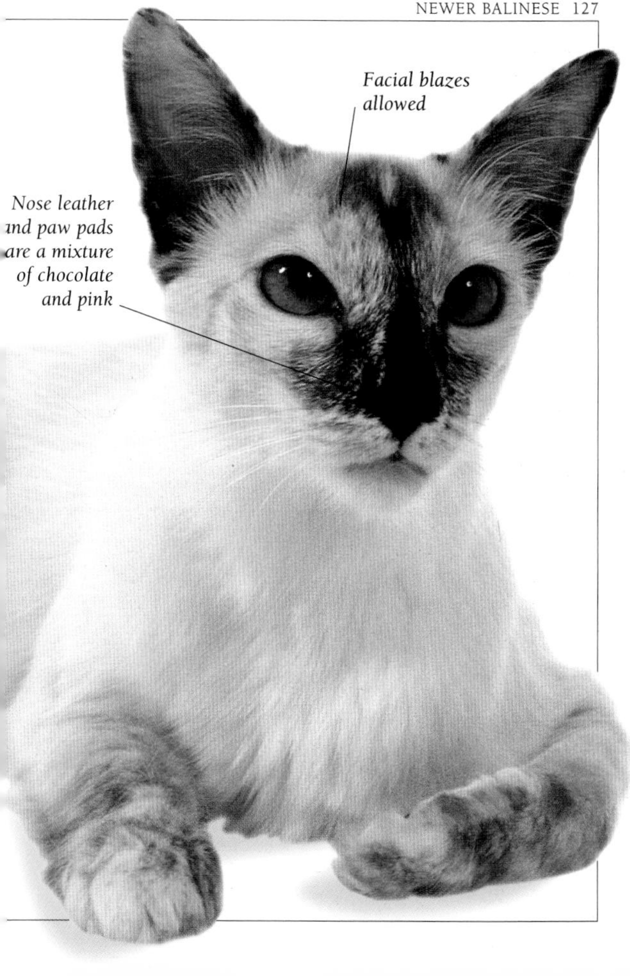
Facial blazes allowed
Nose leather and paw pads are a mixture of chocolate and pink

Seal Tabby Point

The Seal Tabby Point is noticeably shaded, with a cream body shading to a warm fawn color over the back. There should be no vestige of tabby markings on the body. The legs, tail, and face should show clear tabby markings.

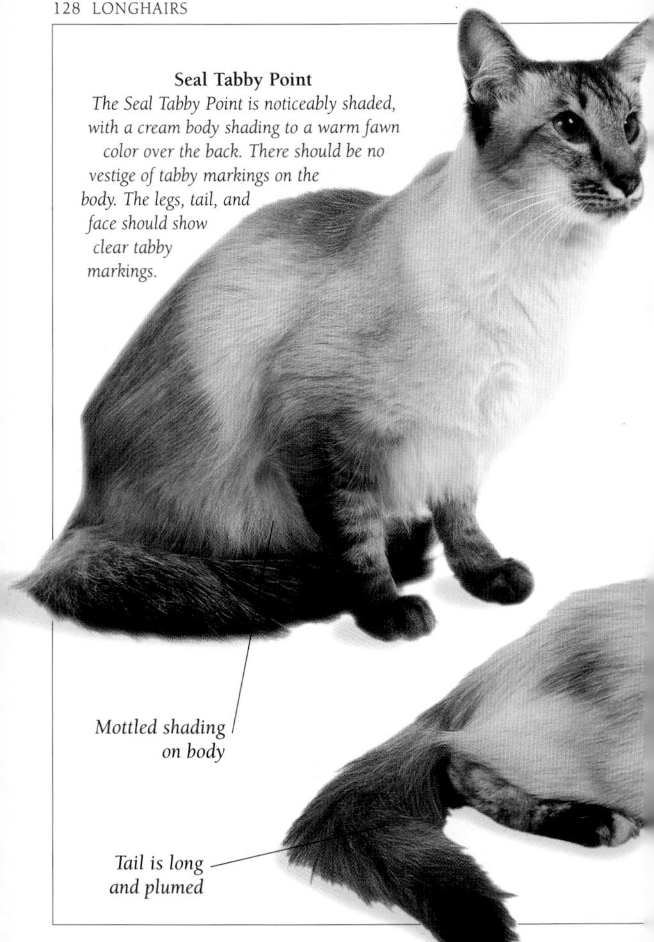
Mottled shading on body
Tail is long and plumed

Blue Tabby Point

A Blue Point must have a blue nose, but a Blue Tabby Point may have a pink nose outlined in blue. The eyes must follow the same standard as self points. The "thumb" marks on the backs of the ears may be less apparent in a Blue Tabby Point than in other tabby points.

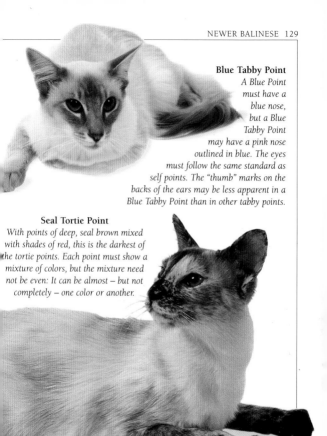

Seal Tortie Point

With points of deep, seal brown mixed with shades of red, this is the darkest of the tortie points. Each point must show a mixture of colors, but the mixture need not be even: It can be almost – but not completely – one color or another.

Seal Tortie Tabby Point

All points of a Tortie Tabby Point must show both tabby marks and mingled colors, and body shading should be uneven, as in tabby points. In tabby points and tortie tabby points, the color is not judged as strictly as it is in the self points: Variety of tone is acceptable.

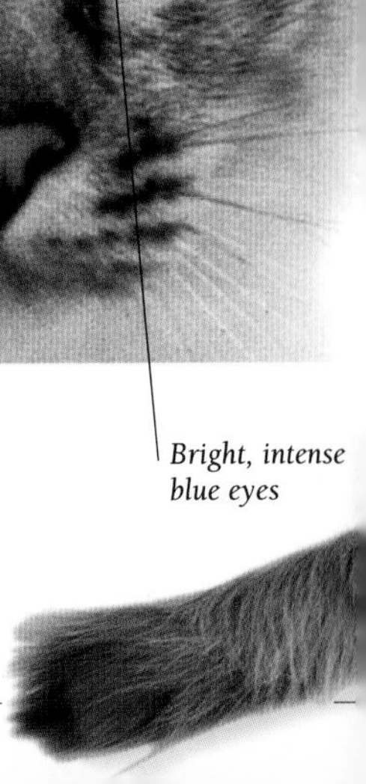

Chocolate Tabby Point

Tabby points must show clear facial markings, with distinctly spotted whisker pads and dark-rimmed eyes. The legs and tail should also be barred or ringed, but it is not possible to distinguish which tabby pattern is present on a pointed cat. Tabby points are called lynx points in North America.

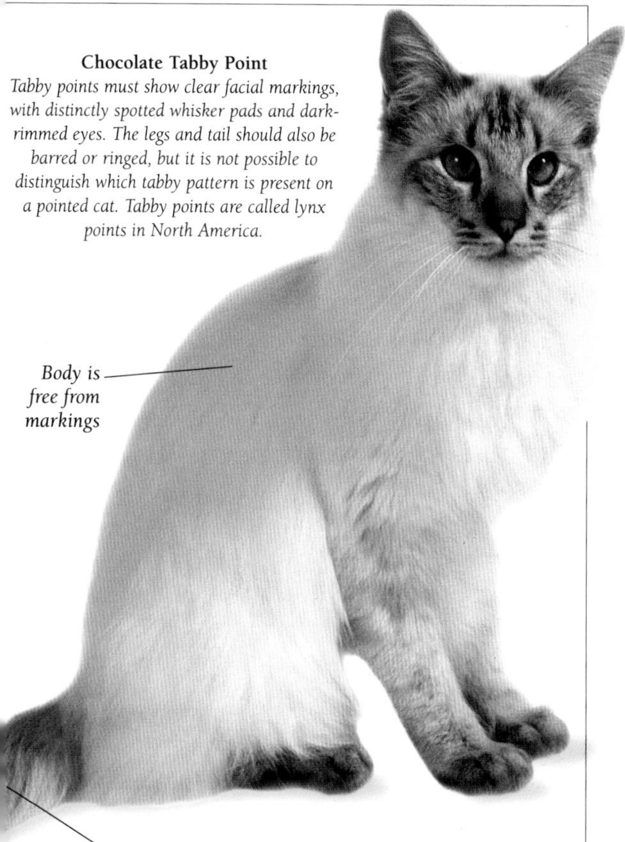
Body is free from markings
Tail is barred or ringed

ANGORA (BRITISH)

The Angora is similar in temperament to other Oriental breeds – lively and inquisitive, and long and lean, with a tail that forms an elegant plume. The fine, silky coat has no woolly undercoat, so this cat is easy to groom. Siamese (*see page 280*), Balinese (*see page 120*), and Oriental Shorthairs (*see page 292*), are all permitted outcrosses in Angora pedigrees. The Angora breed suffers from a profusion of confusing names. Unrelated to the Turkish Angora (*see page 100*), it is called the Javanese in mainland Europe to avoid confusion; however, some North American associations use Javanese for some colors of Balinese. In North America, the Angora has also been called the Oriental Longhair, implying that it is descended from the Oriental Shorthair. However, there is now an Oriental Longhair (*see page 138*) with that descent.

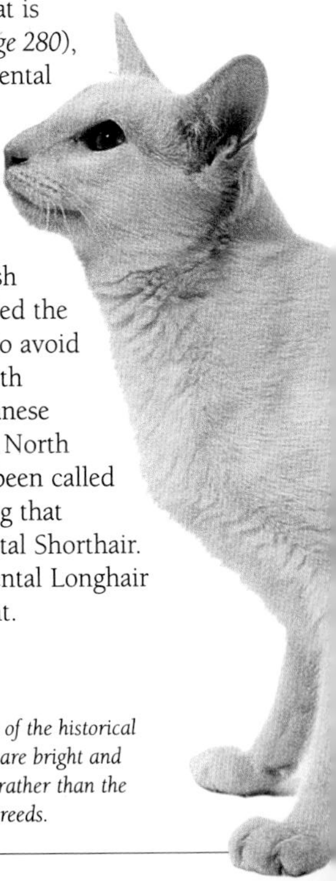

Blue-Eyed White

To many people, this is the classic color of the historical Angora, or French cat. The blue eyes are bright and vivid, similar to those of the Siamese, rather than the paler baby-blue of Western breeds.

Breed Colors

SELF AND TORTIE COLORS
Black, Chocolate, Cinnamon, Red, Blue, Lilac, Fawn, Cream, Caramel, Apricot, White (Blue-, Green-, Odd-Eyed), Tortoiseshell, Chocolate Tortoiseshell, Cinnamon Tortoiseshell, Blue Tortoiseshell, Lilac Tortoiseshell, Fawn Tortoiseshell, Caramel Tortoiseshell

SMOKE, SHADED, SILVER SHADED, AND TIPPED
Colors are as for self and tortie colors, with the exception of White

TABBIES (ALL PATTERNS)
Brown, Chocolate, Cinnamon, Red, Blue, Lilac, Fawn, Cream, Caramel, Tortie, Chocolate Tortie, Cinnamon Tortie, Blue Tortie, Lilac Tortie, Fawn Tortie, Caramel Tortie

SILVER TABBY COLORS (ALL PATTERNS)
Colors are as for standard tabbies

CHOCOLATE TORTIE TABBY

CINNAMON TORTIE TABBY

CARAMEL TORTIE

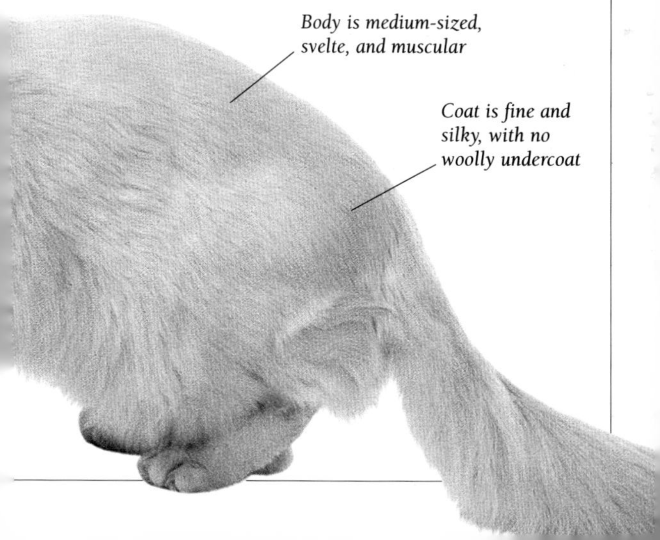
Body is medium-sized, svelte, and muscular
Coat is fine and silky, with no woolly undercoat

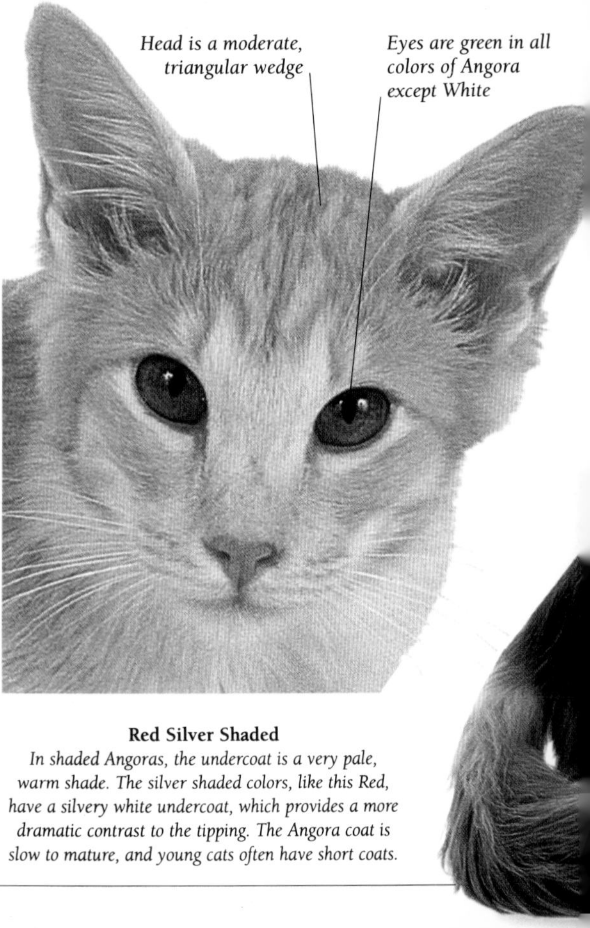
Head is a moderate, triangular wedge
Eyes are green in all colors of Angora except White

Red Silver Shaded

In shaded Angoras, the undercoat is a very pale, warm shade. The silver shaded colors, like this Red, have a silvery white undercoat, which provides a more dramatic contrast to the tipping. The Angora coat is slow to mature, and young cats often have short coats.

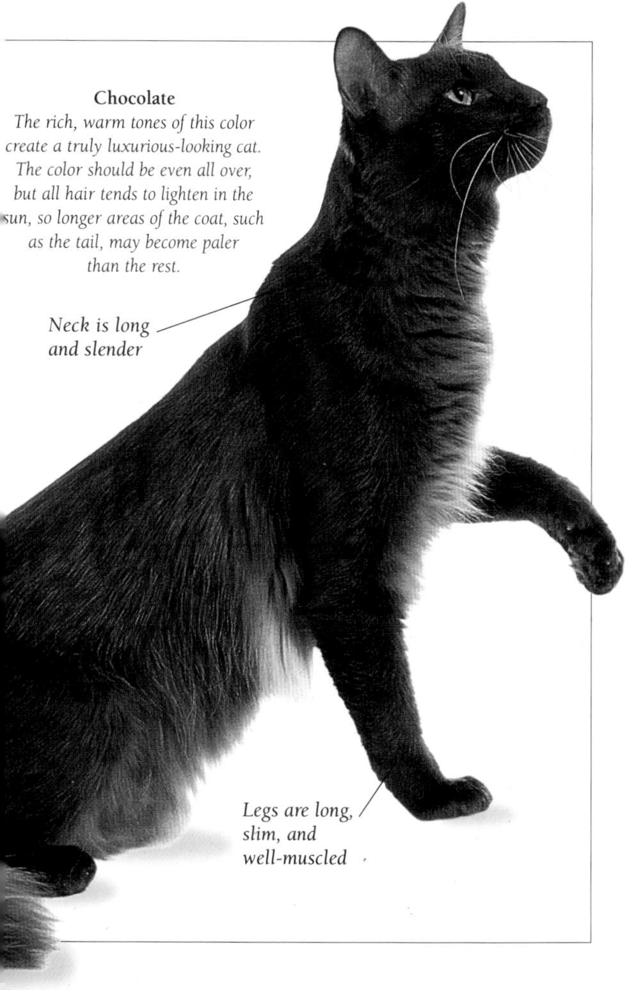
Neck is long and slender
Legs are long, slim, and well-muscled

Chocolate

The rich, warm tones of this color create a truly luxurious-looking cat. The color should be even all over, but all hair tends to lighten in the sun, so longer areas of the coat, such as the tail, may become paler than the rest.

Key Facts

Date of origin 1970s

Place of origin Britain

Ancestry Siamese/Abyssinian crosses

Outcross breeds Siamese, Balinese, Oriental Shorthair

Other name Javanese (Europe), previously Oriental Longhair (United States), Mandarin

Weight range 5–11 lb (2.5–5.5 kg)

Temperament Energetic exhibitionist

Cinnamon

The first Angora, Cuckoo, *was a Cinnamon. The gene for this color came from the Abyssinian parentage, where it is known as Sorrel. The tone should be warm, and eye rims and nose leather should match the coat.*

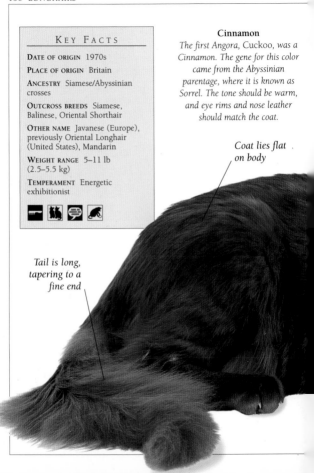

Coat lies flat on body
Tail is long, tapering to a fine end

Breed History The Angora was developed in Britain by Maureen Silson, who mated a Sorrel Abyssinian (*see page 232*) to a Seal Point Siamese in the mid-1960s, attempting to produce a Siamese with ticked points. The descendants inherited both the cinnamon trait, producing cinnamon Oriental Shorthairs, and also the gene for long hair, which led to the creation of the Angora. Descendants of this mating resulted in the majority of today's British Angoras. The breed is not related to the 19th-century Angora, or to the revived Turkish Angora.

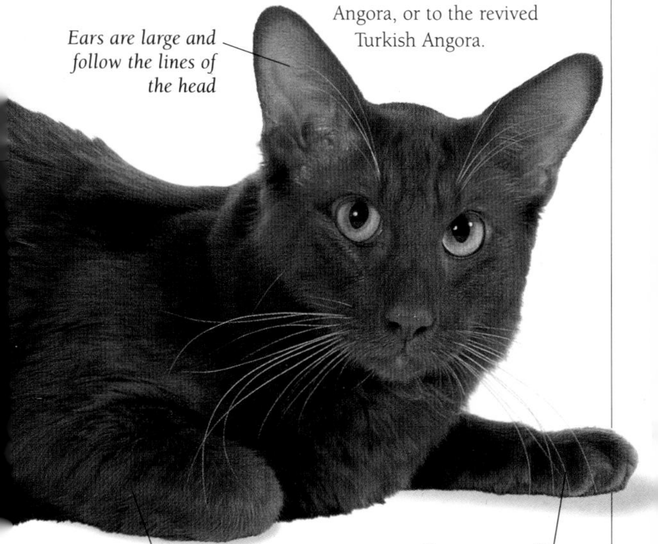
Ears are large and follow the lines of the head
Forelegs are shorter than hindlegs
Paws are small and oval

Oriental Longhair

This beautiful, fully colored, semi-longhaired version of the Oriental Shorthair completes the quartet of Oriental breeds. Just as the Siamese (*see page 242*) has a semi-longhair counterpart in the Balinese (*see page 120*), the Oriental Shorthair (*see page 292*) has its own silky alternative in the Oriental Longhair. The coat of the Oriental Longhair lacks an undercoat and tends to lie flat against the body. In summer, but for the plumed tail, it can look similar to shorthairs. This breed reflects its family in all respects: It bears the colors of the Oriental, and the soft coat and plumed tail of the Balinese.

Breed Colors

All colors and patterns, except pointed, sepia, and mink.
All colors and patterns, including pointed, sepia, and mink

BLUE TORTIE TABBY

FAWN AND WHITE

WHITE

BLACK

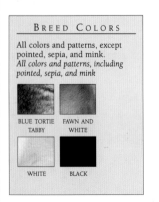

Chestnut

In North America, the colors in the Oriental Longhair breed follow the naming conventions of the Oriental Shorthair. In Britain, Orientals of this color are called Havanas, while in other breeds the color is called chocolate. The coats of Chestnut cats should be a rich, warm brown, somewhat redder than is usual for chocolate.

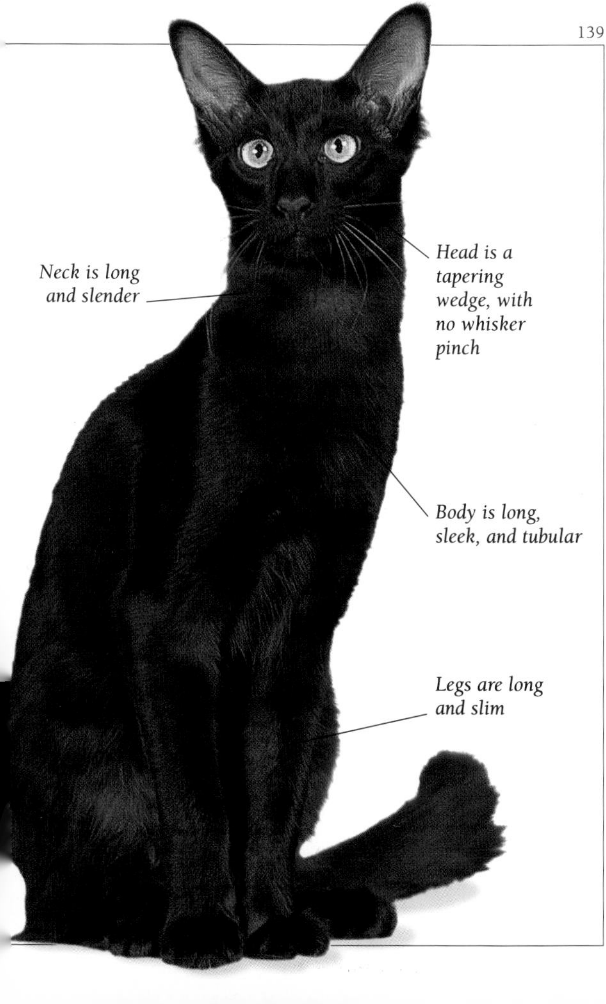
Neck is long and slender
Head is a tapering wedge, with no whisker pinch
Body is long, sleek, and tubular
Legs are long and slim

Breed History In spite of the efforts of breeders to control matings, cats still manage to spring some surprises. In 1985, an Oriental Shorthair and a Balinese at Sheryl Ann Boyle's Sholine cattery conspired to produce a litter of silky, semi-longhaired Orientals. These kittens were much too attractive to be ignored; The breed was then developed, and is now recognized by both TICA and CFA. As with Oriental Shorthairs, the breed associations differ as to the status of pointed kittens. There may occasionally be some confusion in name between this cat and the Angora (see page 132), which has in the past been called an Oriental Longhair in North America; visually and historically, the two are quite distinct.

Key Facts

Date of origin 1985

Place of origin North America

Ancestry Oriental Shorthair, Balinese

Outcross breeds Siamese, Balinese, Oriental Shorthair

Other name None

Weight range 10–13 lb (4.5–6 kg)

Temperament Friendly and inquisitive

Chestnut Silver-Ticked Tabby
The ticked pattern should show clear tabby markings on the face, legs, and tail, and at least one necklace. Silvering reduces the amount of color, and the contrast between the topcoat and undercoat may outshine the ticking's shimmer.

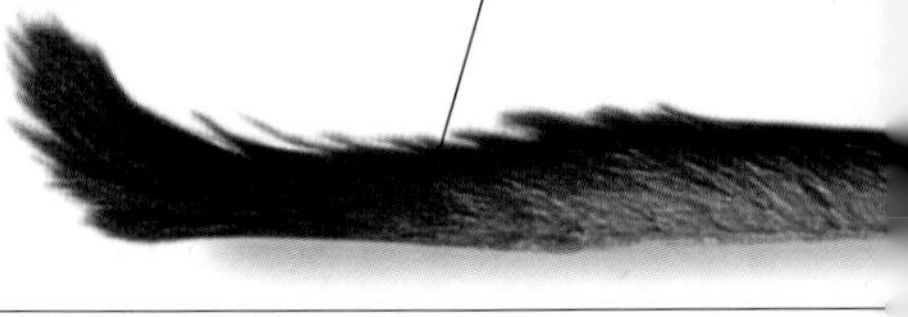
Tail is long, tapering, and softly plumed

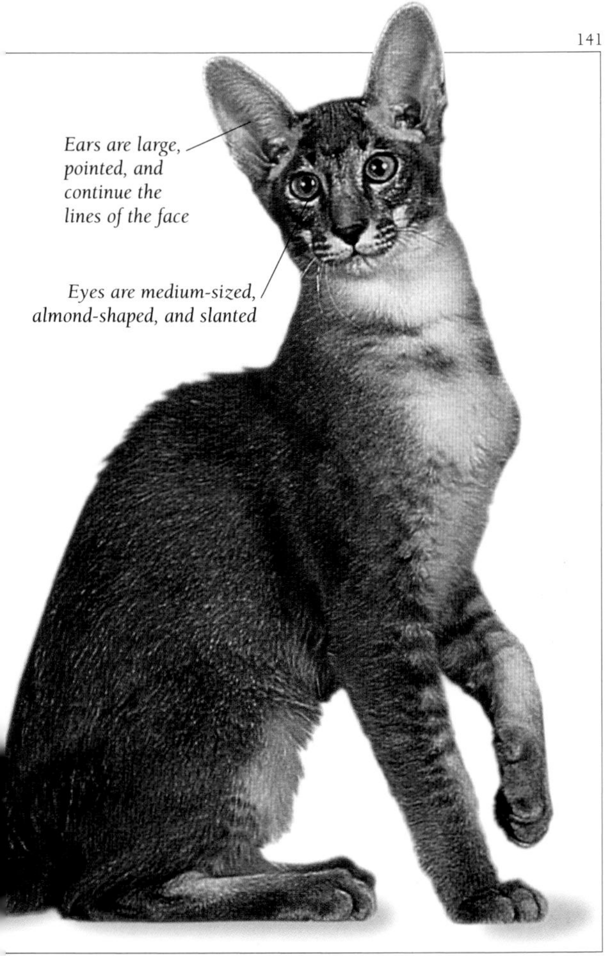
Ears are large, pointed, and continue the lines of the face
Eyes are medium-sized, almond-shaped, and slanted

La Perm

Most of the rexed breeds in existence have originated, and therefore been developed, in shorthairs. The longhaired La Perm and the Selkirk Rex (*see page 82*) are the only longhaired curly cats accepted by major registries. The Bohemian Rex, which is a proposed rexed Longhair, has never achieved recognition, and the rexed Maine Coon (*see page 46*) is also highly controversial. Although La Perms are descended from random-bred American stock, they have a foreign, Oriental appearance, with a wedge-shaped head and lean build. They are outdoor cats who are very active and inquisitive, and so not suitable for owners seeking lap-cats. The breed description reflects their farm-cat ancestry, which notes that they are "excellent hunters".

Breed Colors

All colors and patterns, including sepia, pointed, and mink

WHITE

Red Tabby

The proportion of red cats in the random-bred population varies geographically. However, it is predictable that there are few red selfs because dedicated breeding is usually needed to eliminate tabby markings from this color. In any new breed this work has to begin afresh.

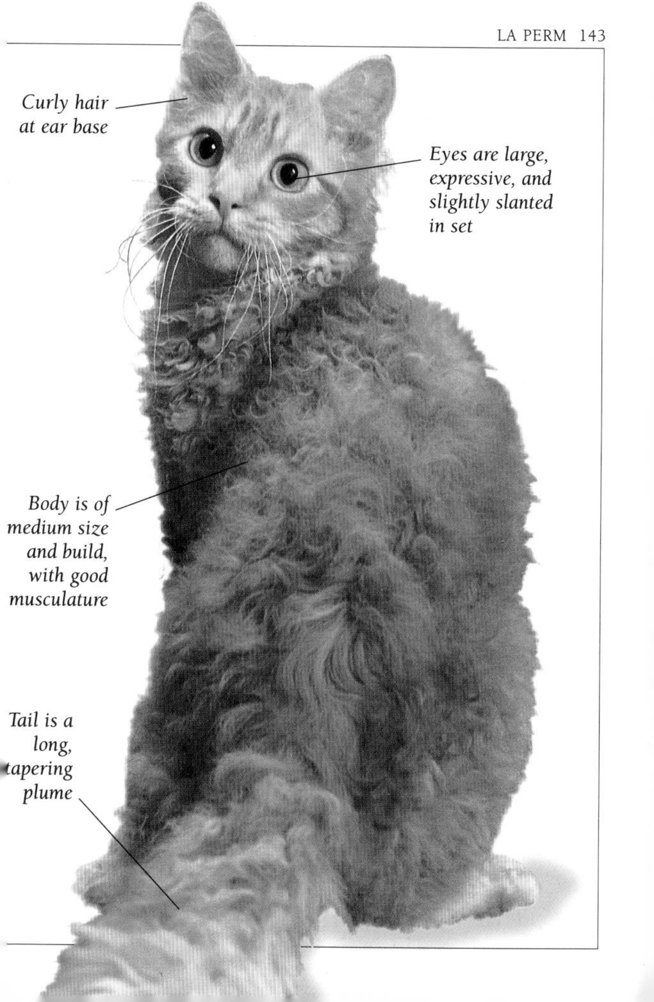
Curly hair at ear base
Eyes are large, expressive, and slightly slanted in set
Body is of medium size and build, with good musculature
Tail is a long, tapering plume

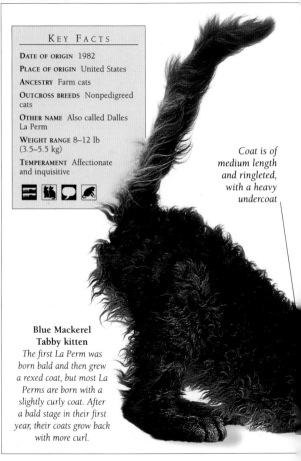

Key Facts

Date of origin 1982

Place of origin United States

Ancestry Farm cats

Outcross breeds Nonpedigreed cats

Other name Also called Dalles La Perm

Weight range 8–12 lb (3.5–5.5 kg)

Temperament Affectionate and inquisitive

Coat is of medium length and ringleted, with a heavy undercoat

Blue Mackerel Tabby kitten
The first La Perm was born bald and then grew a rexed coat, but most La Perms are born with a slightly curly coat. After a bald stage in their first year, their coats grow back with more curl.

Breed History In 1982, a farm cat in The Dalles, Oregon, produced a litter of six kittens that included a single bald kitten. In spite of this disadvantage, the kitten survived, and she eventually grew a coat. Unexpectedly, her coat, unlike that of her litter mates, was curly and soft to the touch. Linda Koehl, the owner and founder of the breed, named this kitten Curly. Over the next five years, Koehl bred a number of curly coated kittens, which were to become the basis of the La Perm breed. The gene is dominant, so wide outcrossing to increase the gene pool can be achieved while still producing reasonable numbers of rexed kittens. Of the major registries, only TICA has recognized the La Perm.

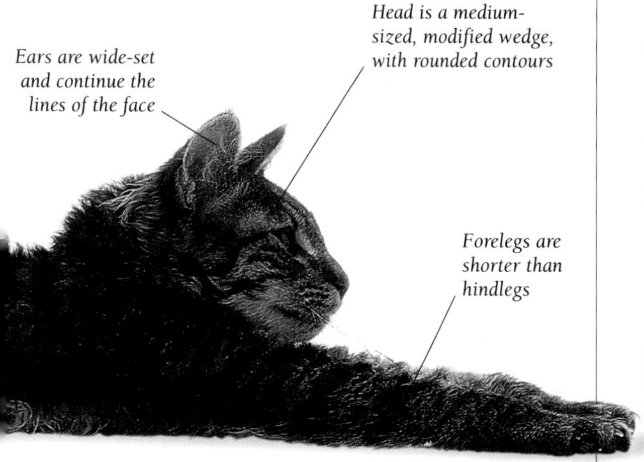

Head is a medium-sized, modified wedge, with rounded contours
Ears are wide-set and continue the lines of the face
Forelegs are shorter than hindlegs

KURILE ISLAND BOBTAIL

Both this breed and its homeland are of uncertain ownership. The Kurile Island chain, running from the easternmost point of the Russian Federation to the tip of Japan's Hokkaido Island, is disputed between the two nations. The Kurile Island Bobtail is of quite a different type to the Japanese Bobtail (*see page 150*), although it has the same short tail. Its coat, conditioned by the harsh winters of its northern home, is longer and thicker than that of its more southerly relation, and its build is sturdier. A relatively small range of colors is recognized by the breed standard. A friendly breed, it nonetheless has an independent character.

Coat is semi-long, with discernible undercoat

Legs are sturdy, but not heavy for build, with round paws

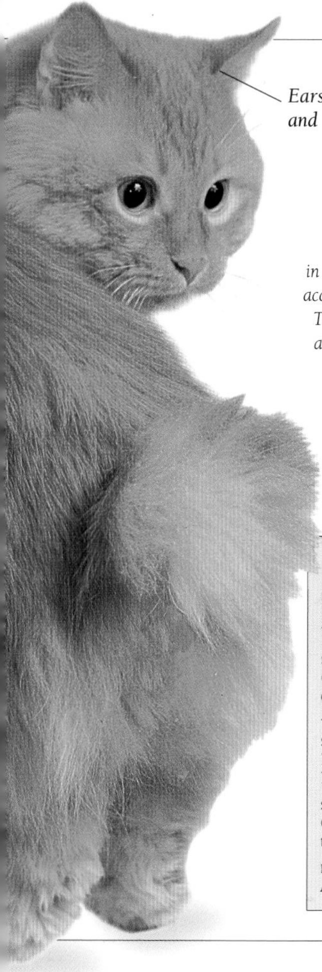

Ears are medium-sized and set upright

Red Self

Sex-linked red is common in cats from this area, and is ideally accompanied by copper-colored eyes. The coat is longest over the throat and in "breeches" on the hindlegs. Males often develop a full face, with clear jowls.

BREED COLORS

SELF AND TORTIE
Black, Red, Blue, Cream, Tortoiseshell, Blue-Cream, White

SMOKE, SHADED, AND TIPPED
Colors are as for self and tortie, except White

TABBIES (CLASSIC, MACKEREL, SPOTTED)
Brown, Red, Blue, Cream, Brown Tortie, Blue Tortie

SILVER TABBIES
Colors are as for standard tabbies

BICOLORS
Any allowed color with White

Key Facts

Date of origin Pre-18th century

Place of origin Kurile Islands

Ancestry Domestic cats

Outcross breeds None

Other name None

Weight range 7–10 lb (3–4.5 kg)

Temperament Busy and friendly

Tail is short, curled, and carried high

Breed History Until recently, only the Japanese Bobtail was widely known among bobtail breeds. With the advent of a more open attitude in the countries of the former Soviet Union, new breeds are emerging, among them some surprises such as the previously obscure Kurile Island Bobtail. This breed represents the same mutation as its Japanese cousin, and has been present on the Kurile Islands for centuries. While this genetic similarity causes no problems to the Russian bodies that register the Kurile, the shared mutation that causes its bobtail might be a barrier to the breed's acceptance in Europe.

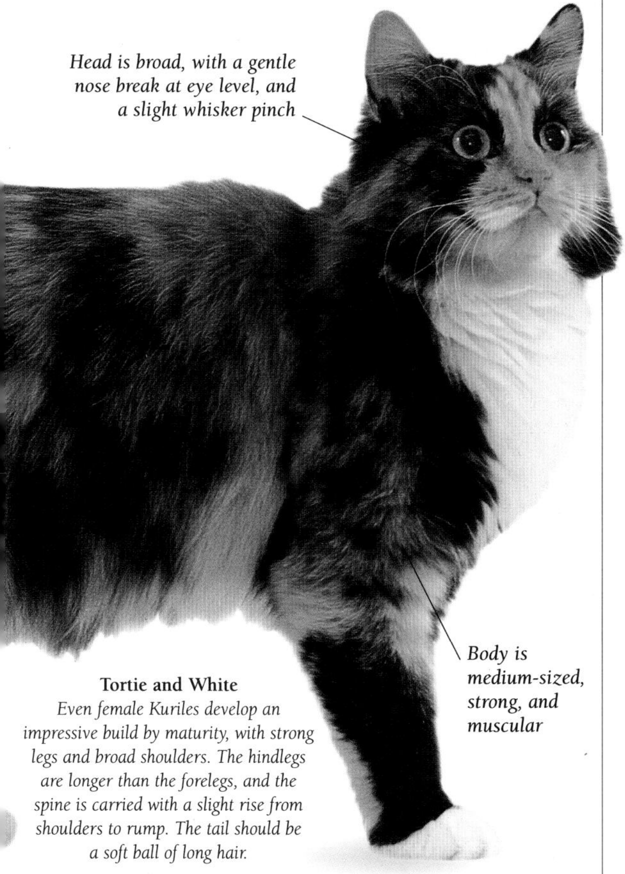
Head is broad, with a gentle nose break at eye level, and a slight whisker pinch
Body is medium-sized, strong, and muscular

Tortie and White
Even female Kuriles develop an impressive build by maturity, with strong legs and broad shoulders. The hindlegs are longer than the forelegs, and the spine is carried with a slight rise from shoulders to rump. The tail should be a soft ball of long hair.

JAPANESE BOBTAIL

Sociable and inquisitive, this longhaired breed exists only in small numbers. The Japanese Bobtail is bred by very few breeders worldwide. This is in part because the longhair gene is masked in longhair-to-shorthair breedings, and the low numbers of longhairs means that mating only longhair-to-longhair could lead to serious inbreeding. In this version of the Bobtail, the short tail makes a full, fluffy pom-pom: This trait does not carry spinal or bone deformities with it.

BREED COLORS

SELF AND TORTIE COLOURS
Black, Red, Tortoiseshell, White
All other self and tortie colors, including pointed, mink, and sepia

TABBY COLORS
All colors in all four tabby patterns

BICOLORS
Black, Red, Tortoiseshell, with White
All other colors and patterns with White

Bobtail face
An almost equilateral triangle, the face has gentle curves and high cheekbones. Odd eyes are prized in Japanese Bobtails, especially in the Tortie and White coat pattern, known as Mi-ke.

BREED HISTORY This cat is a natural variant of the shorthaired Bobtail (*see page 304*). Many examples of both types can be found in Japanese art over the last three centuries. The documented breeding history, however, only dates from 1968, when shorthaired Bobtails were brought to the United States, carrying with them the longhair gene. Now that the shorthaired version is established in North America, the less common longhaired cat is gaining some ground there. It has yet to gain recognition in Britain.

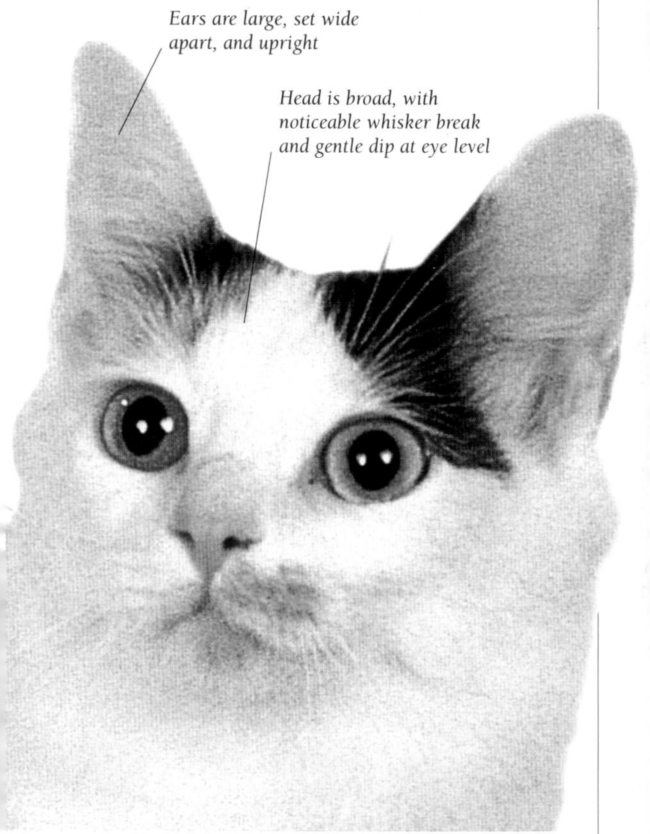
Ears are large, set wide apart, and upright
Head is broad, with noticeable whisker break and gentle dip at eye level

Key Facts

Date of origin 1700s

Place of origin Japan

Ancestry Household cats

Outcross breeds None

Other name None

Weight range 6–9 lb (2.5–4 kg)

Temperament Vibrantly alert

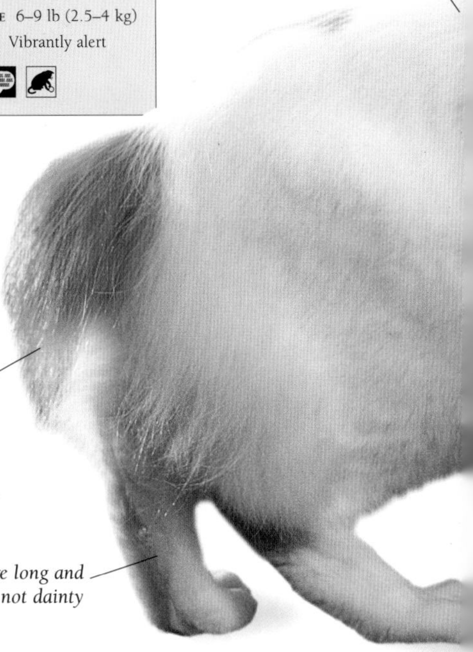
Body is long, straight, and slender, but well muscled
Tail is a short pom-pom, either straight or curled
Legs are long and slender but not dainty

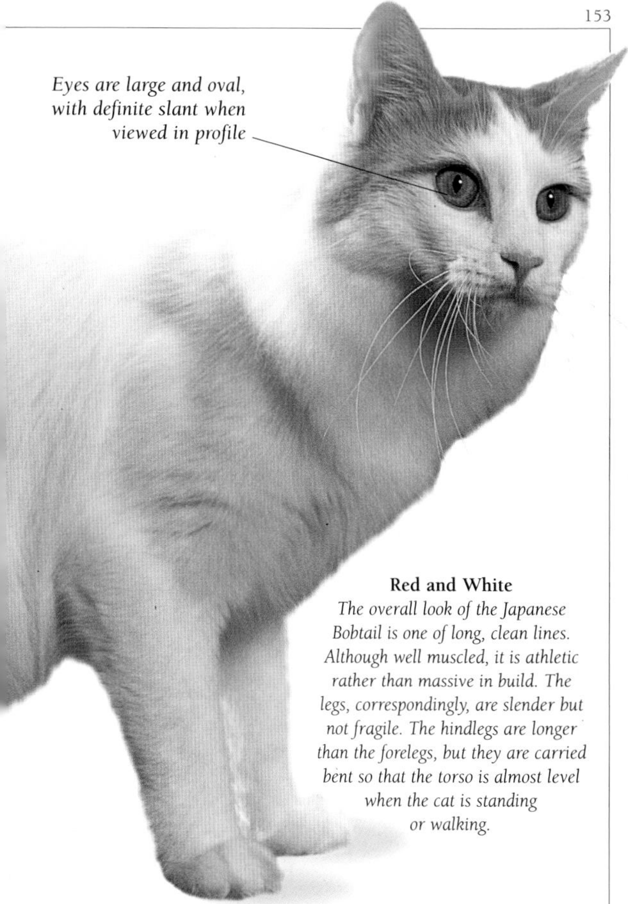

Eyes are large and oval, with definite slant when viewed in profile

Red and White

The overall look of the Japanese Bobtail is one of long, clean lines. Although well muscled, it is athletic rather than massive in build. The legs, correspondingly, are slender but not fragile. The hindlegs are longer than the forelegs, but they are carried bent so that the torso is almost level when the cat is standing or walking.

RANDOM-BRED CATS

By far the most commonly owned domestic cat is the humble, random-bred household pet. Even in countries with many pedigree cats, these self-selected pets outnumber them four to one. While some people want the looks and personality traits of a certain breed, random-bred cats can be as satisfying. A cat's personality depends on its early experiences as much as any inbred traits. Only a few of these "alley cats" have long hair, because it is a recessive trait, but cats with nonpedigreed origins in the style of the Angora or the Maine Coon do occasionally show up.

Blue

Blue, the defining color of several naturally developed breeds, is often found in the feline populations of Mainland Europe. The semi-foreign build of a cat like this indicates a heritage in common with southern European breeds, such as the Turkish Angora.

Cream and White

Creams are less common than reds among random-bred cat populations. In both colors, even selfs almost always show some ghost tabby markings. Breeders of pedigree cats select carefully to minimize these markings and produce consistently clear self coats, but even in random-bred cats the occasional individual shows a surprisingly solid color.

INTRODUCTION TO SHORTHAIRS

Thousands of years ago, domestic cats spread from Egypt across the world. New varieties evolved to suit the new conditions. Survival of the fittest in colder climates favored stocky individuals, with dense undercoats of weatherproof hair to protect them in winter. In northern climates, cats developed "cobby" bodies, a type later developed into the British Shorthair and exported as the foundation stock for many of the world's cats. At the same time, the cat was also spreading east across Asia. In warm climates, natural selection favored thinner coats and a smaller body to increase the surface-area-to-weight ratio, to help lose excess heat. Such cats are now called foreign or, if extremely slender, Oriental types.

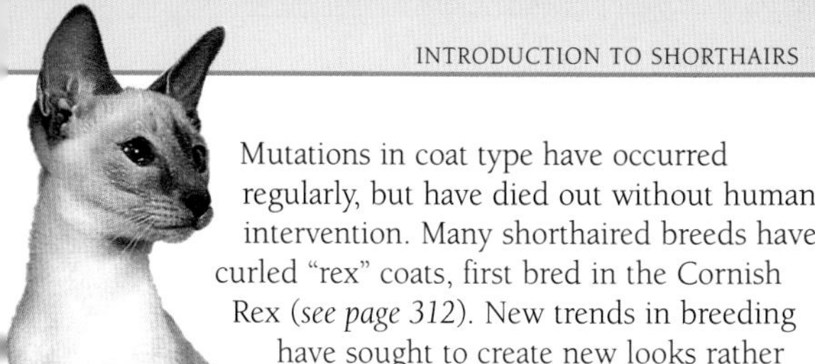

Mutations in coat type have occurred regularly, but have died out without human intervention. Many shorthaired breeds have curled "rex" coats, first bred in the Cornish Rex (*see page 312*). New trends in breeding have sought to create new looks rather than refine what nature has already achieved. Many of these breeds emulate wild cats: the Ocicat is a typical example. The Bengal (*see page 344*) was the first breed produced by mating the domestic cat with a wild cat, the Asian leopard cat.

Siamese

This breed was once defined for most people solely by its pointed pattern. Today, many breeds include this pattern, and the Siamese is recognized more by its extremely fine, elongated type, which has helped to make it one of the more controversial cats among breeders.

European Shorthair

Like its British and American counterparts, this type developed naturally in random-bred cats over many hundreds of years. It has been preserved and perpetuated by breeders in the 20th century.

EXOTIC SHORTHAIR

Genuinely exotic in looks, this shorthaired version of the Persian (*see page 16*) has the gentle personality and voice of its parent breed. Exotics have the conformation of Persians, but a highly original coat: not quite short, but not semi-long either. Outcrossing to bring in the short coat has given the Exotic a livelier and more inquisitive disposition than its antecedents; it has not, however, eliminated the anatomical problems of the face inherited from the Persian. The dense, double coat needs combing twice weekly. The breed remains rare, partly because many litters still contain longhaired kittens.

Brown Mackerel Tabby
While the Persian is recognized only i the classic or blotched pattern, Exoti tabbies may also be mackerel striped or spotted. The facia markings of all three of thes patterns are the same only the body marking vary. The Mackere Tabby should hav narrow vertica stripes coverin the body

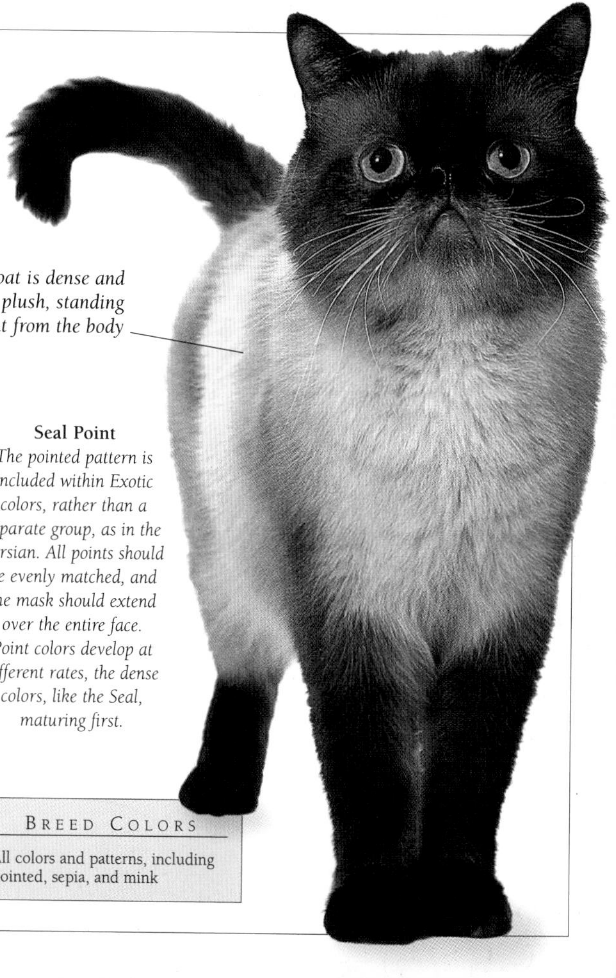
Coat is dense and plush, standing out from the body

Seal Point
The pointed pattern is included within Exotic colors, rather than a separate group, as in the Persian. All points should be evenly matched, and the mask should extend over the entire face. Point colors develop at different rates, the dense colors, like the Seal, maturing first.

Breed Colors

All colors and patterns, including pointed, sepia, and mink

Breed History In the early 1960s, breeders of the American Shorthair (*see page 190*) attempted to introduce the Persian's coat texture into their breed. Instead, they produced cats with the Shorthair's coat on the Persian's compact body. Unintentionally, the "shorthaired Persian" was born, complete with a flattened, "teddy bear" face. To differentiate their cats from American Shorthairs, breeders called them Exotic Shorthairs, and used British Shorthairs (*see page 164*), Burmese (*see page 262*), and even Russian Blues (*see page 224*) in their breed programs. CFA recognized the breed in 1967.

Black

With a coat of lustrous black hair and eyes of brilliant gold, this color might have been the model for many of the lucky black cats produced as toys by companies over the years.

Tail is relatively short

Paws are large, rounded, and fir

Exotic head

The Exotic has inherited some of the Persian's flaws, such as overflowing tear ducts, constricted nostrils, and dental problems. In an effort to breed for health, the British standards call for the upper edge of the nose leather to be below the the lower edge of the eye.

Blue

The color standard for the Blue Exotic is similar to that for the blue British Shorthair. Comparing the two breeds shows how distinct breed conformations can be, even in two stockily built cats. The Exotic is the roundest of all the shorthairs, with a breed standard that calls for rounded lines from the ears to the toes. The cuddly appearance can give a deceptive illusion of softness; beneath the fur, the curves should be of muscle.

Eyes are large and round

Blue-Cream

The standard for all tortie Exotics calls for the colors to be balanced and softly intermingled, and for all four feet and the tail to contain both colors. Some distinct patches of color are allowable, and facial blazes are permitted. Tortie patterning is inherently unpredictable.

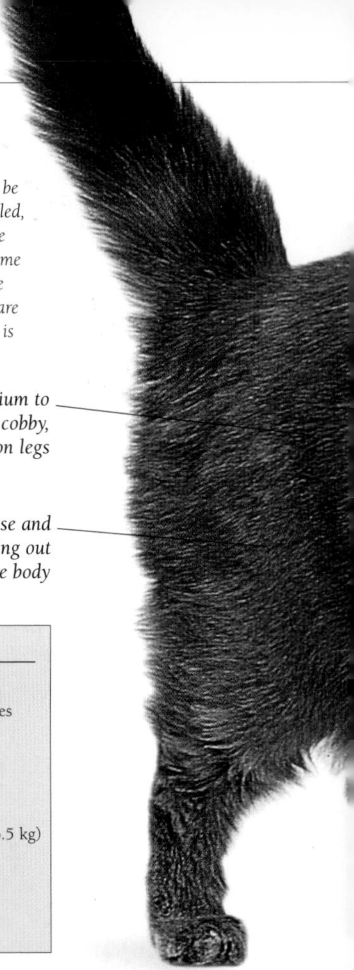

Body is medium to large and cobby, carried low on legs

Coat is dense and plush, standing out from the body

KEY FACTS

DATE OF ORIGIN 1960s

PLACE OF ORIGIN United States

ANCESTRY Persian/American Shorthair

OUTCROSS BREEDS None

OTHER NAME None

WEIGHT RANGE 7–14 lb (3–6.5 kg)

TEMPERAMENT Gentle and inquisitive

Head is round and
ıassive, with full cheeks

BRITISH SHORTHAIR

This impressively built cat is self-possessed and self-reliant. Although undemanding and gentle, British Shorthairs are not tolerant of handling; judges and breeders describe them as "four-feet-on-the-ground" cats. Numerous firm guard hairs give the dense, bouncy coat a distinctive, crisp feel, and the protective undercoat insulates the cat on the coldest day. Thick-legged and well-muscled, this breed is both compact and surprisingly heavy. Large, round eyes suggest a gentle disposition, although it is a very successful hunter.

Red Classic Tabby

The original tabby was the Brown, less common today, but Reds also made an early appearance. Ginger-reds are often seen in the nonpedigreed cats of Britain, but a century of breeding has modified this color to deep, tawny shades.

Ears are medium in size, with rounded tips

Silver Spotted Tabby
This striking pattern was also one of the earliest, appearing in the 1880s. There are silver versions of all the tabby colors and patterns, but the black remains one of the most popular. As in other breeds, the Silvers have hazel, rather than copper, eyes.

BREED COLORS

SELF AND TORTIE COLORS
Black, Chocolate, Red, Blue, Lilac, Cream, Tortoiseshell, Chocolate Tortie, Blue Tortie, Lilac Tortie, White (Blue-, Odd-, Orange-Eyed)

SMOKE AND TIPPED
Colors are as for self and tortie colors, with the addition of Golden Tipped

BICOLORS
All self and tortie colors with white

TABBY (CLASSIC, MACKEREL, SPOTTED)
Brown, Chocolate, Red, Blue, Lilac, Cream, Tortie, Chocolate Tortie, Blue Tortie, Lilac Tortie

SILVER TABBY (CLASSIC, MACKEREL, SPOTTED)
Colors are as for standard tabbies

POINTED COLORS
All self, tortie, and tabby colors

RED SPOTTED TABBY

BLUE SPOTTED TABBY

BLACK SMOKE

BROWN CLASSIC TABBY

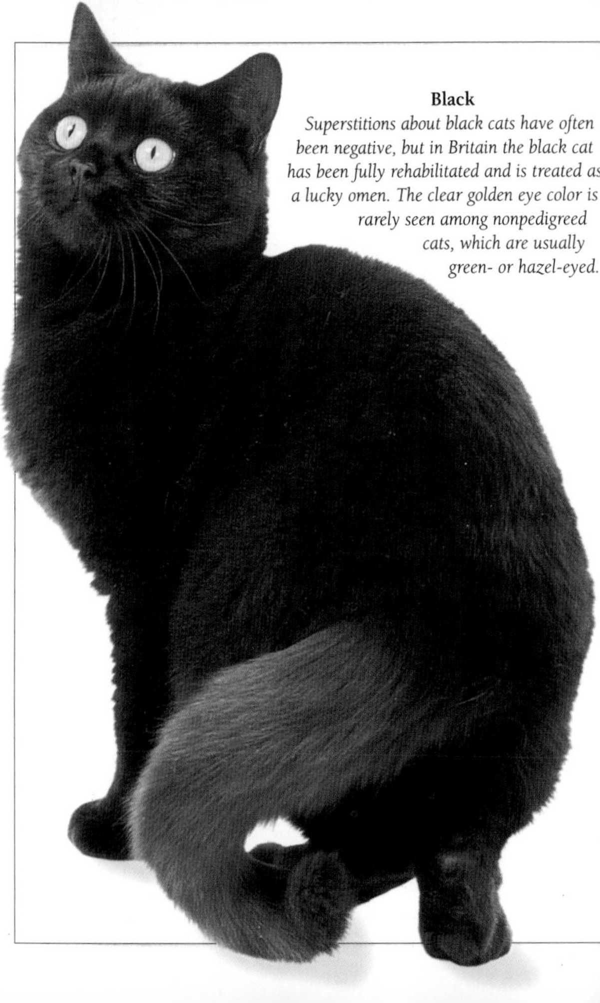

Black

Superstitions about black cats have often been negative, but in Britain the black cat has been fully rehabilitated and is treated as a lucky omen. The clear golden eye color is rarely seen among nonpedigreed cats, which are usually green- or hazel-eyed.

Coat is dense, with a crisp feel

Tortoiseshell

A difficult color to breed, this was nevertheless one of the very first to be recognized. The standard for the Tortoiseshell in this breed calls for an even mingling of colors without obvious patches, in contrast to the Tortoiseshell standard in the American Shorthair. Brindling or tabby markings are faults.

BREED HISTORY British Shorthairs were developed in the 1800s from the farm, street, and household cats of Britain. Although it was the most-shown breed at the first British shows, and Harrison Weir, the "inventor" of the Cat Fancy bred "British Blues," the breed was in decline by the turn of the century, and had almost died out by the 1950s. It was revived by dedicated breeders who exported stock to Ireland and the British Commonwealth. By the 1970s, it had arrived in the United States where, as the British Blue, it gained many admirers. A curious feature separates the breed from most shorthaired cats: About half of all British Shorthairs have Type-B blood, a rare trait.

Blue

This color is the all-time classic British Shorthair. It was one of the earliest colors, and has always been the most popular. For many years, the British Blue was the only British cat recognized in North America. When the breed population fell in World War II, breeders outcrossed first to Oriental cats, and then to Blue Persians, which were closer in type.

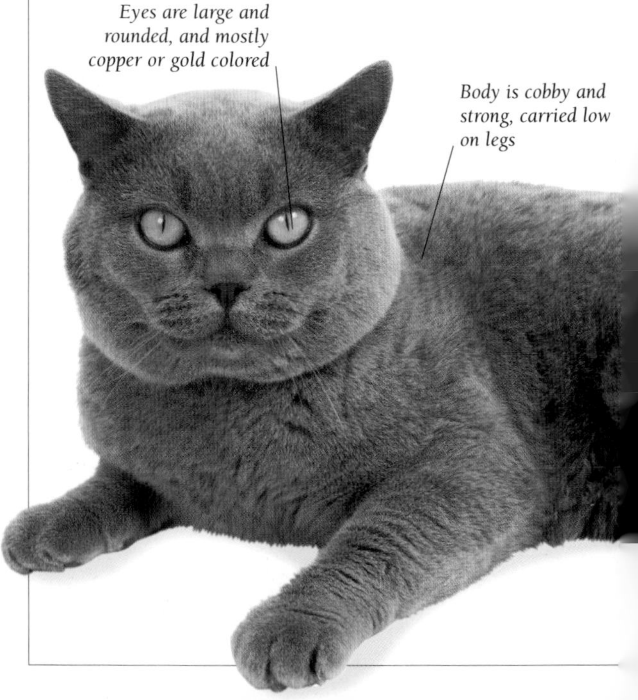
Eyes are large and rounded, and mostly copper or gold colored
Body is cobby and strong, carried low on legs

Orange-Eyed White

This color was developed from the Blue-Eyed White, which appeared at the end of the 19th century. A perfect white with no yellow tinge is rare. Blue- and Odd-Eyed Whites can show a congenital deafness, and the standard requires deep blue eyes in an attempt to avoid the problem; orange-eyed cats rarely suffer from this form of deafness.

Face is round with full cheeks

KEY FACTS

DATE OF ORIGIN 1880s

PLACE OF ORIGIN Great Britain

ANCESTRY Household, street, and farm cats

OTHER NAME Tipped colors once called Chinchilla Shorthairs

WEIGHT RANGE 9–18 lb (4–8 kg)

TEMPERAMENT Genial and relaxed

Newer British Shorthair Colors

Since the breed was first developed, British Shorthairs have increased enormously in range. Some of these appeared before World War II, but recently there has been an even greater development of colors and patterns. In the 1950s, numbers were low, and breeders outcrossed surviving British Shorthairs with Persians to ensure the survival of the blue coat. Although now rare, the Persian influence means British Shorthair matings still occasionally produce kittens with fluffy coats. More recently, adventurous matings with Oriental breeds have created delightful new coat colors. These are not universally accepted outside Britain.

Black and White Bicolor

While there have been many bicolors from the earliest days of the breed, the show standard originally specified that the markings should be symmetrical, a standard almost impossible to meet. A revision allowing less rigid distribution of color in the half-white coat was welcomed.

Black-tipped

This was known until 1978 as the Chinchilla Shorthair because it was developed through matings with Chinchilla Persians. Persian heritage is still apparent in kittens before they acquire their adult coats.

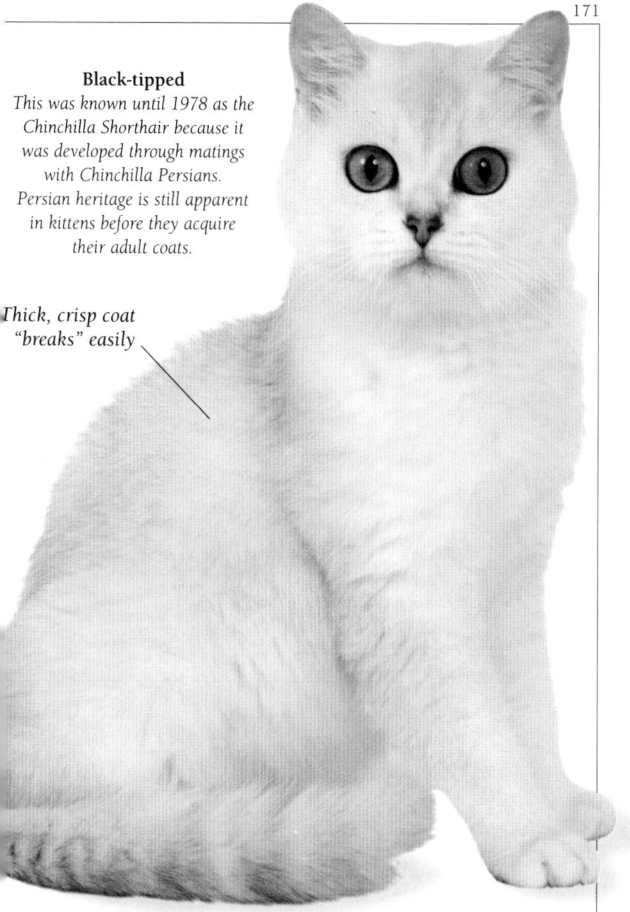

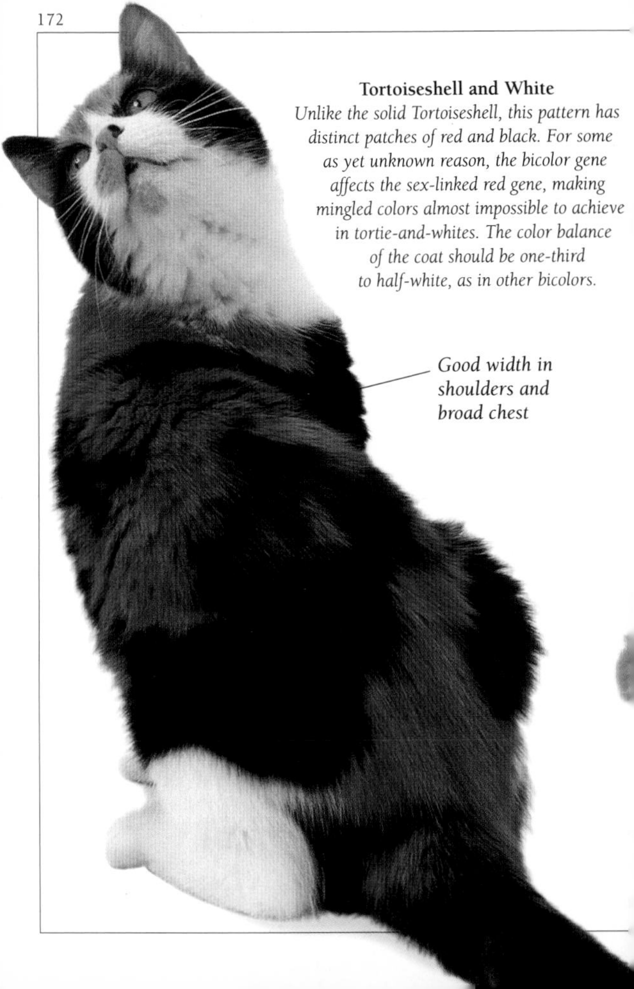

Tortoiseshell and White

Unlike the solid Tortoiseshell, this pattern has distinct patches of red and black. For some as yet unknown reason, the bicolor gene affects the sex-linked red gene, making mingled colors almost impossible to achieve in tortie-and-whites. The color balance of the coat should be one-third to half-white, as in other bicolors.

Chocolate kitten

The gene for this rich brown color originally came from Oriental cats. Crossbreeding brought the color into the Persian breed, from which it was introduced into the British Shorthair. Because of its outcross origins, this color is not universally recognized outside Britain.

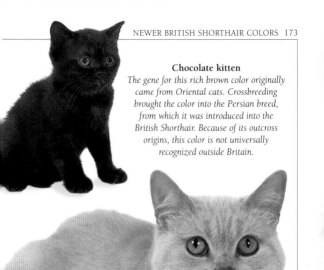

Cream

Creams, which are dilute Red selfs, have been ecognized since the 1920s. Breeders did not know how to produce them, and early Creams were "hot," resembling Reds. Good, "cool" Creams, as ar as possible from red, took a great deal of work.

Paws are compact, firm, and rounded

Seal Colorpointed kitten

These colors have only been fully accepted in Britain during the 1990s. The result of outcrossing to Siamese, they still resemble the British Shorthair in all respects other than their exotic pattern.

Blue-Cream Colorpointed

As with the solid colors, pointed torties should show evenly mingled colors on their points. Ideally, each point shows a mix of colors. Despite the Oriental influence, these cats tend to have the placid nature of their British forebears.

MANX

The lack of a tail is this breed's most obvious visible characteristic, but its "bunny-hop" gait is just as unique. If there is any single word that encapsulates the Manx it is "round" – round-bodied, round-eyed, round-rumped, and round-headed. Slow-maturing Manx come in a huge range of colors and patterns. Cats may be "rumpies" (with no tail, just a dimple at the base of the spine), "stumpies" (with short tails), and "tailies" (with almost natural, usually kinked, tails). Stumpies and tailies make excellent pets, with retiring but friendly personalities, but show cats are all rumpies.

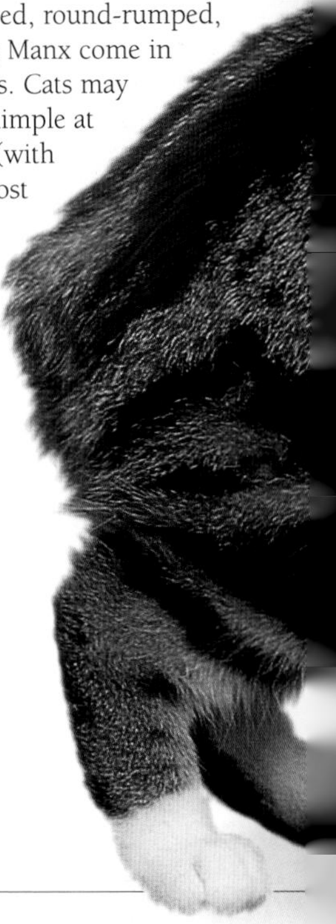

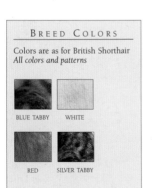

BREED COLORS

Colors are as for British Shorthair
All colors and patterns

BLUE TABBY

WHITE

RED

SILVER TABBY

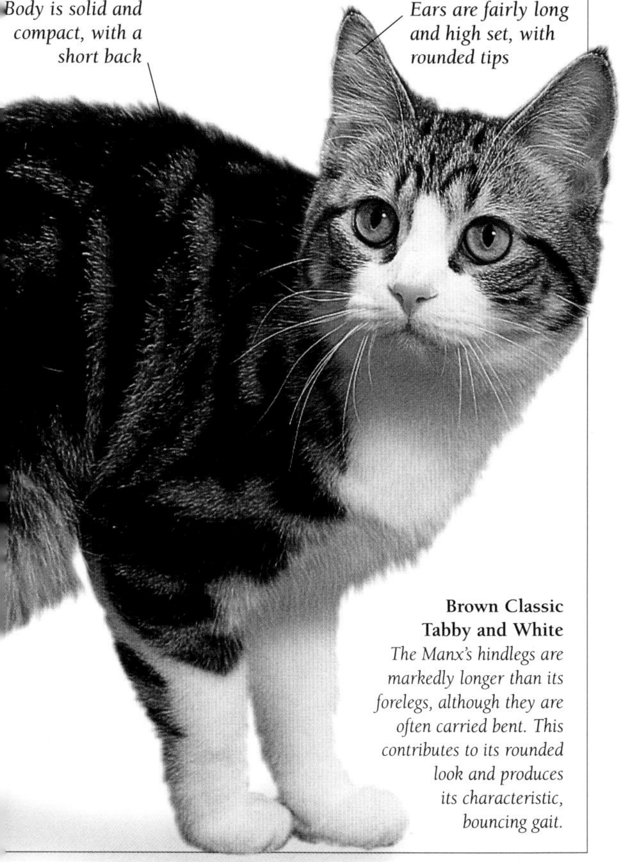
Body is solid and compact, with a short back
Ears are fairly long and high set, with rounded tips

Brown Classic Tabby and White
The Manx's hindlegs are markedly longer than its forelegs, although they are often carried bent. This contributes to its rounded look and produces its characteristic, bouncing gait.

Black and White

A common combination in British cats, this coat must show no blurring or speckling in a show cat. This stumpy is not suitable for showing because of its vestigial tail.

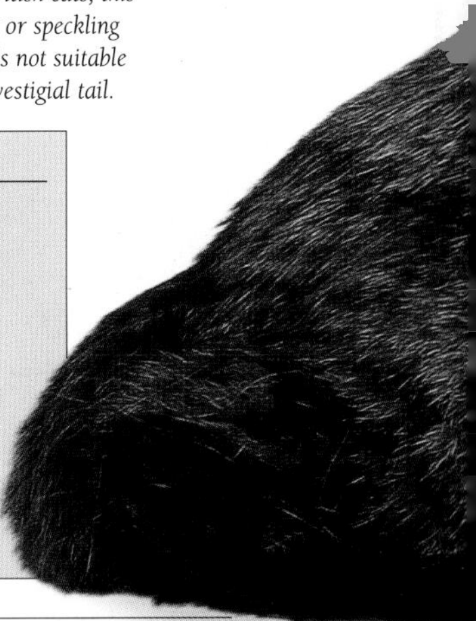

KEY FACTS

DATE OF ORIGIN Pre-1700s

PLACE OF ORIGIN Isle of Man

ANCESTRY Household cats

OUTCROSS BREEDS None

OTHER NAME None

WEIGHT RANGE 8–12 lb (3.5–5.5 kg)

TEMPERAMENT Mellow and even-tempered

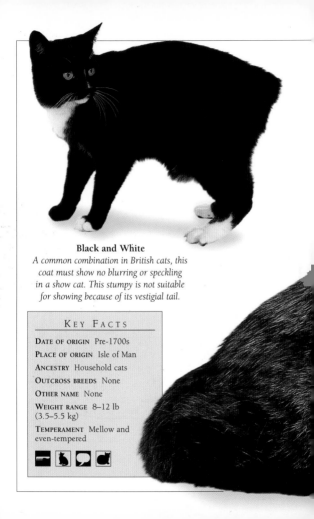

Tortoiseshell

As in all breeds, the British associations prefer a more softly mingled tortoiseshell pattern than the North American registries. This individual is a stumpy, with a short, stubby tail, and is therefore unsuitable for showing in any registry.

Coat is thick and double, with quality more important than pattern

Brown Tortie Tabby

The Manx is one of the stoutest of all cat breeds. The GCCF showing standard calls for the cat to have "good breadth of chest," while the CFA standard states that the proportion of the body to the legs should be such that they describe a square. The show standards of all breed registries call for a completely tailless individual, with a rounded rump.

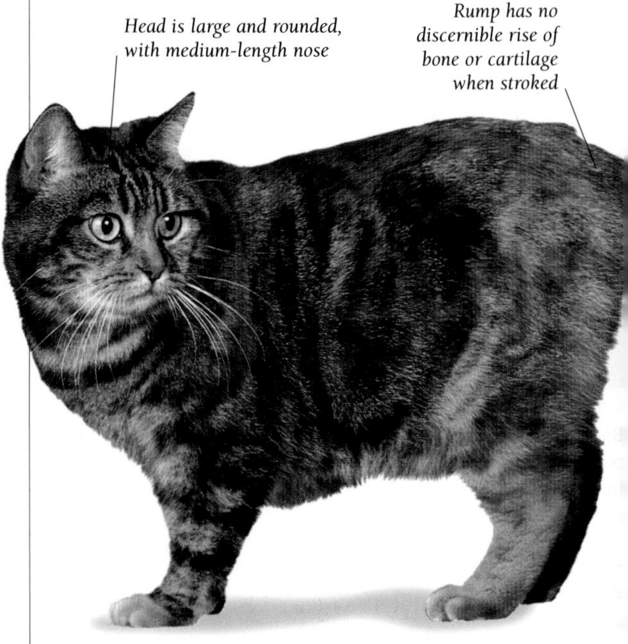

Head is large and rounded, with medium-length nose
Rump has no discernible rise of bone or cartilage when stroked

Manx head
The full-cheeked face of the Manx shows its roots in the typical random-bred British cat. The head should be broad, with a straight nose and a firm chin.

Breed History The Manx originated on the Isle of Man. Taillessness occurs occasionally in feline populations as a spontaneous mutation: in large populations it usually disappears, but in isolated groups, such as those on islands, it can survive. This is how the Manx and Japanese Bobtail (*see page 150*) developed. The traditional Manx was rangier than today; now it is bred for roundness. Manx have been shown in Britain since the late 19th century, and in North America since 1899. It was recognized by CFA in the 1920s.

SELKIRK REX

Rexing is apparent in the soft, thick, plush coat of this breed from the moment a kitten is born, but it then disappears, to reappear at eight to ten months. While the coat, in which all hairs are curled, needs routine grooming, excessive combing and brushing, especially after bathing, straightens the hair. In body conformation, this patient and relaxed breed most closely resembles the British Shorthair, especially in its leg length. It also comes in two versions, the plush shorthair and the more dramatic longhair (*see page* 82). There are known debilitating medical conditions associated with some other rexed breeds, but it is not known yet whether there are any such problems with the Selkirk Rex. The Selkirk is unlike most other Rexes in that the trait is dominant, so outcrossing to broaden the gene pool still produces at least 50 percent rexed litters.

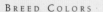

BREED COLORS

All colors and patterns, including pointed, sepia, and mink.

RED TABBY AND WHITE

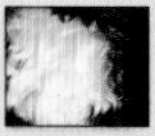

BLACK AND WHITE

SHADED SILVER

Selkirk head

The Selkirk head has a more Western look, rather than the Oriental style dominant in other rexes. The full-cheeked face has heavy jowls, round eyes, and a short muzzle. The whiskers are crinkly and can be fragile.

Ears are medium-sized, pointed, and set well apart
Head is rounded, with distinct stop to the nose

KEY FACTS

DATE OF ORIGIN 1987

PLACE OF ORIGIN United States

ANCESTRY Rescued domestic cat, Persian, Exotic, British and American Shorthairs

OUTCROSS BREEDS Longhair, Exotic, British and American Shorthairs

OTHER NAME None

WEIGHT RANGE 7–11 lb (3–5 kg)

TEMPERAMENT Patiently tolerant

Black Smoke

Like other rexed breeds, the Selkirk shows smoke and shaded colors to great advantage. Outcrossing to pedigree breeds allows a new breed like the Selkirk to take advantage of the decades of breeding that have gone into producing traits such as deep copper eyes, achieving them in a shorter time.

BREED HISTORY There is always the possibility that new mutations will arise unexpectedly, and, when there is enough interest, new breeds will be developed from this. The Selkirk Rex is one of the latest additions to the list of cat breeds. In 1987, a female Calico kitten was born at For Pet's Sake, a pet rescue center in Montana. This kitten, one of a litter of seven, was the only one to have curly hair and curly whiskers. Miss DePesto of NoFace, as she was called by Jeri Newman, her breeder, was bred, and three in her litter of six had curly coats, indicating that the rexed coat was genetically dominant. It is assumed that Pest herself was the source of this genetic mutation. Further breedings, including one back to her son, revealed that she carried the recessive genes for long hair and pointing. Jeri named the breed after the nearby Selkirk Mountains, and it is recognized by TICA.

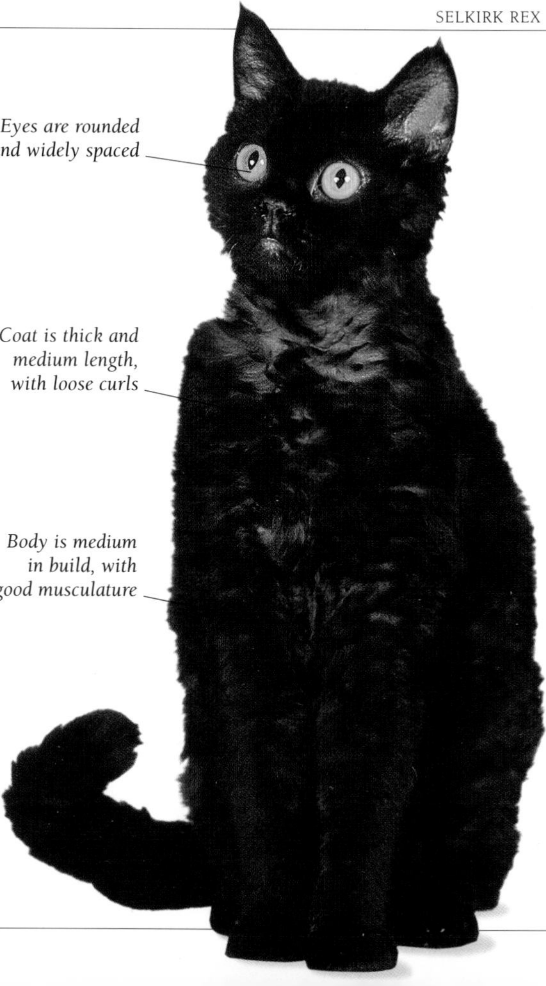
Eyes are rounded and widely spaced
Coat is thick and medium length, with loose curls
Body is medium in build, with good musculature

Scottish Fold

Folded ears ensure that this breed is immediately distinctive, with its rounded look, short neck, round head, and compact body. The unique ears are due to a dominant gene that causes varying degrees of fold. The first Fold had what is now called a "single" fold, where the ears bend forward; today's show cats have tight "triple" folds. Straight-eared cats are still essential for breeding healthy Folds. The breed has a placid personality, and its undemonstrative behavior suits its reserved appearance.

Fold head
The ears of a Scottish Fold should be "set in a cap-like fashion," flat against the head. Small, tightly folded ears are the ideal. The face should have a sweet expression.

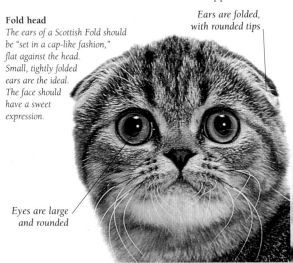

Ears are folded, with rounded tips
Eyes are large and rounded

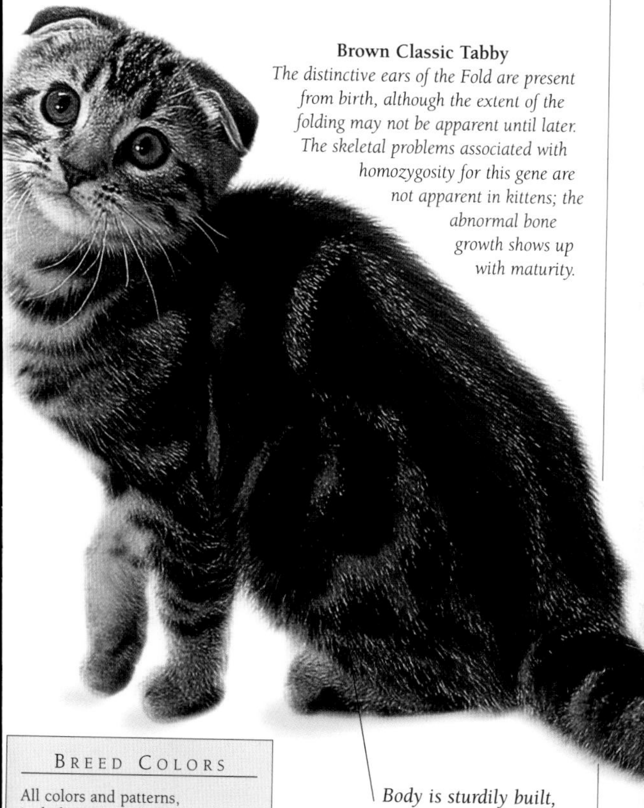

Brown Classic Tabby
The distinctive ears of the Fold are present from birth, although the extent of the folding may not be apparent until later. The skeletal problems associated with homozygosity for this gene are not apparent in kittens; the abnormal bone growth shows up with maturity.

Body is sturdily built, and flexible along spine

Breed Colors

All colors and patterns, including pointed, sepia, and mink

Breed History Folded ears are common in dogs, but rarely seen in cats. Susie, the Fold's founding mother, was a farm cat born in Tayside, Scotland. Local shepherd William Ross and his wife Mary were given one of Susie's kittens, which they named Snooks. Bred with a British Shorthair (*see page 164*), she produced Snowball, a white male who was shown locally. In 1971, Mary Ross sent some Folds to Neil Todd, a geneticist in Newtonville, Massachusetts. Development continued in the United States, using British and American Shorthairs (*see page 190*), and Folds were fully recognized by 1994. In Britain, the problems of crippled homozygous Folds have so far prevented recognition.

Key Facts

Date of origin 1961

Place of origin Scotland

Ancestry Farm cat, British and American Shorthairs

Outcross breeds British and American Shorthairs

Other name None

Weight range 6–13 lb (2.5–6 kg)

Temperament Quietly confident

Blue Tortie Tabby and White

The scoring system for Folds places most of the emphasis on body type. The ears should be folded toward the nose. After the ears, the most important part of the body is the tail; any shortening or stiffness indicates skeletal problems. All aspects of the Fold standard call for a healthy, well-proportioned, supple cat.

Long, tapering tail is preferred

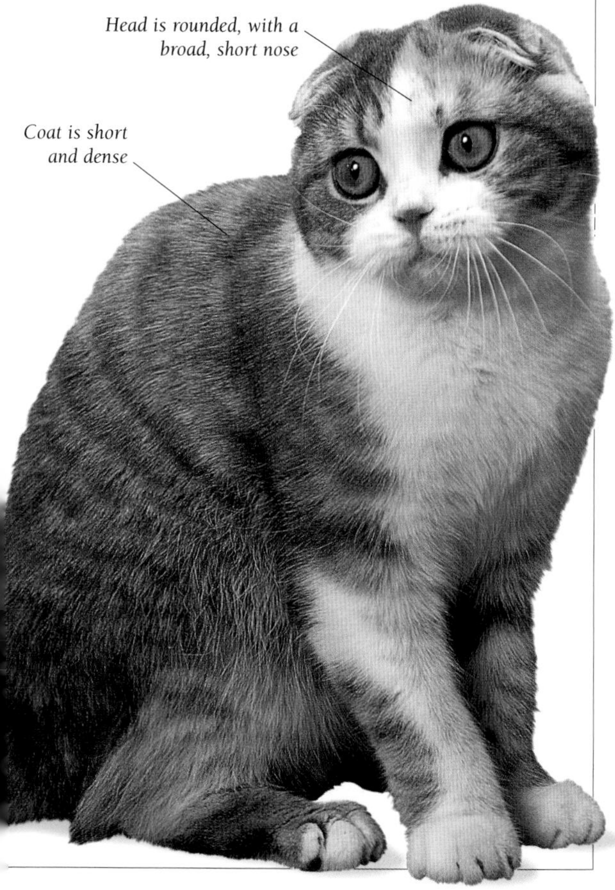
Head is rounded, with a broad, short nose
Coat is short and dense

AMERICAN SHORTHAIR

This self-sufficient cat is popular in both the home and the showring in the United States. American Shorthairs can be quite large, and the full-cheeked face and muscular body exude strength. American Shorthairs still share features with household cats, and breeders aim to produce kittens that have the best of these qualities. Although no longer allowed, for awhile, any nonpedigreed cat that met the standard could be registered, widening the gene pool.

Head is large, and slightly longer than it is wide

Breed Colors

SELF AND TORTIE COLORS
Black, Red, Blue, Cream, White, Tortoiseshell, Blue-Cream
All other self and tortie colors

SMOKE COLORS
Black, Cameo, Blue, Tortoiseshell, Blue-Cream
All other self and tortie colors except White

SHADED AND TIPPED COLORS
Colors are as for self and tortie colors except White
Colors are as for self and tortie colors except White

TABBIES (CLASSIC, MACKEREL)
Brown, Red, Blue, Cream, Brown Patched, Blue Patched
Spotted and ticked patterns, all other self and tortie colors

TABBY BICOLORS
All tabby colors with white

SHADED TABBIES
Colors and patterns are as for standard tabbies

BICOLORS (STANDARD AND VAN)
Colors are as for self and tortie colors except White

SMOKE, SHADED, AND TIPPED BICOLORS
Black Smoke, Cameo Smoke, Blue Smoke, Tortoiseshell Smoke, Shaded Cameo, Shell Cameo with White
All other smoke, shaded, and tipped colors with white

SILVER TABBY BICOLORS
Silver Tabby, Cameo Tabby, Silver Patched Tabby with White
All other silver tabby colors with white

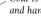

Coat is short, thick, and hard in texture

Brown Classic Tabby kittens
In CFA, only the blotched and striped tabby patterns are accepted, while TICA accepts the spotted and ticked patterns as well. The blotched tabbies were prevalent among the breed's emigrant ancestors: Blotched tabby populations show a high correlation with old trading routes.

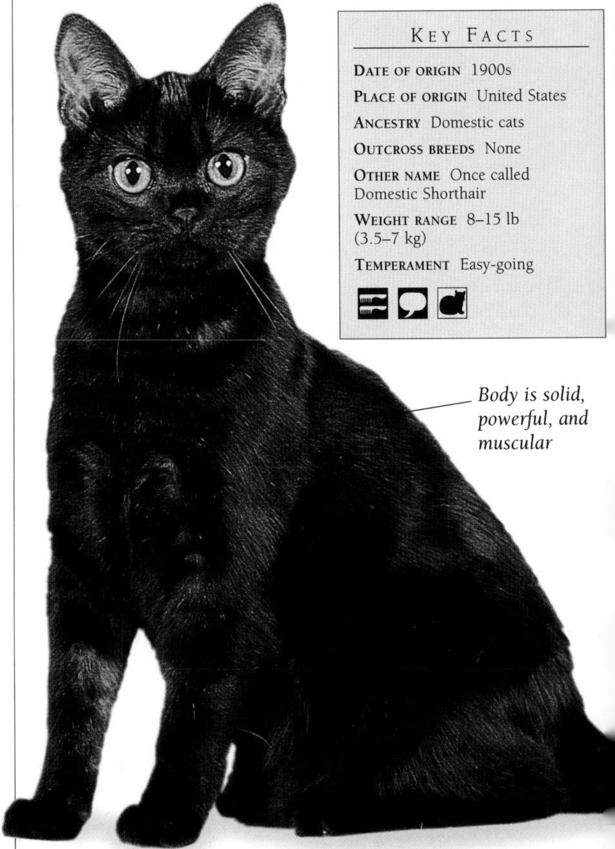

Key Facts

Date of origin 1900s

Place of origin United States

Ancestry Domestic cats

Outcross breeds None

Other name Once called Domestic Shorthair

Weight range 8–15 lb (3.5–7 kg)

Temperament Easy-going

Body is solid, powerful, and muscular

Eyes are large, rounded, and very slightly tilted

Silver Tabby

The Silver Tabby is a popular color, with dense, inky black markings on a background of sterling silver. In 1965, a Silver Tabby won the United States Cat of the Year award, prompting the breed's name change from the original "Domestic Shorthair" to its present "American Shorthair."

Legs are medium length and heavily muscled

Black Smoke

In 1904, Buster Brown, the first all-American cat to be registered in the breed, was a Black Smoke of street origins.

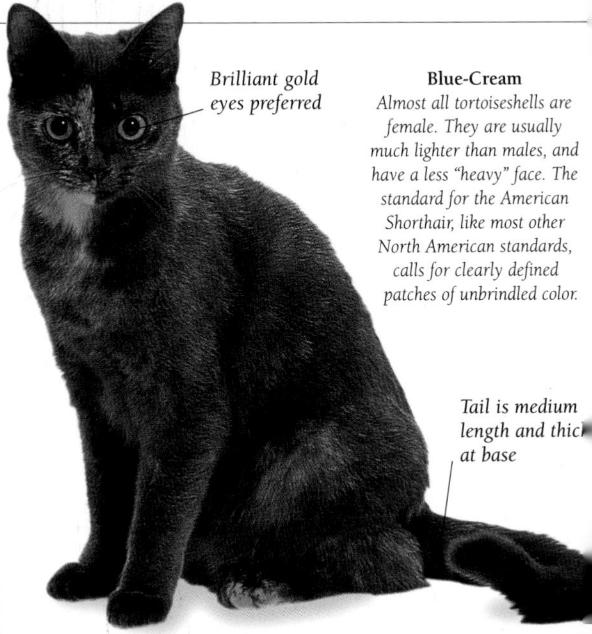

Blue-Cream

Almost all tortoiseshells are female. They are usually much lighter than males, and have a less "heavy" face. The standard for the American Shorthair, like most other North American standards, calls for clearly defined patches of unbrindled color.

Breed History Domestic cats arrived in North America with the first settlers. The new environment bred a new kind of cat, with thick, hard coats that were dense enough to protect them from moisture and cold. With more natural predators around, these cats evolved to be bigger than European felines. Early in the 20th century, some American breeders realized that their domestic cat's marvelous characteristics should be preserved in a breed. The first litter, born in 1904, was from a mating of American and British Shorthairs. The breed acquired its current name in 1965.

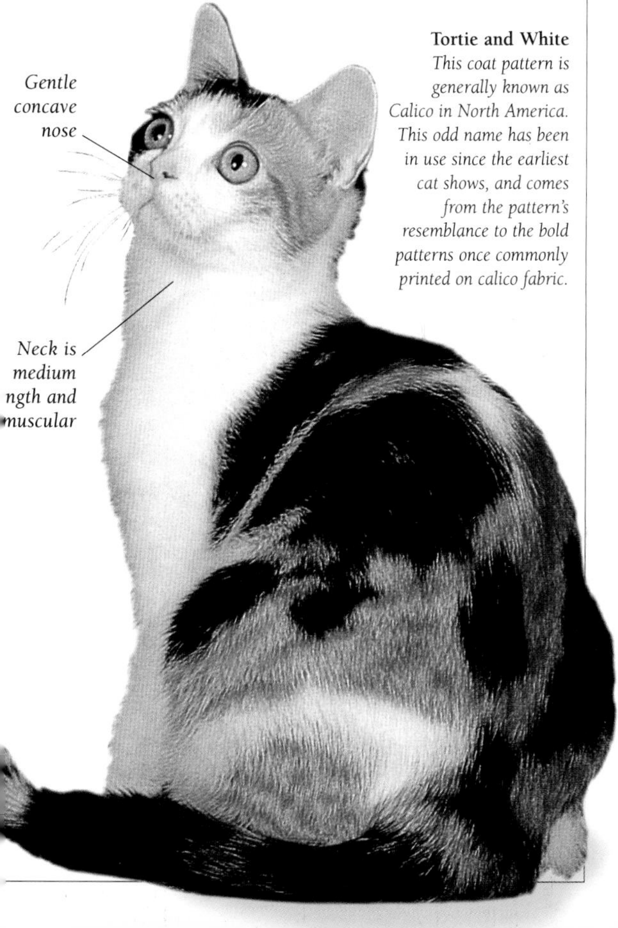

Tortie and White
This coat pattern is generally known as Calico in North America. This odd name has been in use since the earliest cat shows, and comes from the pattern's resemblance to the bold patterns once commonly printed on calico fabric.

AMERICAN WIREHAIR

This breed's most notable characteristic is, of course, its coat. Distinctive to the touch, it feels like stroking an astrakhan hat. Every hair is thinner than usual and crimped, hooked, or bent, giving the overall appearance of "wiring." The most prized coat is dense and coarse, but a kitten born with a coat that appears to have ringlets may have only a wavy coat at maturity, while coats that are only lightly wired early in life may continue to develop throughout the cat's first year. A cat with curly whiskers is highly valued. The American Wirehair is a relaxed and friendly breed. Its advocates say it is rarely destructive and enjoys being handled.

BREED COLORS

SELF AND TORTIE
Black, Red, Blue, Cream,
White (Blue-Eyed, Gold-Eyed,
Odd-Eyed), Tortoiseshell,
Blue Tortie
All other self and tortie colors

SMOKE
Black, Red, Blue
All other self and tortie colors with the exception of White

SHADED AND TIPPED
Shaded Silver, Shaded Cameo,
Chinchilla Silver, Shell Cameo
All other self and tortie colors

TABBIES (CLASSIC, MACKEREL)
Brown, Red, Blue, Cream
All other self and tortie colors

SHADED TABBIES
Silver, Cameo
All other tabby colors

BICOLORS
Self and tortie colors with white
All colors and patterns with white

BROWN TABBY

BLUE

WHITE

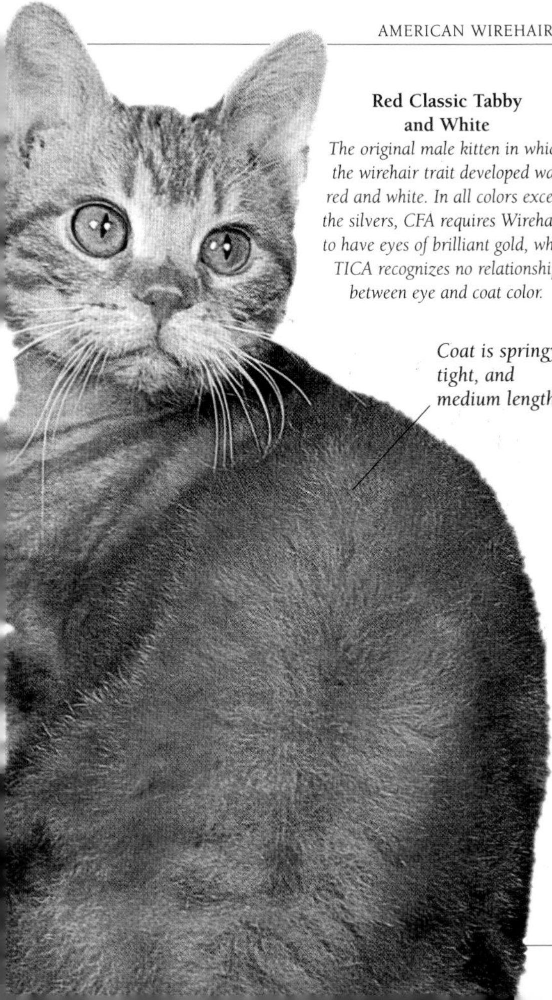
Coat is springy, tight, and medium length

Red Classic Tabby and White

The original male kitten in which the wirehair trait developed was red and white. In all colors except the silvers, CFA requires Wirehairs to have eyes of brilliant gold, while TICA recognizes no relationship between eye and coat color.

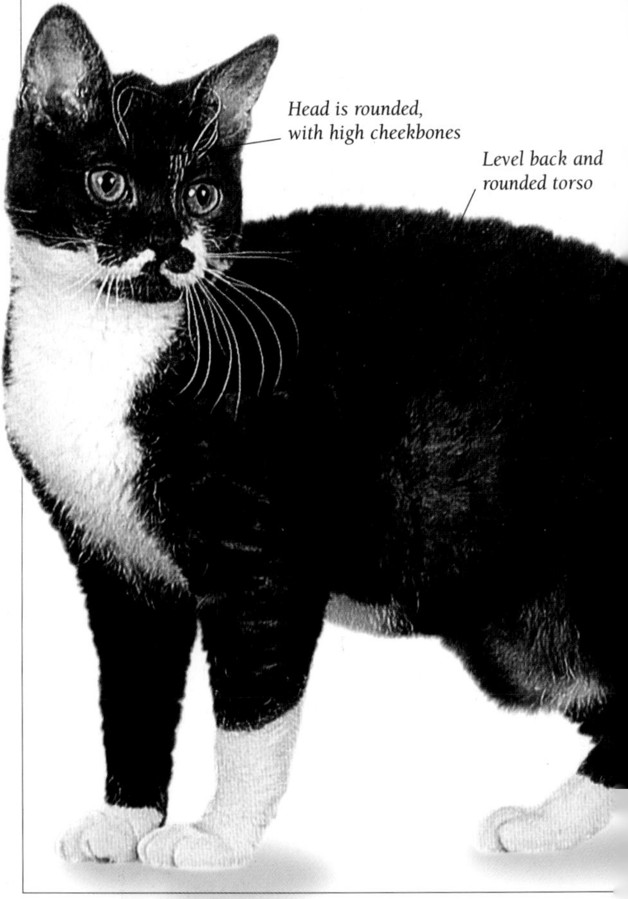
Head is rounded, with high cheekbones
Level back and rounded torso

BREED HISTORY This breed descends from a kitten born in 1966 in New York. Breeder Joan O'Shea obtained both a male kitten and his normal-coated sister. A careful breeding program, determined that this was a dominant mutation. The breed was developed through crossings with American Shorthairs, and a breed standard was written in 1967.

KEY FACTS

DATE OF ORIGIN 1966

PLACE OF ORIGIN United States

ANCESTRY Farm cat, American Shorthair

OUTCROSS BREEDS American Shorthair

OTHER NAME None

WEIGHT RANGE 8–15 lb (3.5–7 kg)

TEMPERAMENT Busy, occasionally bossy

Tapered tail is rounded at the tip, but not blunt
Legs are medium length and sturdy, with compact, rounded paws

Black Smoke and White

Smoke bicolors are softer in contrast than solid bicolors. In most shorthairs, the undercoat is unseen except when the cat moves, but the Wirehair's coat ensures that a little white always shines through.

AMERICAN CURL

This elegant breed includes both long- and short- coat types. The shorthaired American Curl has taken longer to develop, because the original Curls (*see page 70*) were all longhaired: Many shorthaired Curls carry a hidden longhair gene and produce longhaired kittens. The shape of the ears is very important to breeders. The Curl has three grades: Cats with ears just turned back (first degree) become pets; those with more curl (second degree) are used for breeding; and those with full crescents (third degree) are shown.

BREED COLORS

SELF AND TORTIE
Black, Chocolate, Red, Blue, Lilac, Cream, White, Tortoiseshell, Blue-Cream
All other self and tortie colors

SMOKE
Colors as for self and tortie, except White and with the addition of Chocolate Tortie
All other self and tortie colors

SHADED AND TIPPED
Shaded Silver, Shaded Golden, Shaded Cameo, Shaded Tortoiseshell, Chinchilla Silver, Chinchilla Golden, Shell Cameo, Shell Tortoiseshell
All other self and tortie colors

TABBIES (CLASSIC, MACKEREL, SPOTTED, TICKED)
Brown, Red, Blue, Cream, Brown Patched, Blue Patched
All other colors

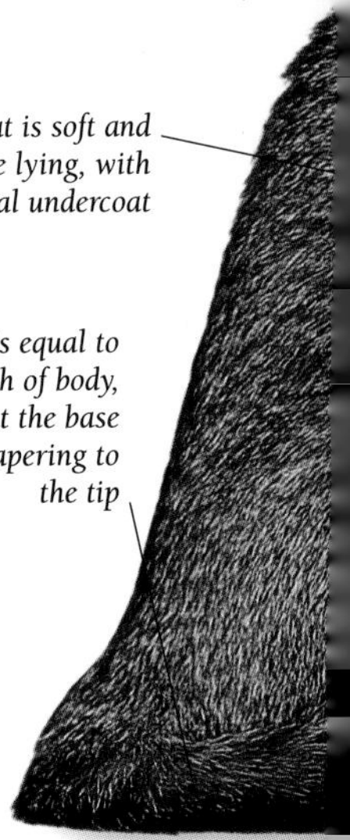

Coat is soft and close lying, with minimal undercoat
Tail is equal to length of body, wide at the base and tapering to the tip

Key Facts

Date of origin 1981

Place of origin United States

Ancestry American household cat

Outcross breeds None

Other name None

Weight range 7–11 lb (3–5 kg)

Temperament Quietly affable

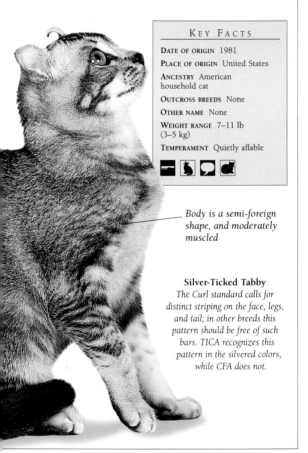

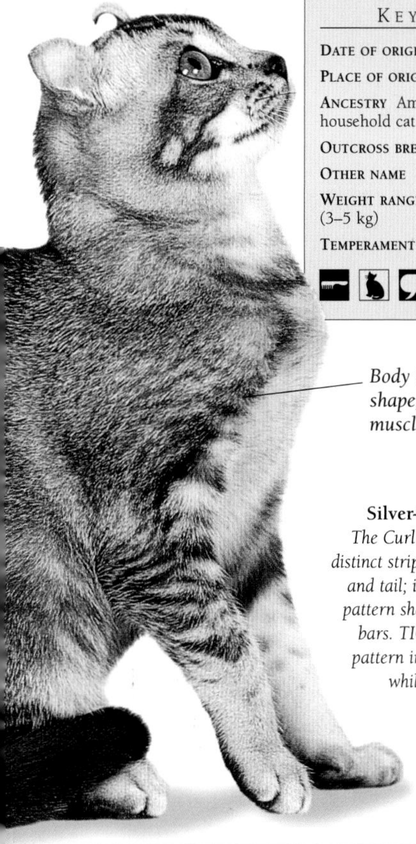

Body is a semi-foreign shape, and moderately muscled

Silver-Ticked Tabby

The Curl standard calls for distinct striping on the face, legs, and tail; in other breeds this pattern should be free of such bars. TICA recognizes this pattern in the silvered colors, while CFA does not.

Breed Colors

SILVER TABBIES (CLASSIC, MACKEREL)
Silver, Chocolate Silver, Cameo, Blue Silver, Lavender Silver, Cream Silver, Silver Patched
All other standard tabby colors, spotted and ticked patterns

BICOLORS (CLASSIC AND VAN)
Black, Red, Blue, Cream, with White, Calico, Dilute Calico
All other colors with white

TABBY BICOLORS
Colors are as for standard tabbies

SELF AND TORTIE POINTS
Seal, Chocolate, Flame, Blue, Lilac, Cream, Tortie, Chocolate Tortie, Blue-Cream, Lilac-Cream
All other colors, sepia, and mink patterns

LYNX (TABBY) POINTS
As for self and tortie points, except Red
All other colors, sepia, and mink patterns

Curl development
All American Curls are born with straight ears. When they are two to ten days old, the tips begin to curve; they then curl and uncurl until they "set" permanently at about four months.

BREED HISTORY For over a decade, the cat has been North America's most popular pet, and California is where the most active breeding programs exist. This new breed is the result of a genetic mutation that occurred in a black, longhaired, stray kitten named Shulamith. Half of her kittens also showed this unusual feature, a genetically dominant characteristic, and were distributed to form a breeding program. All members of this shorthaired breed descend, like their longhaired cousins, from this mother and her kittens, and are accepted on a showing standard that differs from the Persian only in coat.

Ears curve at least
90° in a smooth arc

MUNCHKIN

Although breeders claim that the dwarfism of these cats causes no problems, the Munchkin, a short-legged cat in longhair *(see page 74)* and shorthair versions, has caused unprecedented controversy. The breed has had to undergo rigorous health investigations to gain acceptance, but many breeders still feel that Munchkins are "uncatlike." While their playful personalities are unmistakably feline, it cannot be denied that the breed represents a radical departure from normal feline anatomy. Those who see the cat as a lovable pet may well come round to this breed.

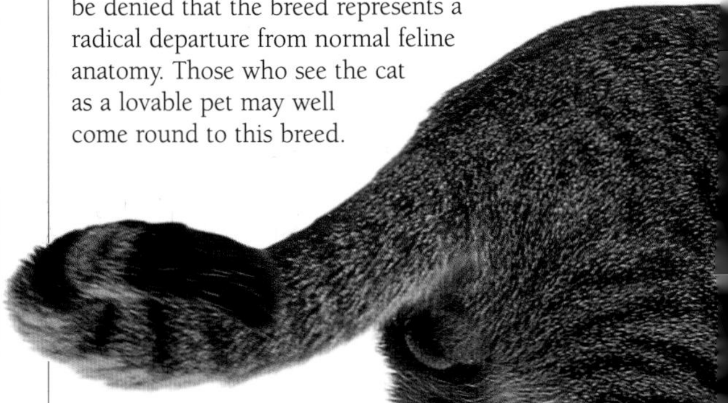

BREED COLORS

All colors and patterns, including pointed, sepia, and mink

RED CLASSIC TABBY

TORTIE AND WHITE

BLACK

Brown Spotted Tabby

Color and pattern are relatively unimportant in the breed standard. Build alone accounts for half the points. Part of the Munchkin's appeal may be that an adult cat's proportions resemble those of a kitten, whose legs are usually fairly short in relation to the body.

Head is triangular, with a medium-length nose
Neck is thick and firmly muscled
Legs are short but not misshapen, and well-muscled
Paws are rounded, compact, and pointing outward

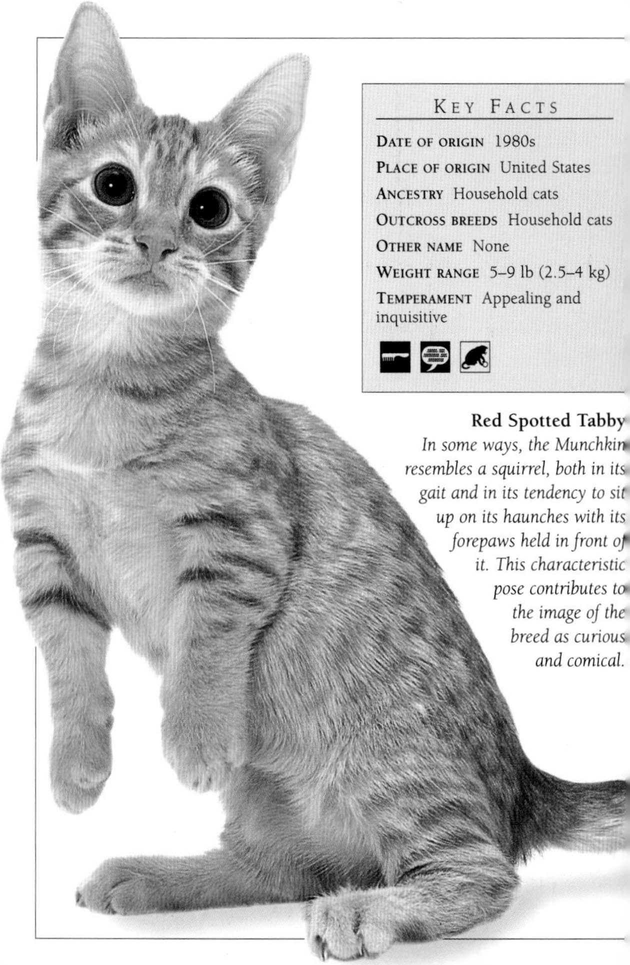

KEY FACTS

DATE OF ORIGIN 1980s

PLACE OF ORIGIN United States

ANCESTRY Household cats

OUTCROSS BREEDS Household cats

OTHER NAME None

WEIGHT RANGE 5–9 lb (2.5–4 kg)

TEMPERAMENT Appealing and inquisitive

Red Spotted Tabby
In some ways, the Munchkin resembles a squirrel, both in its gait and in its tendency to sit up on its haunches with its forepaws held in front of it. This characteristic pose contributes to the image of the breed as curious and comical.

Ears are moderately large, wide at the base, and upright
Eyes are walnut-shaped, large, and slightly tilted

Munchkin head

The breed standard is for a cat of moderation. The head should be neither rounded and jowly nor angular and foreign. All colors and patterns are allowed.

Breed History The Munchkin has been bred for ten years in North America. After health investigations, the breed was recognized by TICA in 1995. Some breeders are working with pedigreed breeds, producing rexed and curled-ear Munchkins, but these programs are not widely approved and the results have not been recognized.

SNOWSHOE

Named for its characteristic white mittens, this breed combines the pointing of the Siamese (*see page 280*) with white spotting, giving it crisp white paws. Two patterns exist: the mitted, with limited white; and the bicolor, with more white on the face and body. The white mittens may be inherited from the breed's American Shorthair (*see page 190*) ancestry, or they may come from its Siamese side; white toes were a known fault in early Siamese. Snowshoes are gregarious and affectionate, and although they are talkative, they have soft voices.

KEY FACTS

DATE OF ORIGIN 1960s

PLACE OF ORIGIN United States

ANCESTRY Siamese, American Shorthair

OUTCROSS BREEDS Solid eumelanistic Siamese, traditional eumelanistic solid, and bicolor American Shorthairs

OTHER NAME None

WEIGHT RANGE 6–12 lb (2.5–5.5 kg)

TEMPERAMENT Active and friendly

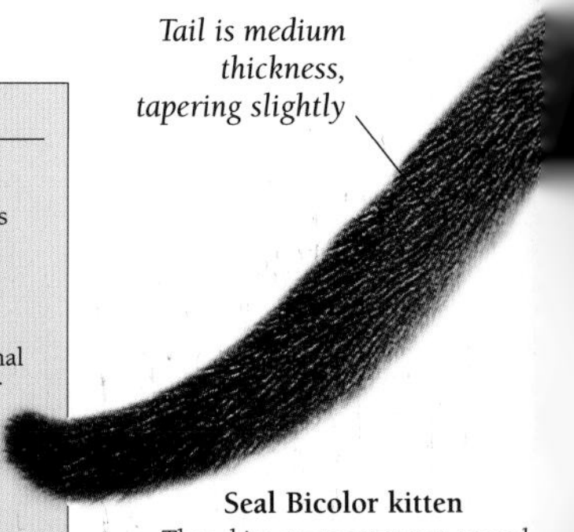
Tail is medium thickness, tapering slightly

Seal Bicolor kitten

The white areas must not exceed two-thirds of the total body area. Th body should be colored, showing subtle shading to lighter underpart with no isolated white spots.

Breed Colors

MITTED COLORS
Seal, Chocolate, Blue, Lilac

BICOLORS
All mitted colors with white

Head is a broad, modified wedge, with a slight stop in profile
Body is moderate in size and musculature, with a semi-foreign build

Snowshoe face
The facial pattern decides if a Snowshoe is mitted or bicolor. An inverted "V" of white makes the cat a bicolor, while anything less makes it a mitted. The amount of white on the body determines whether it is a good or bad example of either pattern.

Breed History In the 1960s, Philadelphia breeder Dorothy Hinds-Daugherty began to cross her Siamese with American Shorthairs. The resulting hybrid faced some opposition from Siamese breeders at first, partly due to fears that the spotting might find its way into Siamese bloodlines after many decades of breeding to eradicate this early fault. The dramatic pointing pattern was also a trademark of the Siamese breed at that time, although it is recognized in a variety of breeds today. The Snowshoe remained little known until the 1980s, when it was recognized by TICA. It has since gained wider popularity, but remains rare. It is not recognized by any of the other major registries.

Mitted Blue

The mitted pattern is the "classic" Snowshoe. White paws ideally stop at the ankles on the forelegs and below the hocks on the hindlegs; the amount of white must not exceed one-third of the body. There may be some white on the face. Sex-linked red colors and cinnamon colors do not occur in the Snowshoe.

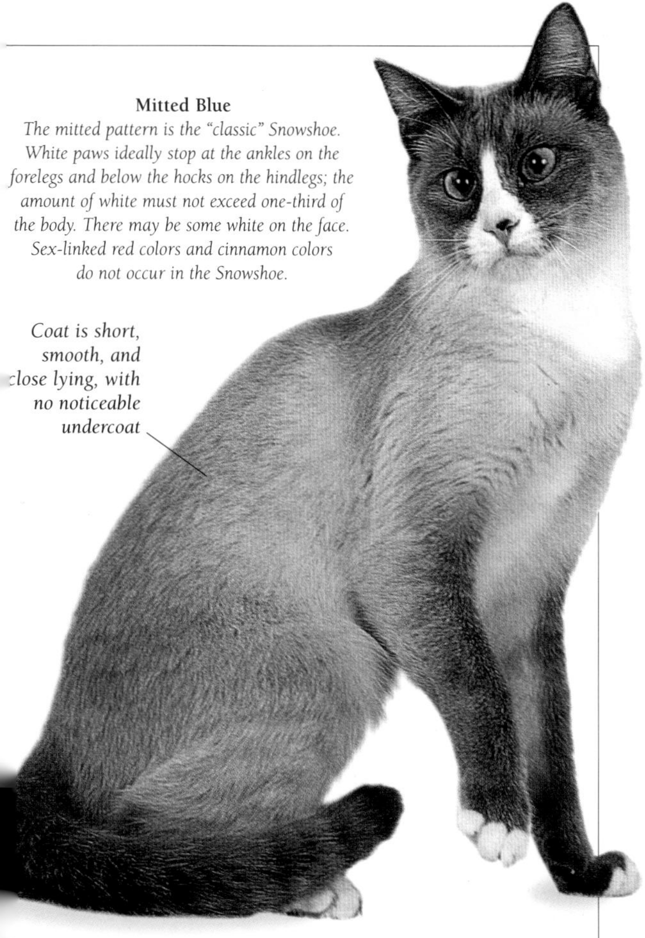
Coat is short, smooth, and close lying, with no noticeable undercoat

European Shorthair

A cat with a whole continent to call home might easily be assumed to be widely popular, but the European Shorthair is less known than either its British Shorthair or American Shorthair counterparts. Over the years since the breed was established, it has become less cobby than the British type, with a slightly longer and less heavily jowled face, perhaps reflecting the typical feline type of warmer mainland European countries more than it did in the past. It has many of the same basic traits as the British cats, however, being a strong, hardy animal with an all-weather coat. Its personality tends to be calm and affectionate, and it is a relatively quiet breed.

Breed Colors

SELF AND TORTIE COLORS
Black, Blue, Red, Cream, Tortie, Blue Tortie, White (Blue-, Odd-, Orange-Eyed)

SMOKE COLORS
Colors are as for self and tortie, except White

TABBY COLORS (CLASSIC, MACKEREL, SPOTTED)
Brown, Blue, Red, Cream, Tortie, Blue Tortie

SILVER TABBY COLORS (CLASSIC, MACKEREL, SPOTTED)
Colors are as for standard tabbies

BICOLORS (STANDARD AND VAN)
Self and tortie colors with white
Smoke, tipped, and tabby colors with white

BROWN TABBY

BLUE-CREAM AND WHITE

SEAL POINT

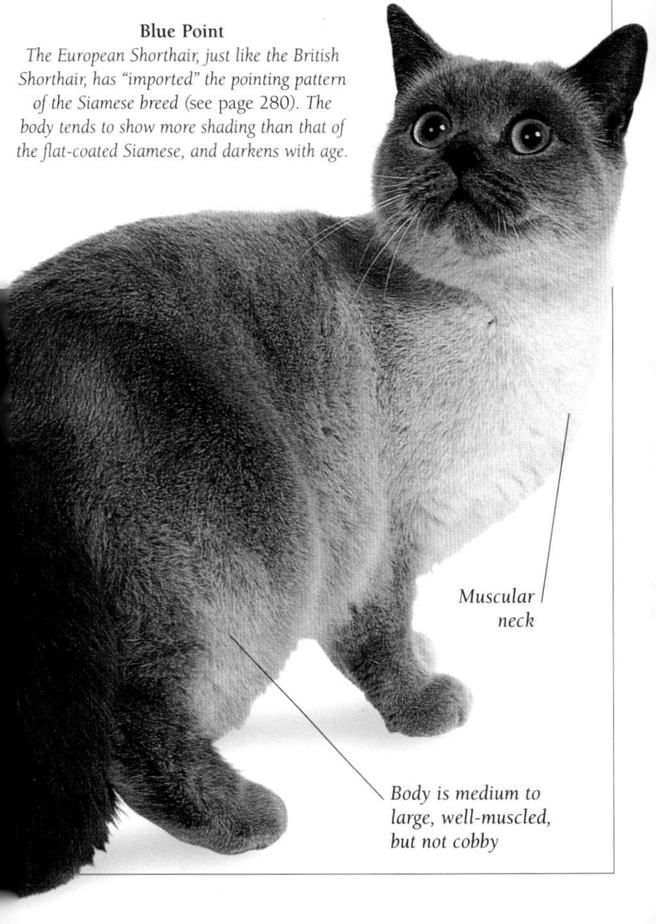

Blue Point

The European Shorthair, just like the British Shorthair, has "imported" the pointing pattern of the Siamese breed (see page 280). *The body tends to show more shading than that of the flat-coated Siamese, and darkens with age.*

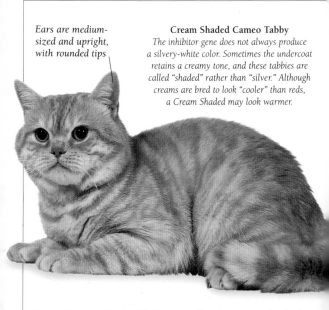

Ears are medium-sized and upright, with rounded tips

Cream Shaded Cameo Tabby

The inhibitor gene does not always produce a silvery-white color. Sometimes the undercoat retains a creamy tone, and these tabbies are called "shaded" rather than "silver." Although creams are bred to look "cooler" than reds, a Cream Shaded may look warmer.

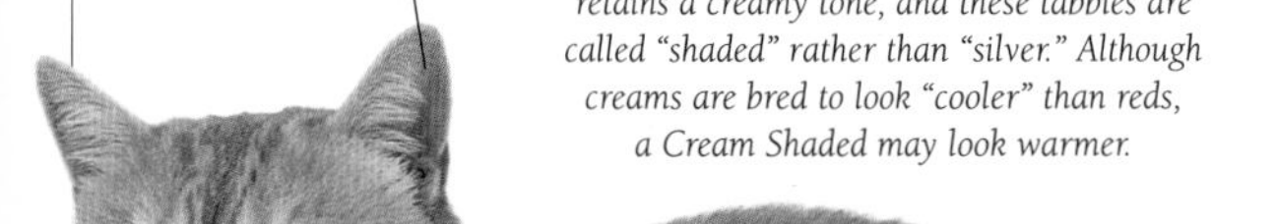

Breed History Until 1982, European Shorthairs were classified with British Shorthairs. FIFé then gave the breed its own category, and it began effectively as a "ready-made" breed, with a full range of colors, established type, and breeding stock with known histories. Despite this advantage, or maybe because it is so similar to the British and American Shorthairs, the European Shorthair does not seem to have caught the imagination of breeders, and remains rare. The breed is now being selectively bred, with no British Shorthair crosses permitted in the pedigree. It is not recognized by GCCF or major breed registries outside Europe.

Black Silver Mackerel Tabby
This breed has three "traditional" tabby patterns of classic, mackerel, and spotted. The Black Silver Tabby is popular because of the contrasting colors in its coat. The markings should be symmetrical on both sides of the body.

Eyes are large, rounded, and well spaced, with colors to match coat
Coat is short and dense, standing away from the body

Red Silver Mackerel Tabby
In the Silver Tabby colors, the undercoat is a pure, glistening white, giving a cool tone to the color.

Key Facts

Date of origin 1982

Place of origin European mainland

Ancestry Household cats, British Shorthair

Outcross breeds None

Other name None

Weight range 8–15 lb (3.5–7 kg)

Temperament Intelligent and reserved

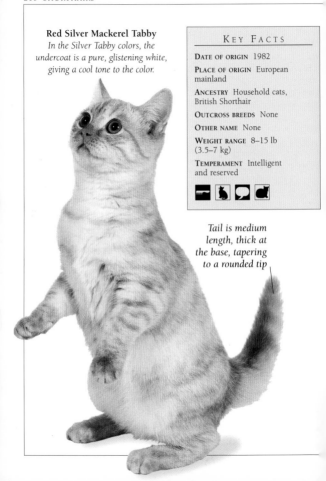

Tail is medium length, thick at the base, tapering to a rounded tip

Tortoiseshell Smoke

In the European Shorthair, the patches of black, red, and cream in the tortoiseshell pattern should be broken into clearly defined patches, rather than subtly intermingled. Because the coat does not lie flat, the white undercoat of a Smoke can be seen and has the effect of "watering down" the colors slightly.

Head is triangular to rounded, with a well-defined muzzle

CHARTREUX

A keen observer of life, rather than an impulsive participant, the Chartreux is a tolerant breed, less talkative than most, with a rather high-pitched meow and an infrequently used chirp. Its short legs, stockiness, and dense, close coat mask its true size. This is a big, powerful, late-maturing cat. Although a good hunter, it is not a fighter: Individuals tend to withdraw from conflicts rather than become aggressive. There is an intriguing naming system for Chartreux: Each year is designated by a letter (omitting K, Q, W, X, Y, and Z), and cats' names begin with the letter determined by the year of birth. For example, cats born in 1997 have names beginning with N.

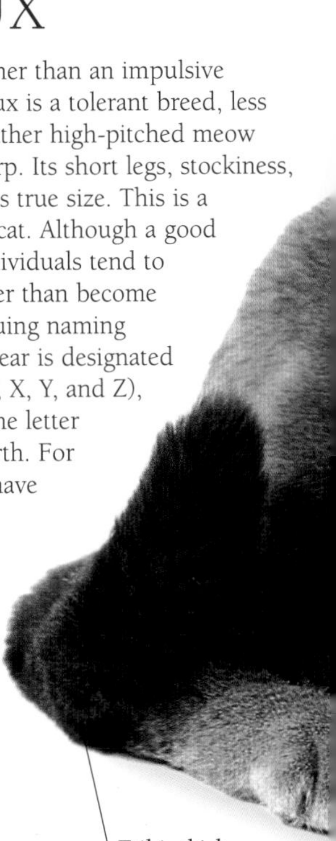

Blue male

Male Chartreux are much larger than females, with a heavier build, although they should never become cobby. They also develop pronounced jowls with age, which adds to the broadness of the head.

Tail is thick at the base, tapering to a rounded tip

BREED COLORS
SELF COLORS Blue

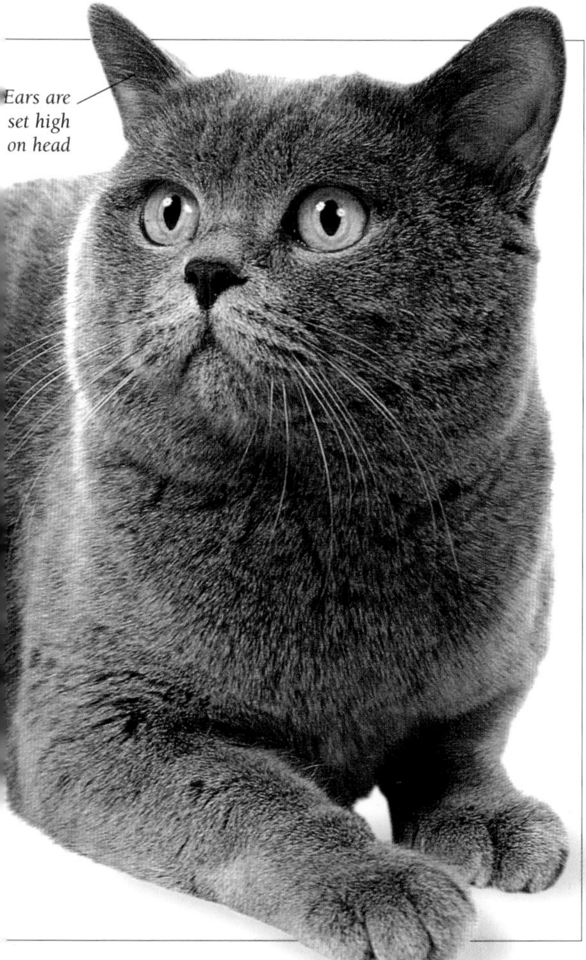
Ears are set high on head

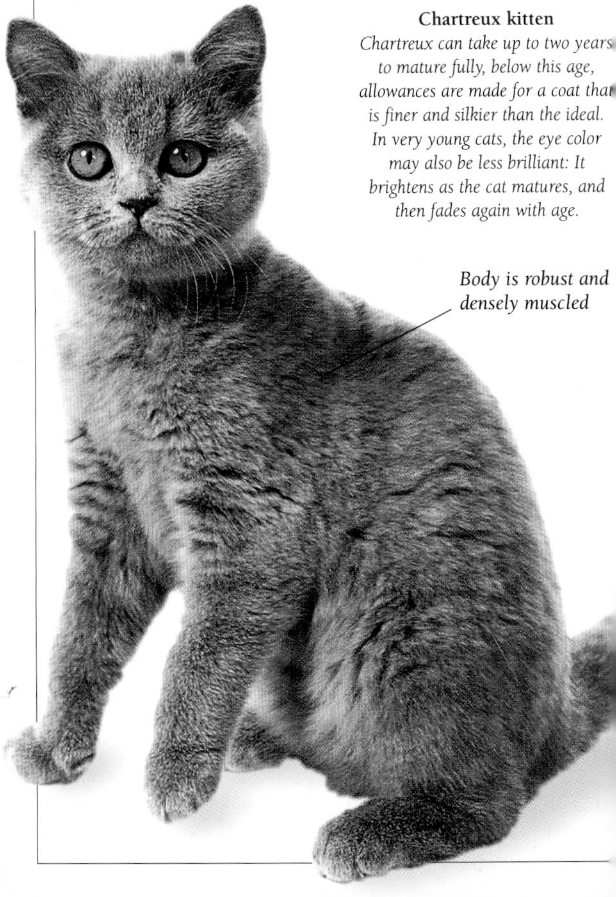

Chartreux kitten

Chartreux can take up to two years to mature fully, below this age, allowances are made for a coat that is finer and silkier than the ideal. In very young cats, the eye color may also be less brilliant: It brightens as the cat matures, and then fades again with age.

Body is robust and densely muscled

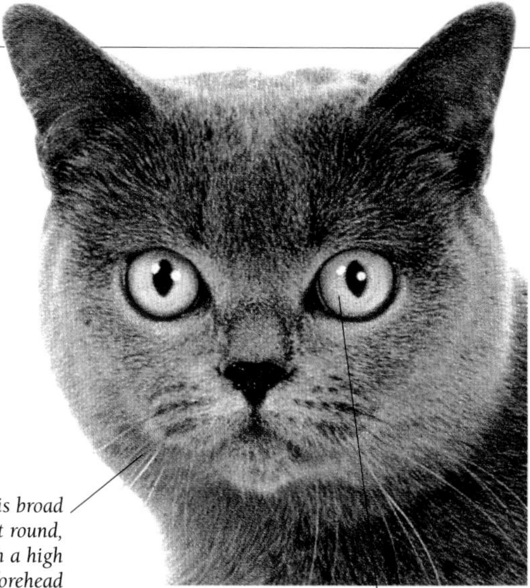
Head is broad but not round, with a high forehead
Eyes are large and round, and gold or copper in color

Chartreux head
The Chartreux head is broad, but stops just short of becoming a sphere. The muzzle is relatively narrow, but the rounded whisker pads and heavy jowls prevent it from looking too pointed. The expression should be sweet, with a slight smile.

Key Facts

Date of origin Pre-18th century

Place of origin France

Ancestry Household cats

Outcross breeds None

Other name None

Weight range 7–17 lb (3–7.5 kg)

Temperament Calmly attentive

Breed History Possibly originating in Syria, the Chartreux's ancestors would have arrived in France by ship. By the 1700s, the breed was described by the naturalist Buffon as the "cat of France" and given a Latin name, *Felis catus coeruleus*. After World War II it became almost extinct, and was reestablished by outcrossing survivors with blue Persians (*see page 16*) and British Blues (*see page 168*). The Chartreux reached North America in the 1970s, but is not bred in many European countries. FIFé assimilated the Chartreux and British Blue under the name Chartreux during the 1970s, and all British and European Blues were described as Chartreux for a time, but these breeds are again treated as distinct.

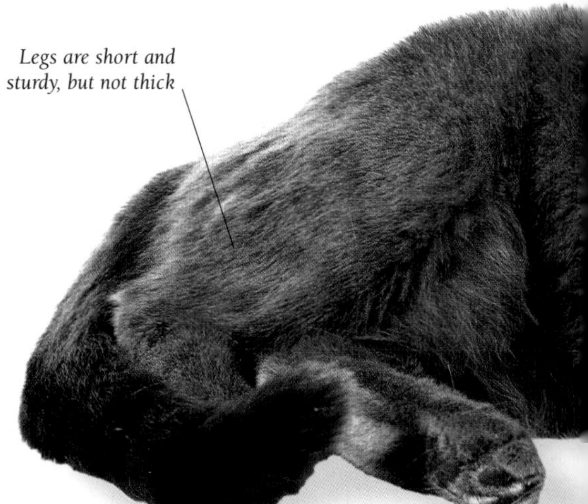

Legs are short and sturdy, but not thick

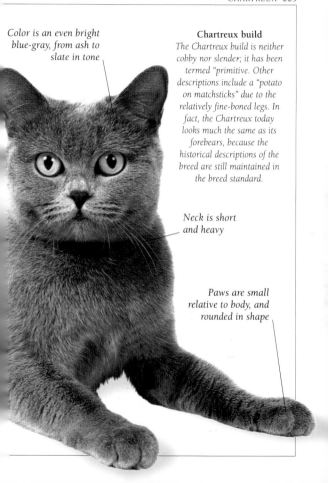

Color is an even bright blue-gray, from ash to slate in tone
Neck is short and heavy
Paws are small relative to body, and rounded in shape

Chartreux build

The Chartreux build is neither cobby nor slender; it has been termed "primitive. Other descriptions include a "potato on matchsticks" due to the relatively fine-boned legs. In fact, the Chartreux today looks much the same as its forebears, because the historical descriptions of the breed are still maintained in the breed standard.

RUSSIAN SHORTHAIR

The original of this group is the slightly reserved and immensely dignified Russian Blue. A cautious cat, it is sensitive to changes in its environment and controlled in its response to strangers. Its most vivid features are its thick, lustrous coat and its emerald-green eyes. The soft, dense, insulating, double coat is unique in feel, and described in the British breed standard as "the truest criterion of the Russian." The Russian's trademark eye color has a more recent origin: the first Russian Blues exhibited in the West, at the Crystal Palace show in England in 1871, had yellow eyes. It was not until 1933 that breed standards called for eye color to be "as vividly green as possible." This is among the least destructive of all breeds, and an ideal indoor cat.

KEY FACTS

DATE OF ORIGIN Pre-1800s

PLACE OF ORIGIN Possibly Russian port of Archangel

ANCESTRY Domestic cats

OUTCROSS BREEDS None

OTHER NAME Archangel Cat, Foreign Blue, Maltese Cat, Spanish Blue, Russian Shorthair

WEIGHT RANGE 7–12 lb (3–5.5 kg)

TEMPERAMENT Reserved and wary

Russian Blue

The original, and to some the only, Russian, this color is an eve blue with a silvery sheen. This sheen gives the coat a luminous appearance, and many breeders s that the less the cat is brushed, th more radiant the coat becomes.

Head is longer from ears to eyes than from eyes to nose
Eyes are large and almond-shaped, and widely spaced
Body is well-muscled, but never cobby or heavy
Legs are long but not delicate

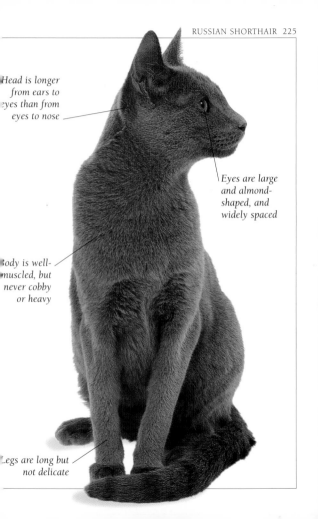

Breed History Legend says that the Russian Blue descends from ships' cats brought from the Russian port of Archangel to Britain in the 19th century. Russian Blues are mentioned by name in Harrison Weir's 1893 book *Our Cats*, but from the Russian Revolution in 1917 until 1948, they were known as Foreign Blues. The modern Russian Blue contains bloodlines from British Blues (*see page 168*), and even from Blue Point Siamese (*see page 281*), consequences of Swedish and British efforts to revive the breed in the 1950s. Black and white versions have been developed in New Zealand and Europe; these are accepted in Britain, but not by FIFé or any North American organizations.

Tail is moderate in length and in thickness, tapering to a rounded tip

Russian Black

The Russian Blue bred true for centuries because the dilute color is recessive, never masking other colors. Black and White Russians are a recent development, and regarded by many as controversial. Least welcome of all are the blue-pointed "Russians," a result of past Siamese outcrosses.

BREED COLORS

SOLID COLORS
Black, Blue, White

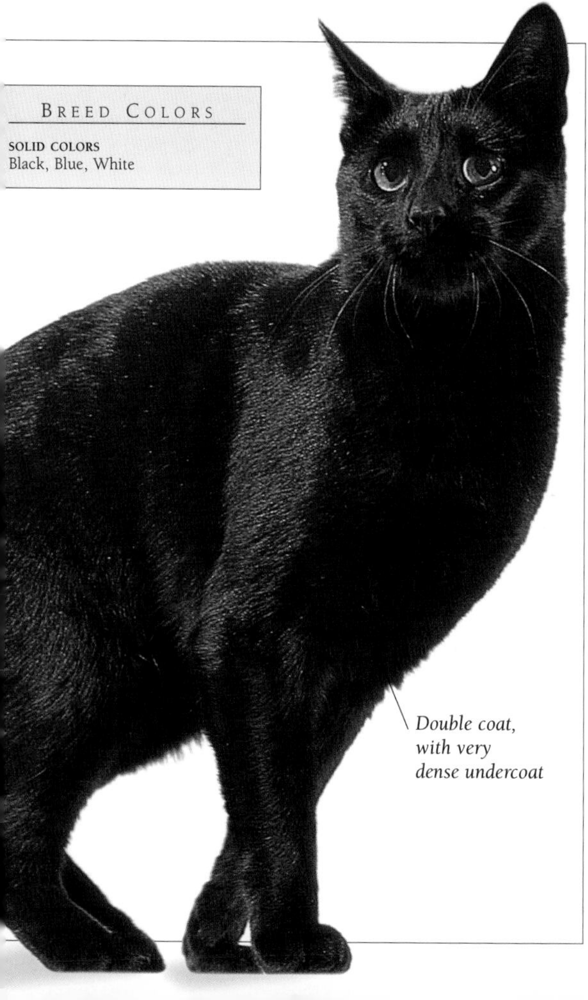

HAVANA BROWN

Elegant and graceful in its outward appearance, the Havana Brown is a very physical breed. Havanas love to play hide-and-seek, and treat leaping out from behind furniture to surprise people as a wonderful game; they are also excellent climbers. Although its origins are the same as those of the Oriental Shorthair (*see page* 292), it has developed to resemble the Russian Blue (*see page* 224). The Havana Brown stands high on its legs for such a moderately sized animal, and is heavy. Kittens and young adults have ghost tabby marks that disappear with age, leaving an even, rich shade of brown, tending toward mahogany.

Tail is of a medium length and thickness

BREED COLORS

SOLID COLORS
Chocolate, *Lilac*

Chocolate

The standard for this shade of brown varies considerably from breed to breed. In the Havana Brown, it is defined as a warm brown, tending toward red-brown. A dark, sable-type coat is a serious fault.

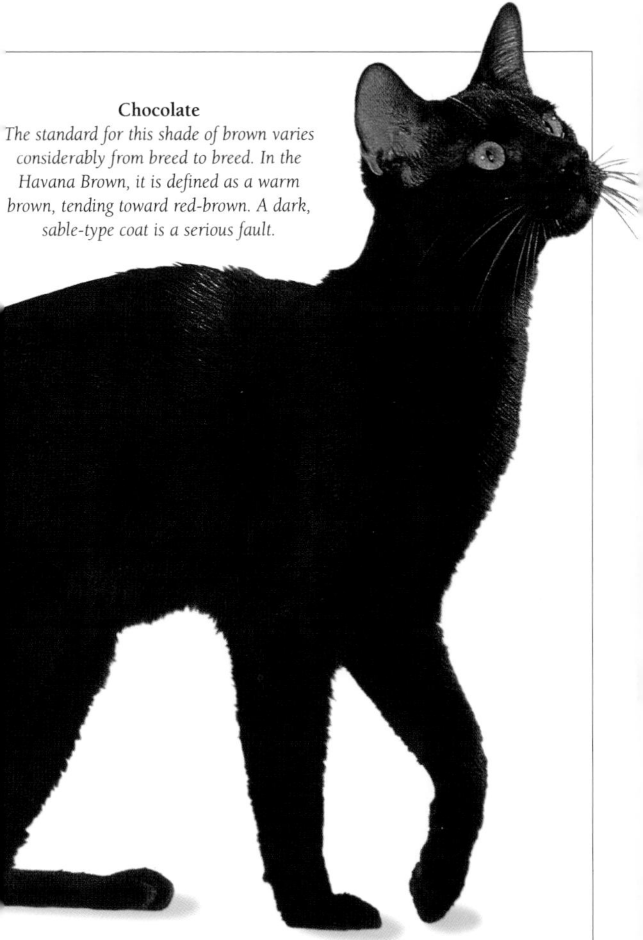

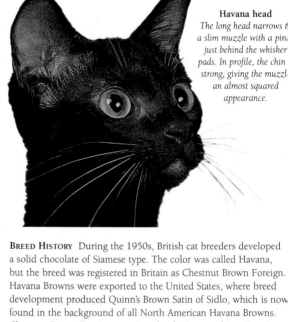

Havana head

The long head narrows t[o] a slim muzzle with a pin[ch] just behind the whisker pads. In profile, the chin [is] strong, giving the muzzl[e] an almost squared appearance.

Breed History During the 1950s, British cat breeders developed a solid chocolate of Siamese type. The color was called Havana, but the breed was registered in Britain as Chestnut Brown Foreign. Havana Browns were exported to the United States, where breed development produced Quinn's Brown Satin of Sidlo, which is now found in the background of all North American Havana Browns. Chestnut Brown Foreigns continued to be imported into America and registered as Havana Browns until 1973, when CFA accepted the Oriental Shorthair breed: From then on, these imports were registered as Chestnut Oriental Shorthairs. Ironically, the Oriental Shorthair color called Chestnut in North America is now called Havana in Britain, leading to some confusion.

Key Facts

Date of origin 1950s

Place of origin Great Britain and the United States

Ancestry Chocolate Point Siamese, Russian Blue

Outcross breeds None

Other name None

Weight range 6–10 lb (2.5–4.5 kg)

Temperament Sweet and sociable

Lilac

Russian Blues were used in the creation of the Havana Brown, introducing the recessive dilute trait, which led to the occasional Lilac cat.

Body is medium in length, carried level

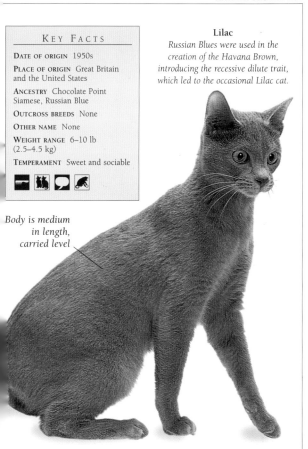

ABYSSINIAN

The almost translucent coat pattern of this breed is due to a single gene, first noted in the Abyssinian. This gene gives each hair several dark bands, evenly dispersed on a lighter background, resulting in a striking "ticked" coat pattern. Abyssinians' ears sometimes have caracal-like tufts, which add to their striking appearance. Although often silent, Abyssinians' personalities are far from quiet; they become attached to their owners, and demand attention and play. They are natural athletes, climbing and investigating anything available: curtains, people, or, if allowed out, fences and trees. They can suffer inherited forms of retinal atrophy, a blindness more common in dogs.

BREED COLORS

TABBIES (TICKED)
Ruddy, Red, Blue, Fawn
Chocolate, sex-linked Red, Lilac, Cream, Chocolate Tortie, Cinnamon Tortie, Blue Tortie, Lilac Tortie, Fawn Tortie

SILVER TABBIES (TICKED)
All standard ticked tabby colors

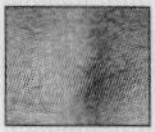

CREAM

CHOCOLATE

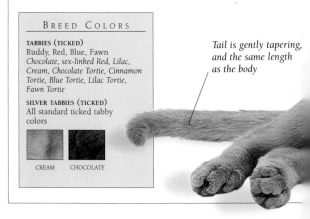

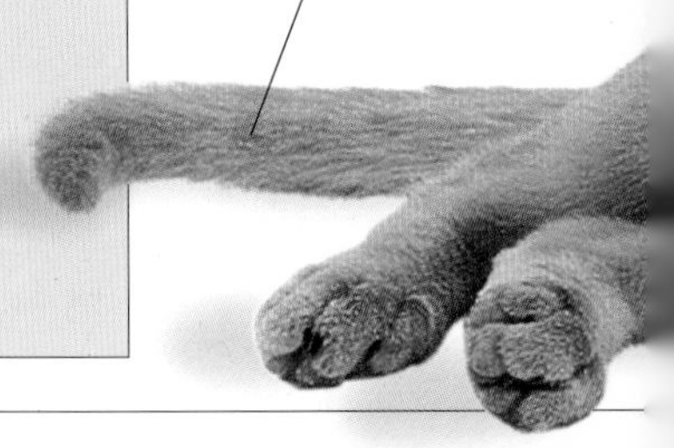

Tail is gently tapering, and the same length as the body

Lilac kitten

One of the newer additions to the range of Abyssinian colors, the Lilac is the dilute shade of the Chocolate. Both colors were introduced through outcrosses to Oriental cats in the 1970s, and they are still not accepted by the more traditional registries.

Eyes have a dark rim set in spectacles of lighter hair

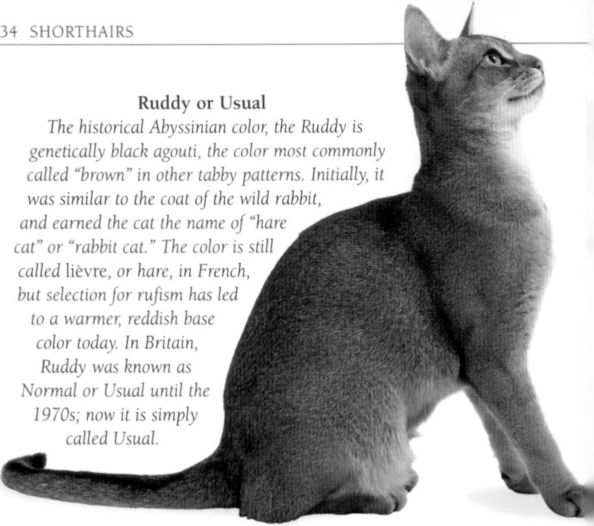

Ruddy or Usual

The historical Abyssinian color, the Ruddy is genetically black agouti, the color most commonly called "brown" in other tabby patterns. Initially, it was similar to the coat of the wild rabbit, and earned the cat the name of "hare cat" or "rabbit cat." The color is still called lièvre, *or hare, in French, but selection for rufism has led to a warmer, reddish base color today. In Britain, Ruddy was known as Normal or Usual until the 1970s; now it is simply called Usual.*

Abyssinian head

The face (below left) *is a wedge. A slight nose break is seen in profile* (below right). *Rounded, almond-shaped eyes are green, hazel, or amber.*

Ears are large and cupped, with tufted tips

Key Facts

Date of origin 1860s

Place of origin Ethiopia

Ancestry Ethiopian household and street cats

Outcross breeds None

Other name Color names vary internationally

Weight range 9–16 lb (4–7.5 kg)

Temperament Attention seeking

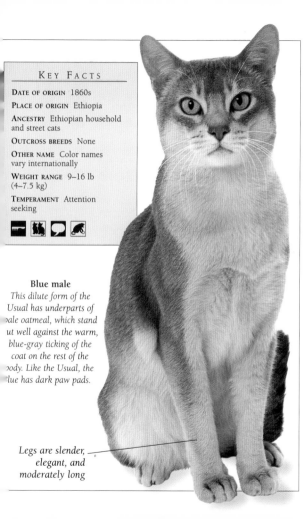

Blue male

This dilute form of the Usual has underparts of ɔale oatmeal, which stand ut well against the warm, blue-gray ticking of the coat on the rest of the ɔody. Like the Usual, the ·lue has dark paw pads.

Legs are slender, elegant, and moderately long

Fawn kitten

This color is the dilute version of the Sorrel and was once called Cream, but it is generally less bright in appearance than a true sex-linked Cream. In some associations only these colors are accepted, but in Britain true reds and creams are accepted for showing.

Coat is close-lying, fine but not soft

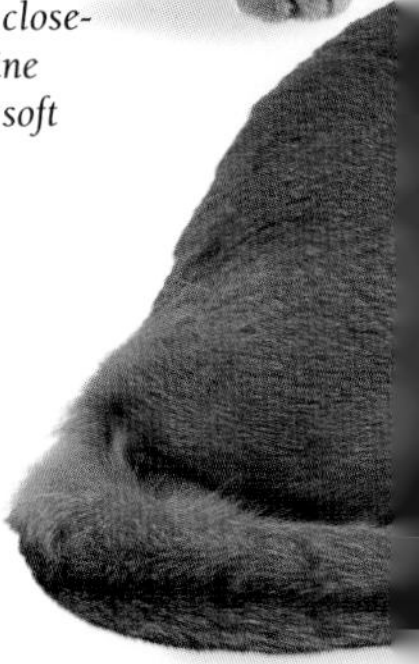

Red or Sorrel

Once called Red in all registries, this color is now more usually called Sorrel in Britain. It is not, however, the true sex-linked Red, but the recessive light brown that is more commonly known as cinnamon in other breeds.

Breed History The Abyssinian's ticking is a perfect camouflage in the dry, sun-scorched habitat of North Africa. The founding cats, including one called Zula, were brought to Britain from Abyssinia (now Ethiopia) after the Abyssinian War in 1868. There is a strong similarity between these first Abys and some ancient Egyptian feline images, suggesting that the ticked mutation occurred thousands of years ago. Accepted in 1882, the breed was almost extinct in Britain by the early 20th century, but by the 1930s it was established in the United States and France. Today, it is most popular in North America. Standards differ internationally: European Abys have a more foreign shape and a wider range of colors.

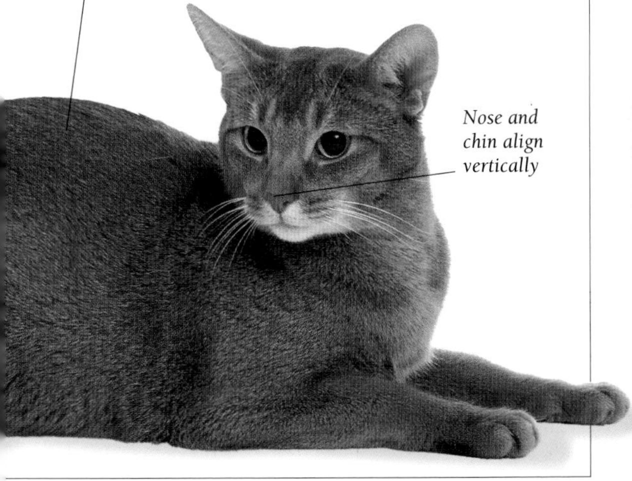
Body is medium-sized and muscular
Nose and chin align vertically

SPOTTED MIST

This is the first breed that has been developed entirely in Australia. The Spotted Mist has been bred to have a playful and home-loving nature. Gentleness of spirit is prized, and the standard penalizes any aggression on the show bench. Similar in some ways to the Asian Ticked Tabby (*see page 260*), its appearance is moderate: medium in size, foreign in build but not extremely so, with a short, but not close-lying coat. The rather delicate markings create a misty appearance and account for the breed's name; the background ticking is essential to this effect. The breed is recognized in six colors. Full color takes a year to develop, and in some colors the delicate spots can be hard to see.

Gold

One of the colors brought in from the Abyssinian ancestry, this is genetically a cinnamon. The mixture of genetic influences in the Spotted Mist has transmuted the coat to gold and bronze markings on a cream ground.

Body is medium sized with moderate muscling

BREED COLORS

TABBY (SPOTTED AND TICKED TOGETHER)
Blue, Brown, Chocolate, Gold, Lilac, Peach

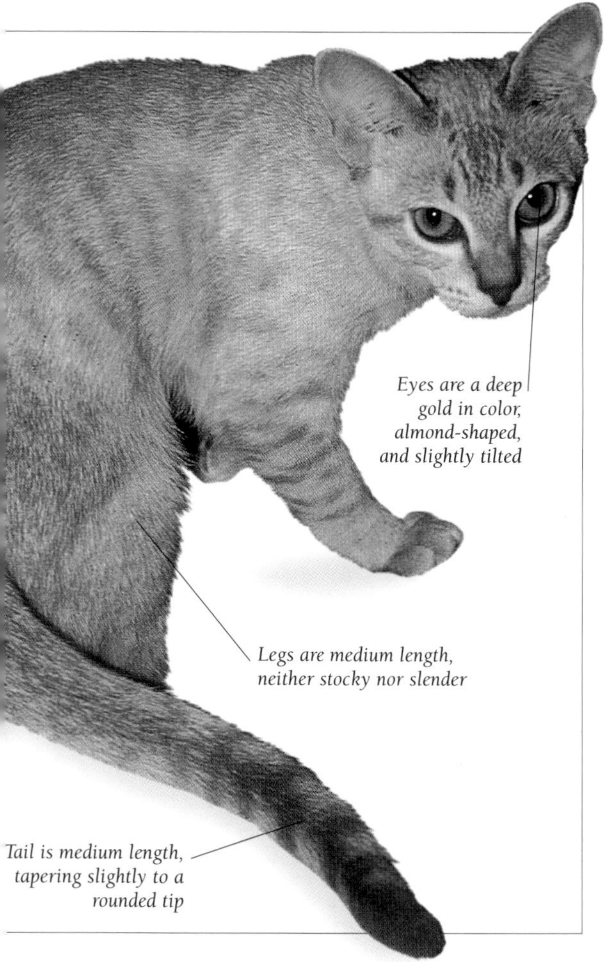
Eyes are a deep gold in color, almond-shaped, and slightly tilted
Legs are medium length, neither stocky nor slender
Tail is medium length, tapering slightly to a rounded tip

Breed History Dr. Truda Staede in New South Wales, Australia, developed a program to produce an indoor-loving, people-oriented breed, with the Burmese shape and a spotted tabby coat. The Burmese contributed conformation, companionability, and four of the six Spotted Mist colors. The Abyssinian added two more colors, the essential ticking, and a lively disposition. Domestic tabbies gave the spots and offset the tendency towards early sexual maturity. In January 1980, the first half-Burmese, quarter-Abyssinian, quarter-domestic tabby kittens were born. A recognized breed in Australia, the Spotted Mist is still very rare and remains unknown elsewhere.

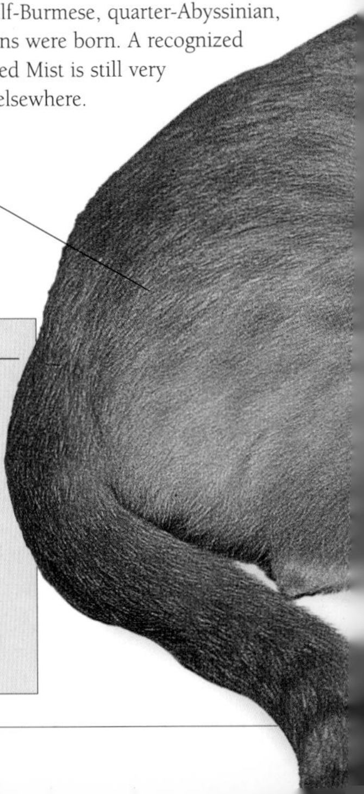

Coat is short, and stands out softly from body

Key Facts

Date of origin 1975

Place of origin Australia

Ancestry Abyssinian, Burmese

Outcross breeds None

Other name None

Weight range 8–13 lb (3.5–6 kg)

Temperament Lively and harmonious

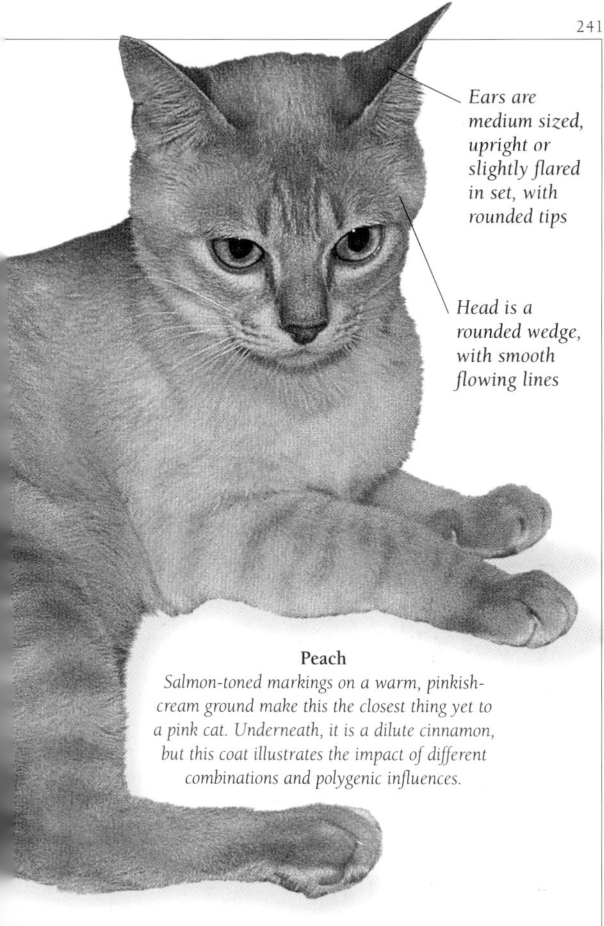
Ears are medium sized, upright or slightly flared in set, with rounded tips
Head is a rounded wedge, with smooth flowing lines

Peach

Salmon-toned markings on a warm, pinkish-cream ground make this the closest thing yet to a pink cat. Underneath, it is a dilute cinnamon, but this coat illustrates the impact of different combinations and polygenic influences.

SINGAPURA

Peaceful, even retiring, by temperament, these cats are at the smaller end of the feline range. Singapuras are distinctive in their one recognized coat, a ticked tabby in a color called Sepia. The Singapura's temperament and physical attributes are widely reputed to be a natural result of selective pressures. In Singapore, most cats are feral and nocturnal. Cats that attract the least attention are more likely to breed successfully, leading to small size, a quiet voice, and a retiring disposition. Western cats are larger than Singapore's "drain cats," either because of genetic differences or better diet. On the basis of this and other factors, some people believe that Singapore's feral stock was the inspiration for the breed, rather than its sole genetic founders.

KEY FACTS

DATE OF ORIGIN 1975

PLACE OF ORIGIN Singapore and the United States

ANCESTRY Disputed

OUTCROSS BREEDS None

OTHER NAME None

WEIGHT RANGE 4–9 lb (2–4 kg)

TEMPERAMENT Affectionate and introspective

Singapura kittens

The coats of Singapura kittens seldom meet the breed standard for adults: they are longer in relation to their small bodies, and also show less developed ticking. Even quite young kittens, however, show the "cheetah lines" that run from the inner corner of the eye to the whisker pads.

BREED COLORS

TABBY (TICKED)
Sepia Agouti

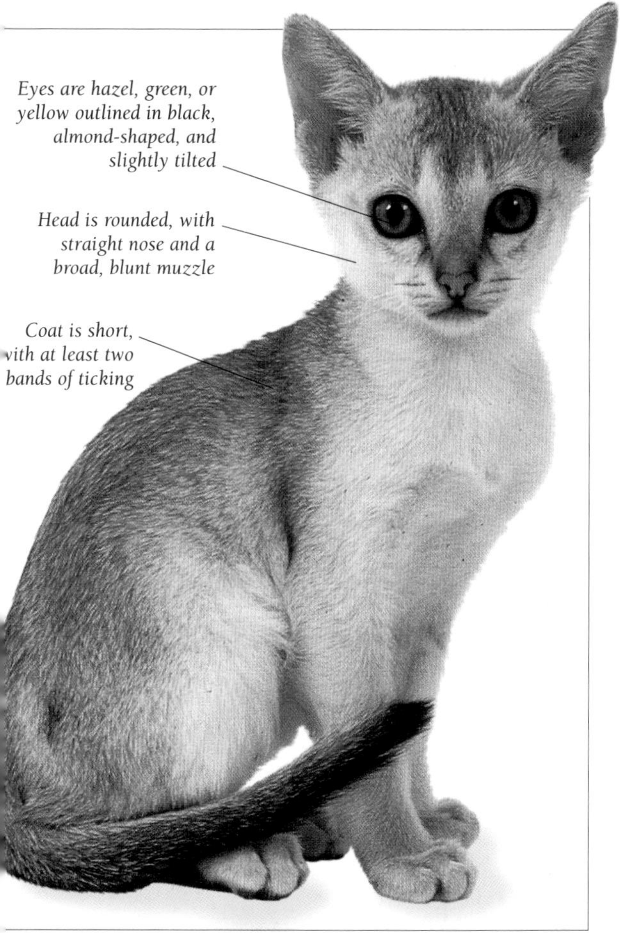
Eyes are hazel, green, or yellow outlined in black, almond-shaped, and slightly tilted
Head is rounded, with straight nose and a broad, blunt muzzle
Coat is short, vith at least two bands of ticking

Ears are wide and deeply cupped, set at a slightly outward angle
Body is of medium length and build

Breed History This new breed's name derives from the Malay word for Singapore, from where Hal and Tommy Meadows brought cats to the United States in 1975; all registered Singapuras today originate from the Meadows' breeding program. The Singapura received its first formal championship recognition in 1988. The breed has reached Europe, but neither FIFé nor the GCCF recognize it, and there is still controversy surrounding its origins. Tommy Meadows also bred Burmese (*see page* 262) and Abyssinians (*see page* 232), and there are claims that these were used to create the Singapura. There are still less than 2,000 Singapuras, and some people believe that the closed register could work to its detriment.

Sepia Agouti
This is the only color in which the Singapura is bred. Genetically, it is a sable ticked tabby, a combination uniting the Burmese allele with the tabby pattern first known in the Abyssinian.

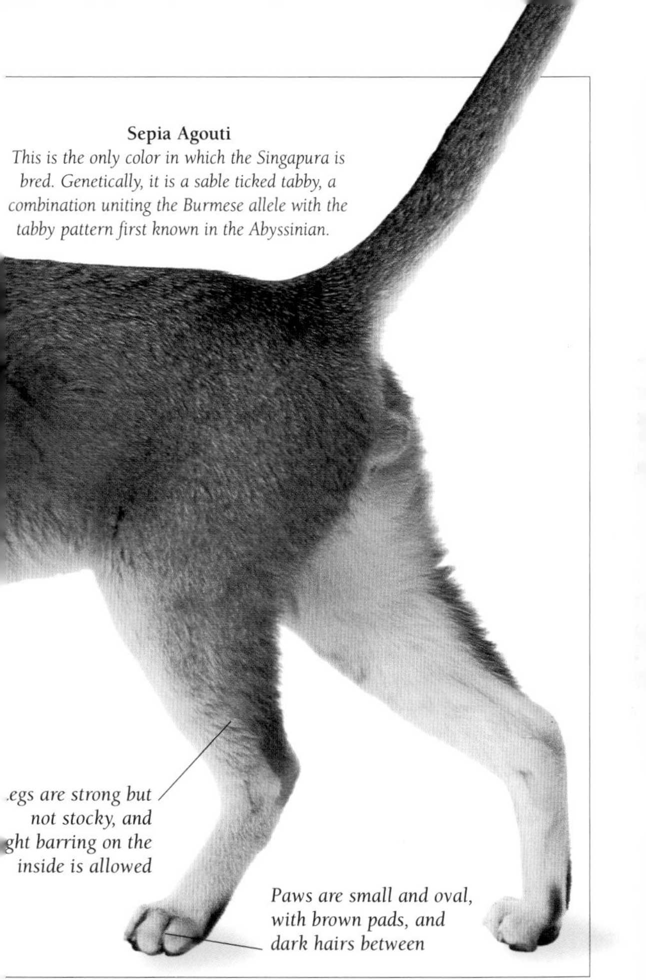
.egs are strong but not stocky, and ght barring on the inside is allowed
Paws are small and oval, with brown pads, and dark hairs between

KORAT

Medium-sized, with a semi-cobby body and a silver-blue coat, the Korat is similar to the Russian Blue (*see page 224*) in size and color. Korats, however, are a densely muscled and rounded breed, with a single rather than double coat and peridot-green rather than emerald-green eyes. The large, prominent eyes give it an innocent expression, but this is a strong-willed, even pushy, cat. While gregariousness makes Korats playful and trainable, they do thrive on having their own way. They have an excellent capacity to grumble and, without attention, can become demanding, stubborn, and territorial. Very rarely, individuals may carry neuromuscular disorders, called GM1 and GM2: these can be established by blood tests.

BREED HISTORY The *Cat Book Poems*, a product of the Ayutthaya Kingdom (AD 1350–1767) in Thailand, describes the silver-blue Si-Sawat from Korat, a remote, high plateau in the northeast of the country. The first Korat in the West may have been entered in English cat shows in the 1880s as a solid blue Siamese (*see page 280*). Modern Korats were introduced into the United States by Mrs. Jean Johnson in 1959; they were recognized there in 1965. The first pair was imported into Britain in 1972, and the breed was recognized in 1975. It remains rare everywhere.

BREED COLORS

SELF COLORS
Blue

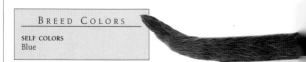

Blues only allowed

As is to be expected from a breed that developed in a warm climate, the Korat has dispensed with the unnecessary insulation of an undercoat, and the single, silver-blue coat is short. Some lilacs have been bred in mainland Europe, but they are unlikely ever to be accepted.

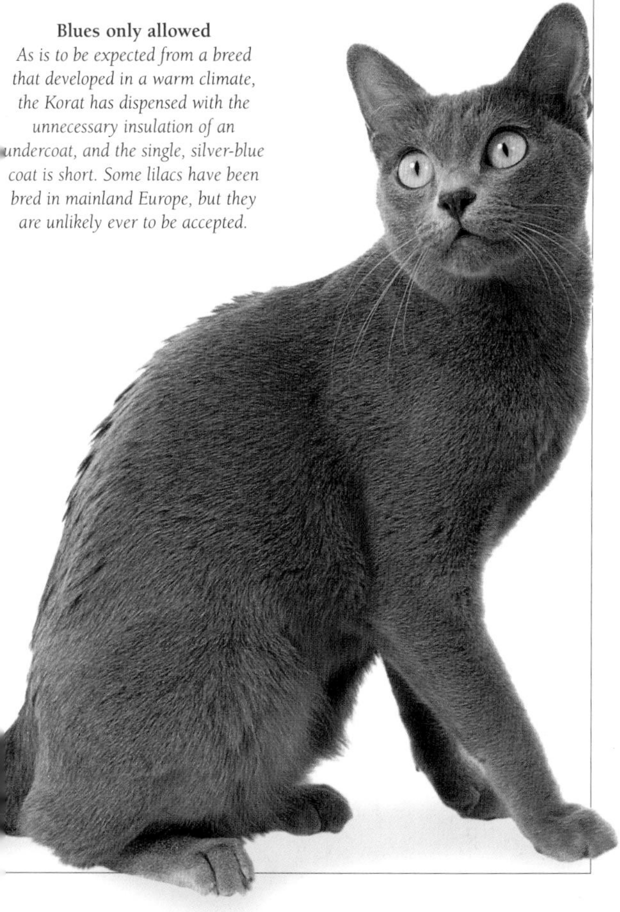

Head is large, with a flat forehead and rounded muzzle
Eyes are luminous, prominent, and rounded

Korat head

Oversized eyes and a heart-shaped face described by gentle curves give the Korat a much softer appearance than its compatriot breeds, but it has every bit as much personality.

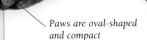

Key Facts

Date of origin Pre 1700s

Place of origin Thailand

Ancestry Household cats

Outcross breeds None

Other name Si-Sawat

Weight range 6–11 lb (2.5–5 kg)

Temperament Demanding and opinionated

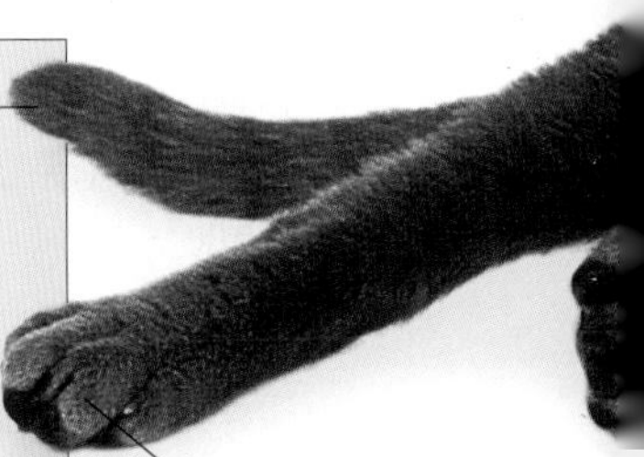
Paws are oval-shaped and compact

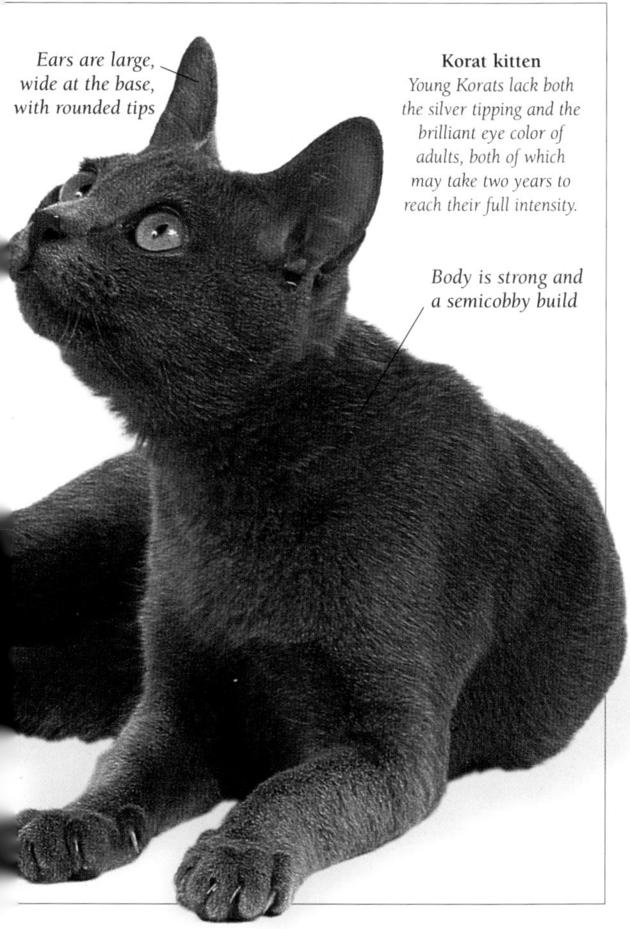
Ears are large,
wide at the base,
with rounded tips
Body is strong and
a semicobby build

Korat kitten
Young Korats lack both the silver tipping and the brilliant eye color of adults, both of which may take two years to reach their full intensity.

BOMBAY

This majestic breed has a coat like jet-black patent leather, a pleasant and distinctive voice, and a gregarious personality. Like its Burmese forebear, the Bombay thrives on human company. It is a real heat-seeker, most often found in the lap of a heat-emitting human. The coat needs little maintenance: an occasional rubdown with a chamois, or even your hand, is all that is needed to keep its sheen and texture. The brilliant copper eye color required by the breed standard can be difficult to develop, and can fade or turn green with age. Litters are large, but the Bombay remains rare outside North America.

Bombay kitten
The full depth of color and texture of the Bombay coat can take up to two years to develop, and allowance is made for this in the breed standards.

Ears are wide at the base with rounded tips
:yes are large, rounded, and widely spaced
Head is rounded in all aspects, with a short to medium-length muzzle

Bombay head

Development of the breed has led some breeders to feel that the head is now close to the American Shorthair. Because of the Burmese heritage, some Bombay lines suffered the Burmese head malformation: breeding to avoid this may account for the present look.

Breed Colors

Self colors
Black, *Sable*

Bombay Black

The glossy, Black Bombay has always had a unique look. The type came from its Burmese heritage, and the solid, even color from its American Shorthair antecedents. Because the sepia pointing gene of the Burmese is recessive, Sable kittens still occasionally appear.

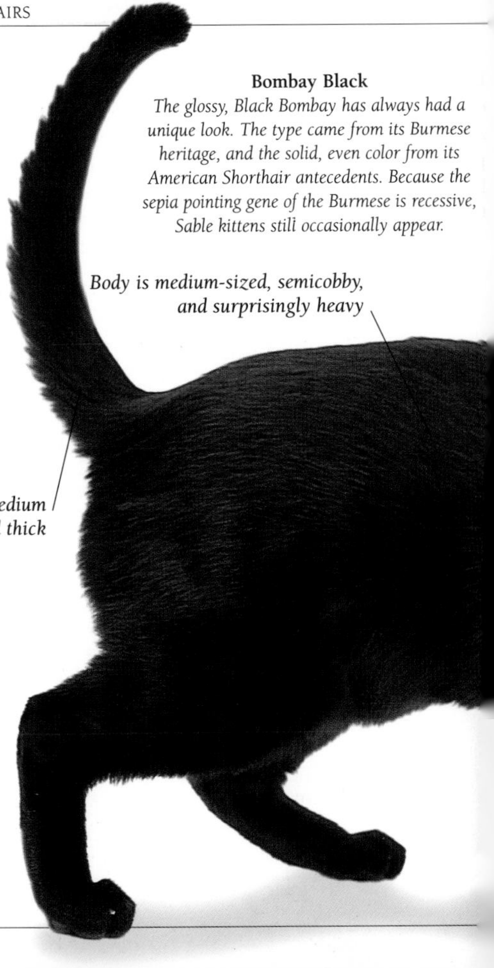

Body is medium-sized, semicobby, and surprisingly heavy
Tail is medium length and thick

REED HISTORY In the 1950s, Kentucky breeder Nikki Horner mbarked on an attempt to create a "mini black panther" from black .merican Shorthairs and Sable Burmese. By the 1960s, she had roduced cats with shiny black coats, muscular bodies, rounded eads, and copper eyes. The Bombay was first recognized in 1976.)ver the years the look has diverged from that of the Burmese, and the Bombay is no longer a "black Burmese." Litters still produce sable-brown kittens with sepia pointing, although these are now rare.

Coat is close lying with satinlike texture
Legs are medium length and sturdy

KEY FACTS

DATE OF ORIGIN 1960s

PLACE OF ORIGIN United States

ANCESTRY Black American Shorthairs and Sable Burmese

OUTCROSS BREEDS None

OTHER NAME None

WEIGHT RANGE 6–11 lb (2.5–5 kg)

TEMPERAMENT Actively inquisitive

THE ASIAN GROUP

Although they share the same origins for the most part, shaded, smoke, self, tabby, and Tiffanie Asians (*see page 116*) have sufficiently distinct breeding for GCCF to designate them a group rather than a breed. Asians had the first breed standard that allowed points to be awarded for temperament. While their ancestry is both Burmese and Chinchilla Longhair, Asians are less boisterous than Burmese, and more sociable than Persians.

Lilac Silver Shaded

The Burmilla, or Asian Shaded, includes both shaded and tipped cats, although the coat should not be so lightly tipped that it appears white. The undercoat should be pale, almost white in Silvers. Tabby markings are restricted to the face, legs, and tail, and broken necklaces.

Shading varies from medium-heavy to tipping

BREED COLORS

BURMILLA OR SHADED (SOLID, SEPIA)
Black, Chocolate, Red, Blue, Lilac, Cream, Caramel, Apricot, Tortoiseshell, Chocolate Tortie, Blue Tortie, Lilac Tortie, Caramel Tortie

SILVER SHADED
Colors and patterns are as for shaded

SMOKE (SOLID, SEPIA)
Black, Chocolate, Red, Blue, Lilac, Cream, Caramel, Apricot, Tortoiseshell, Chocolate Tortie, Blue Tortie, Lilac Tortie, Caramel Tortie

SELF (SOLID)
Bombay, Chocolate, Red, Blue, Lilac, Cream, Caramel, Apricot, Tortoiseshell, Chocolate Tortie, Blue Tortie, Lilac Tortie, Caramel Tortie, Sepia colours

TABBY (ALL PATTERNS IN SOLID, SEPIA)
Brown, Chocolate, Red, Blue, Lilac, Cream, Caramel, Apricot, Tortoiseshell, Chocolate Tortie, Blue Tortie, Lilac Tortie, Caramel Tortie

SILVER TABBIES
Colors and patterns are as for standard tabbies

Brown Silver Shaded
A striking characteristic of the Burmilla is its natural dark "eyeliner." Noting also the line of color around the nose and the red, rather than pink, nose leather, these cats tend to look like they have just returned from a full make-over.

Breed History In 1981, an alliance took place in London between a Burmese and a Chinchilla Persian, resulting in attractive shaded silver kittens. After consultation with the relevant bodies, a breeding program was initiated. The original litter was of Burmese type, and initial policy was to breed back to Burmese every other generation. Both in Britain and Europe, other Burmese–Chinchilla crosses were made: backcrossing still helps to enlarge the genetic base. The Burmilla was recognized by GCCF in 1989 and by FIFé in 1994.

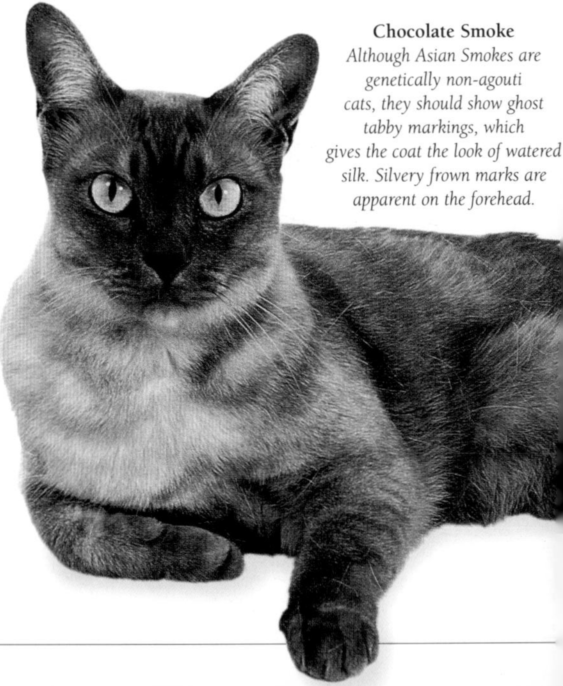

Chocolate Smoke
Although Asian Smokes are genetically non-agouti cats, they should show ghost tabby markings, which gives the coat the look of watered silk. Silvery frown marks are apparent on the forehead.

Black Smoke

n many cases it can be hard to tell a sepia Smoke from a solid Smoke, because Smokes naturally tend to be darker on the short hair of their "point" areas. Black Smokes, however, are not sepia pointed; if they were, the color would also be affected, becoming a deep sable-brown.

oat is short, fine, and close lying

Tail is medium length to long, tapering to a rounded tip

Head is gently rounded on top

Key Facts

Date of origin 1981

Place of origin Great Britain

Ancestry Burmese, Chinchillas, non-pedigrees

Outcross breeds Burmese, Chinchillas with restrictions

Other name Smokes were once called Burmoires

Weight range 9–15 lb (4–7 kg)

Temperament Relaxed and engaged

Bombay

Characterized by a sleek black coat, the Bombay is one of the original Asian selfs. This color should not be confused with the North American breed (see page 250) with which it shares its name. The type of the British Bombay resembles that of the European Burmese; the American Bombay stands alone as both breed and type.

Ears are medium sized to large, widely spaced, and angled slightly outward
Legs are medium length with oval paws

Black Tortie

As in the Burmese, the standard for tortoiseshell Asians allows for colors to be either subtly mingled or dramatically blotched. Distinct facial blazes and solid legs and tails are all accepted. The eye color may range from gold to green.

Black Ticked Tabby

Ticked tabbies are allowed in both standard and silvered coats, in all the Asian colors. The Asian Ticked Tabby standard allows no unbroken necklaces, but it does call for tabby markings on the legs and tail. The intensity of the color may be reduced in silver tabbies, but there should always be at least two bands of darker ticking on every hair. Underparts are paler than the rest of the coat, but should harmonize in color.

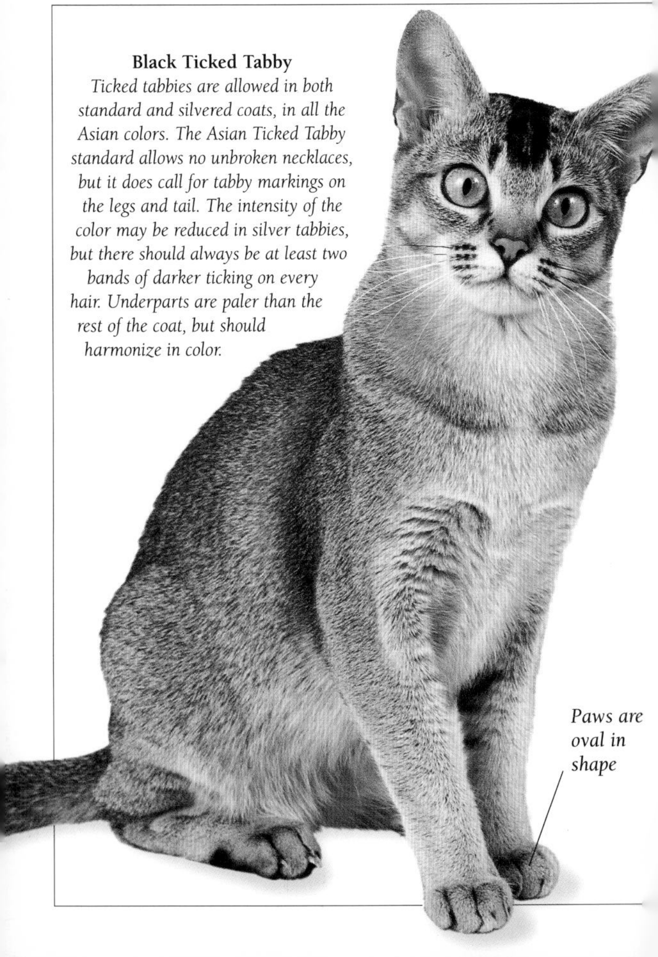

Blue Ticked Tabby kitten

The blue in Asian standards is medium to dark, rather than the light color preferred in many other breeds. This helps to provide good contrast in the tabby colors. The ticked pattern is the most commonly found tabby pattern in Asians, and tabbies are less common than the other coat types.

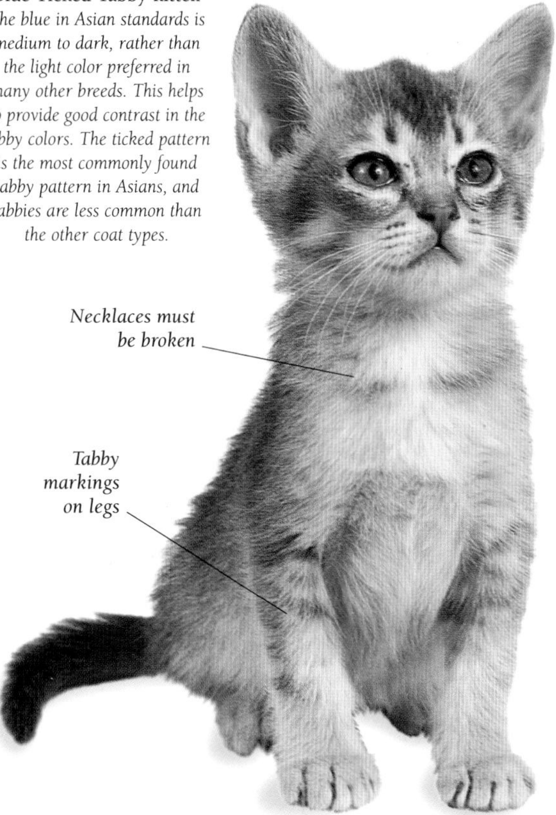
Necklaces must be broken
Tabby markings on legs

AMERICAN BURMESE

Richly colored and wide-eyed, this breed has been described as "bricks wrapped in silk." Although they are fond of human company, Burmese are less vocal or demonstrative than other Oriental breeds. The North American·Burmese differs from its European counterpart (*see page 268*): the standard emphasizes roundness, notably in the shape of the head. The extremely round "contemporary" look was born out of Good Fortune Fortunatus in the 1970s; unfortunately, so was the Burmese head fault, an inherited deformity of the skull that is often lethal or requires euthanasia. As late as the 1980s, Sable was the only color universally accepted. Other colors had occurred since early breeding programs, but were known within CFA as Mandalays. TICA recognizes a much wider range of colors.

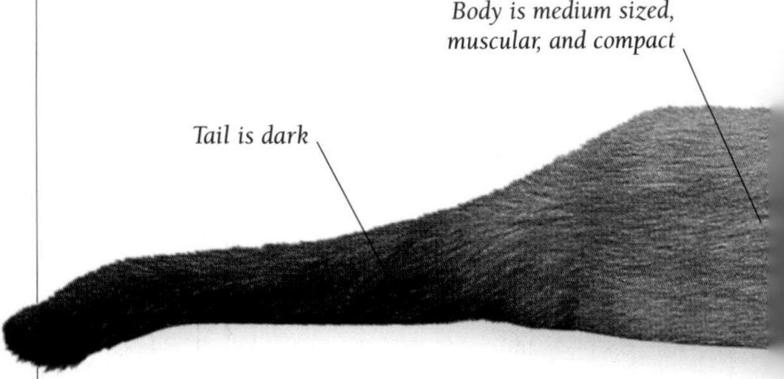
Body is medium sized, muscular, and compact
Tail is dark

Breed Colors

SEPIA
Sable, Champagne, Blue, Platinum
All other self and tortie colors

SABLE TORTIE (NOT CFA)

RED (NOT CFA)

CARAMEL (NOT CFA)

CINNAMON (NOT CFA)

Champagne

In the slightly idiosyncratic terminology of the Burmese colors, CFA puts this color in its "dilute" category; it is in fact the brown more generally referred to as chocolate in other breeds. Some degree of darkening in the mask area is almost unavoidable in this color; the main coat is a warm, even, honey brown.

Eyes are rounded in shape and golden in color
Head is pleasingly rounded with full cheeks

Breed History The Burmese began with Wong Mau, a brown female cat from Rangoon in Burma (now Myanmar), brought to the United States by US Navy psychiatrist Joseph Thompson in 1930. She was to found a breed of which, ironically, she was not a member. Thompson bred Wong Mau to a Siamese (*see page 280*), the most similar breed, and bred the kittens back to Wong Mau. Three distinct types emerged: Siamese-pointed; dark brown with minimal pointing (the first true Burmese); and a dark body and darker points, similar to Wong Mau. She herself was a Burmese–Siamese hybrid, and a natural Tonkinese (*see page 274*).

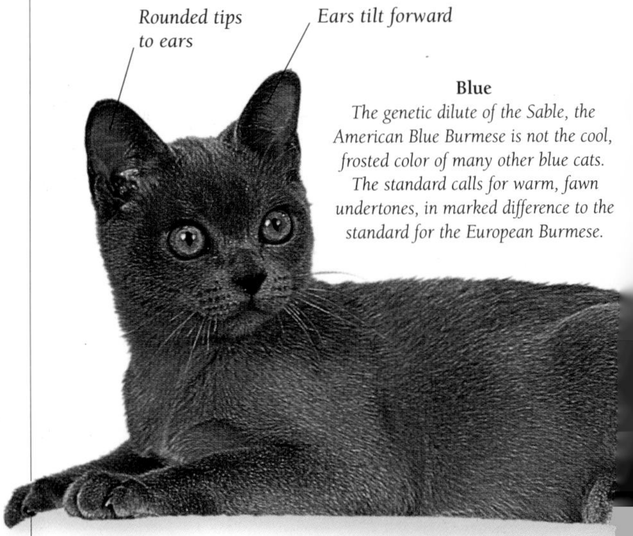

Blue

The genetic dilute of the Sable, the American Blue Burmese is not the cool, frosted color of many other blue cats. The standard calls for warm, fawn undertones, in marked difference to the standard for the European Burmese.

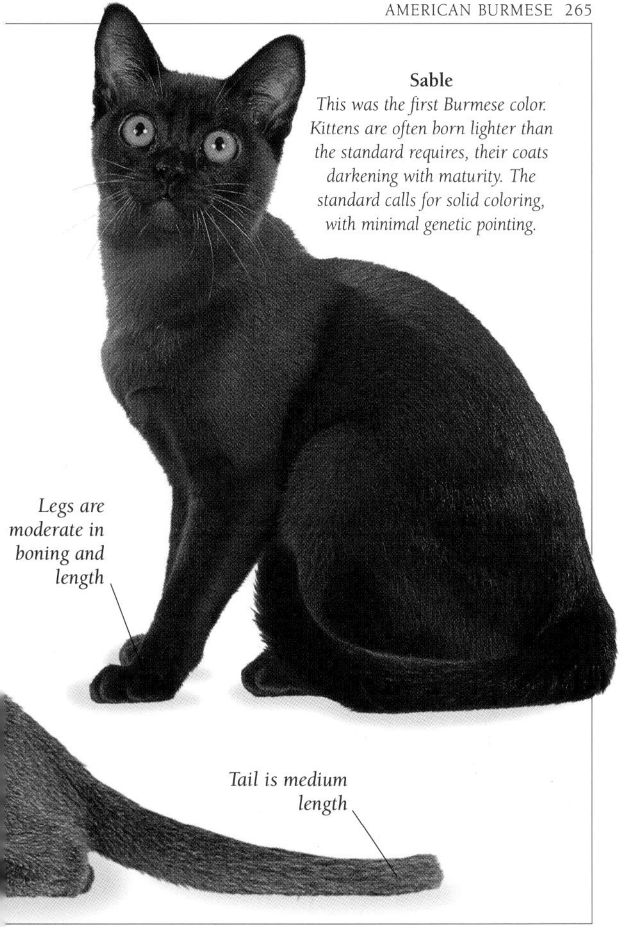
Legs are moderate in boning and length
Tail is medium length

Sable

This was the first Burmese color. Kittens are often born lighter than the standard requires, their coats darkening with maturity. The standard calls for solid coloring, with minimal genetic pointing.

Frost or Platinum

This is the color referred to in other cats as lilac or lavender: the Burmese names for it are unique to this breed. As with the Blue, the tone of the color is warmer in the Burmese than other breeds, with pale fawn undertones. The shade is also lighter than in other breeds, accounting for the metallic name, which is less used today.

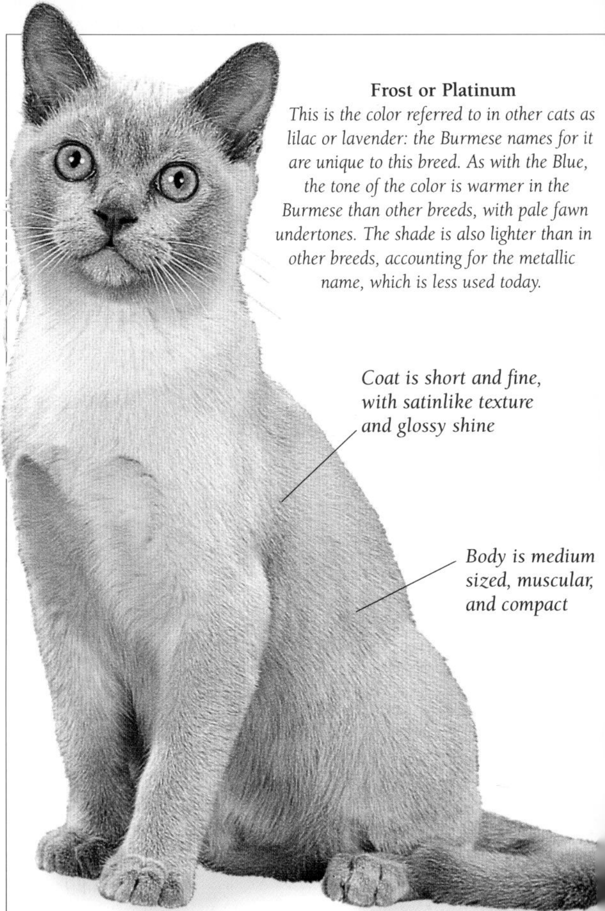

Coat is short and fine, with satinlike texture and glossy shine
Body is medium sized, muscular, and compact

Ears are medium sized and widely spaced
Muzzle is short and broad with a rounded chin

Burmese head

In spite of carrying the Burmese head fault, the contemporary look ruled CFA until 1995. In that year, their top three cats were of the less rounded "traditional" type, which does not carry the fault.

Key Facts

Date of origin 1930s

Place of origin Burma (now Myanmar)

Ancestry Temple cats, Siamese crosses

Outcross breeds None

Other name Some colors previously called Mandalay

Weight range 8–14 lb (3.5–6.5 kg)

Temperament Friendly and relaxed

EUROPEAN BURMESE

The Burmese has diverged into two types, almost two breeds, on either side of the Atlantic. While the American side of the family (*see page* 262) has developed into a rounded cat, European breeders, followed by those in South Africa, New Zealand, and Australia, have opted for a well-muscled but more angular shape. This more Oriental look has a moderately wedge-shaped head, oval eyes, and long legs. Matings have expanded the color range to ten: more than CFA recognizes, but lacking the Cinnamon and Fawn accepted by TICA. Regardless of color or type, the Burmese is ideally suited to living in active households.

Head is a short, blunt wedge

Burmese head

This Lilac shows the typical European Burmese head and eyes. Burmese eye color can appear very different in different lights. A golden yellow is much preferred: South African and Australian cats are particularly noted for their excellent eye color.

Blue

The British breed standard recognizes the Burmese as a pointed cat, but requires that the shading be slight and confined to the face. The underparts can be lighter than the body. The standard for the Blue calls for a soft color, with a silver sheen on rounded areas of the body.

Breed Colors

SELF AND TORTIE COLORS
Brown, Chocolate, Red, Blue, Lilac, Cream, Brown Tortie, Chocolate Tortie, Blue Tortie, Lilac Tortie.

CHOCOLATE TORTIE

CREAM

BROWN

LILAC

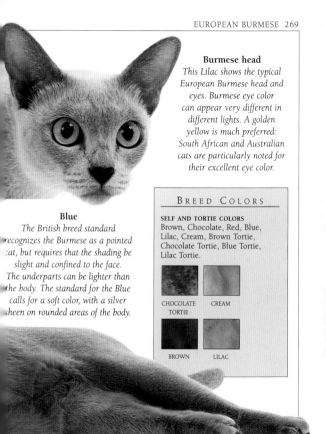

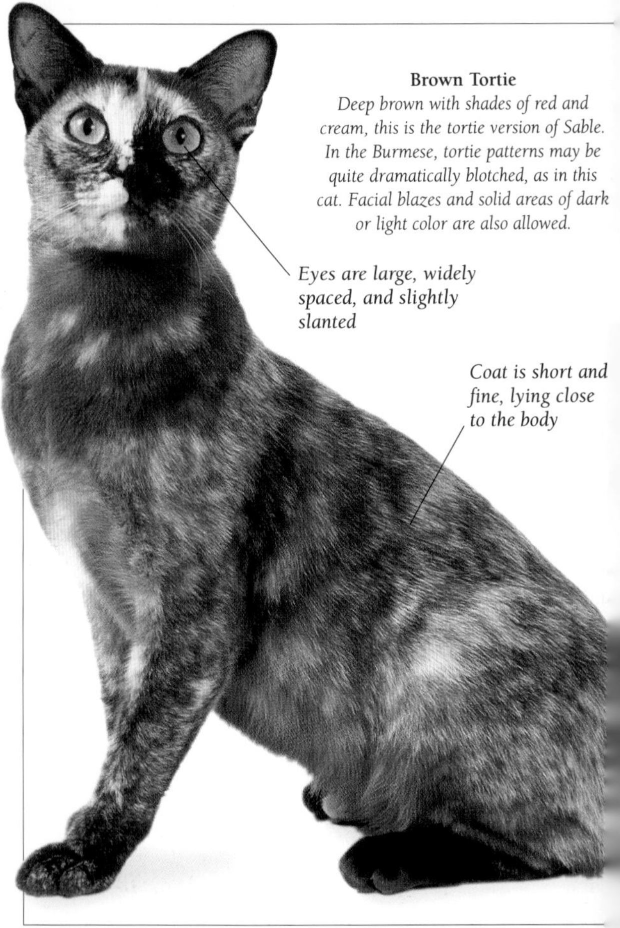

Eyes are large, widely spaced, and slightly slanted
Coat is short and fine, lying close to the body

Brown Tortie

Deep brown with shades of red and cream, this is the tortie version of Sable. In the Burmese, tortie patterns may be quite dramatically blotched, as in this cat. Facial blazes and solid areas of dark or light color are also allowed.

Red

A tangerine shade is preferred in Burmese, with less rufousing than other breeds. Exposed skin may show some freckling, and tabby markings are tolerated on the face. The short Burmese coat will not cover vestigial tabby markings, so a good Red is to be prized.

BREED HISTORY The European Burmese is descended from the American breed: American cats were imported into Europe after World War II, and the brown was recognized in 1952 by GCCF. However, the Europeans preferred a more Oriental look, and wanted a wider range of colors. GCCF, for example, took only eight years to recognize the Blue, while in North America CFA took decades to do so. This seems to have started a trend: the wide range of colors seen in the European breed was developed by the introduction of the red gene, and in the 1970s this range was broadened to create tortie versions of all the recognized colors. A further change came in 1996, when FIFé amended its breed standard to allow green eyes.

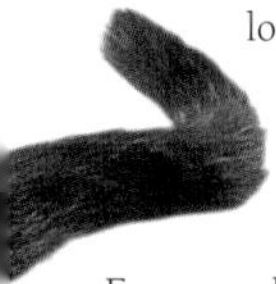

Chocolate

This color is more accurately detailed as a shade of "milk chocolate" in the breed standard. An even overall color is preferable, but elusive. Although the nose leather matches the coat, the paw pads are pink, shading to brown.

Body is strong, muscular, and surprisingly heavy

Underparts may be slightly lighter than rest of coat

Slender legs are in proportion to body

Lilac Tortie

This subtly mingled lilac-and-cream coat is not rated above the more blotched mixtures in the Burmese, although it would be in other breeds in Britain.

Key Facts

Date of origin 1930s

Place of origin Burma (now Myanmar)

Ancestry Temple cats, Siamese cat crosses

Outcross breeds None

Other name None

Weight range 8–14 lb (3.5–6.5 kg)

Temperament Friendly and relaxed

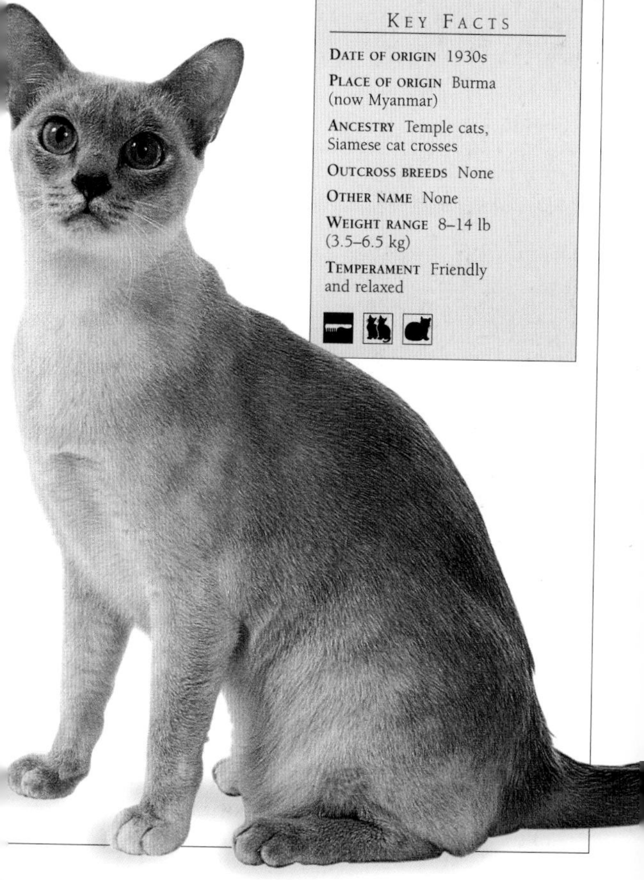

TONKINESE

Some breeders dispute whether these cats can be called a breed: as a hybrid of the Burmese (*see page 262*) and the Siamese (*see page 280*), Tonkinese inevitably produce variants in the pointing patterns of both their parent breeds. But this is hardly the first breed to produce variants, and the softly pointed "mink" pattern is not their only distinguishing feature. Their type is a blend of their parent breeds, less angular than one but lighter than the other, and their temperament has all the lively curiosity and affection of an Oriental breed. With its attractive looks and friendly manner, the "Tonk" is already one of the more popular breeds.

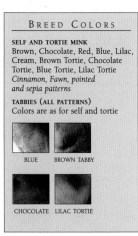

BREED COLORS

SELF AND TORTIE MINK
Brown, Chocolate, Red, Blue, Lilac, Cream, Brown Tortie, Chocolate Tortie, Blue Tortie, Lilac Tortie
Cinnamon, Fawn, pointed and sepia patterns

TABBIES (ALL PATTERNS)
Colors are as for self and tortie

BLUE

BROWN TABBY

CHOCOLATE

LILAC TORTIE

Brown or Natural

Called Sable in the Burmese and Seal in the Siamese, this color has two names in the Tonkinese, being called Natural in North America and Brown elsewhere. It should be a light brown with darker seal points and matching seal nose leather and paw pads. The Tonk is well muscled and medium-foreign in shape. There is a slight difference between North American and European cats, perhaps reflecting the difference in Burmese type: European Tonks tend to be slightly more angular than their transatlantic counterparts.

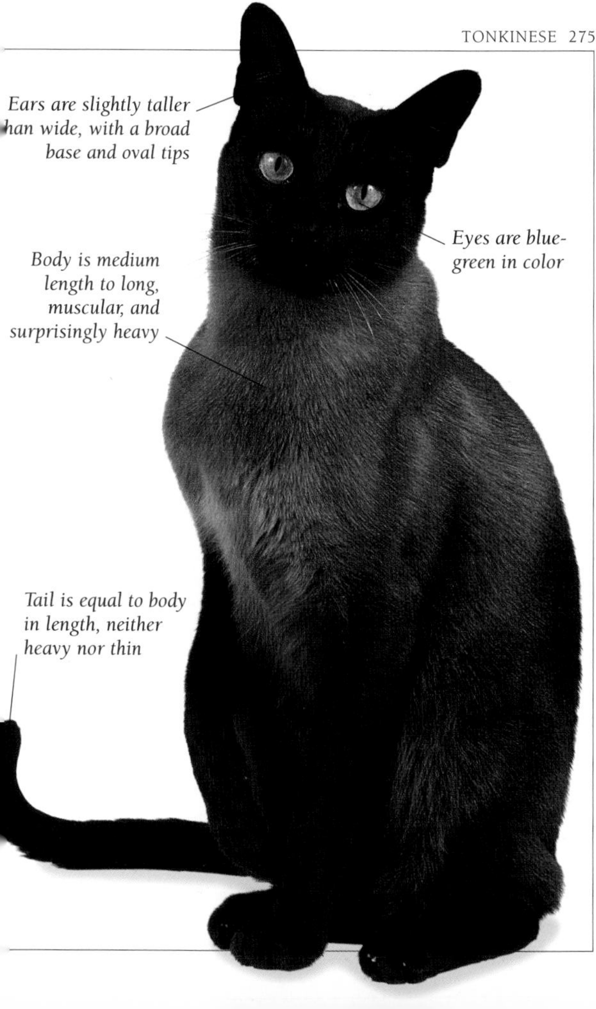
Ears are slightly taller than wide, with a broad base and oval tips
Eyes are blue-green in color
Body is medium length to long, muscular, and surprisingly heavy
Tail is equal to body in length, neither heavy nor thin

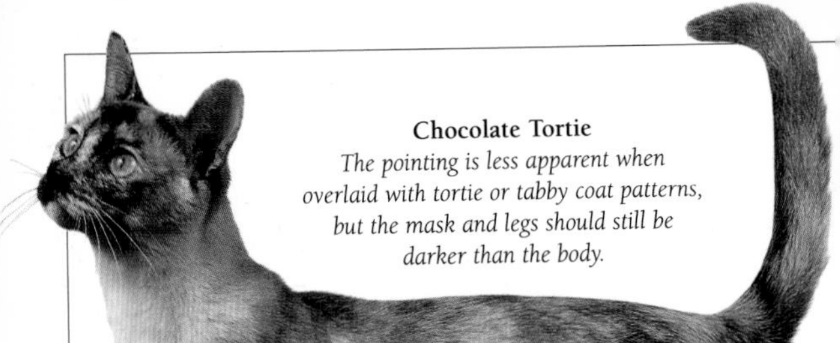

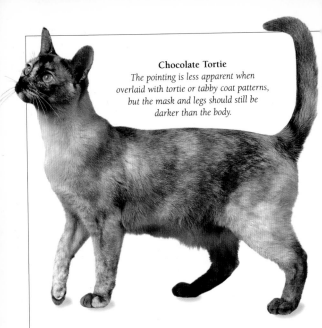

Chocolate Tortie

The pointing is less apparent when overlaid with tortie or tabby coat patterns, but the mask and legs should still be darker than the body.

Breed History Some breeders believe that the "Chocolate Siamese" of the 1880s were in fact Tonkinese-type Siamese–Burmese hybrids but this is unprovable. The first documented Tonkinese seen in the West was Wong Mau, the mother of the Burmese breed imported from Rangoon (*see page 264*). Her natural hybrid characteristics were bred out of her offspring, however, and not until the 1950s did work begin to recreate this blend through breeding programs. Early work was carried out in Canada, and the breed was first recognized by the Canadian Cat Association. Today it is accepted by all major registries, although there is still considerable variation in the acceptance of colors.

Cream

The standard for this color in the Tonkinese calls for a "rich, warm" tone, shading to paler cream. The points may be less even than in other colors, with the legs being lighter than the mask and tail. As in all breeds, it is difficult to eliminate tabby markings completely from Creams and Reds, and slight markings are allowed in cats that are excellent in other respects.

Darker points merge
ently into a lighter body
Coat is short, silky, and close-lying

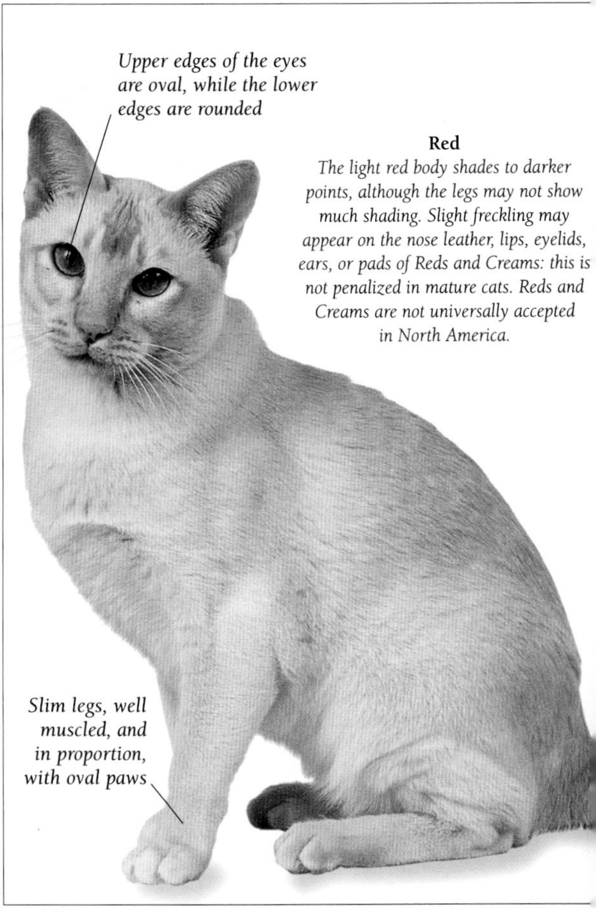

Upper edges of the eyes are oval, while the lower edges are rounded
Slim legs, well muscled, and in proportion, with oval paws

Red

The light red body shades to darker points, although the legs may not show much shading. Slight freckling may appear on the nose leather, lips, eyelids, ears, or pads of Reds and Creams: this is not penalized in mature cats. Reds and Creams are not universally accepted in North America.

Moderate wedge-shaped head with slight nose break and whisker pinch

Lilac

The body of the Lilac is a pale, dove gray with a pinkish cast, and the points are a darker shade of the same color. Kittens are often lighter than adults, although they should develop distinct pointing fairly early. Eye color can range from light blue to the green seen in this individual, but any tinge of yellow is unacceptable. The exact shade is not related to the coat color.

Key Facts

Date of origin 1960s

Place of origin United States and Canada

Ancestry Burmese and Siamese

Outcross breeds Burmese and Siamese

Other name Once called Golden Siamese

Weight range 6–12 lb (2.5–5.5 kg)

Temperament Sociable and intelligent

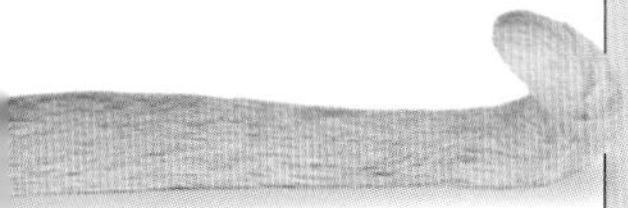

SIAMESE

Possibly the world's most instantly recognizable cat breed, the Siamese is also one of the more controversial. The first cats often had crossed eyes and kinked tails; the early breed standards even required these traits, as well as legs that were "a little short." Since then, selective breeding has altered the cat considerably – crossed eyes and kinked tails are now rare – but the build of the cat is a matter of dispute. GCCF Siamese have a svelte body, long, slim legs, and a long head with slanting eyes and a fine muzzle; North American cats take this look to greater extremes. All Siamese still have the gregarious, chatty nature for which they are famous.

BREED COLORS

SIAMESE POINT COLORS
Seal, Chocolate, Blue, Lilac

COLORPOINT SHORTHAIR POINT COLORS (IN CFA)
Red, Cream, tortie and tabby versions of all colors
Cinnamon, Fawn, Smoke, Silver and particolor versions

CHOCOLATE TORTIE POINT

CREAM TABBY POINT

LILAC TORTIE TABBY POINT

CHOCOLATE TABBY POINT

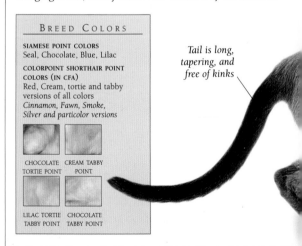

Tail is long, tapering, and free of kinks

Blue Point

Records of Blue Points go back at least as far as 1903: given that Thailand's other famous cat, the Korat (see page 246) is blue, it is likely that the dilute gene came to the West with the Thai cats, rather than being introduced after their arrival. The blue of the Siamese points is lighter than that found in solid-colored coats.

Body is medium sized, long, and svelte
Points are dense and matching in shade

Chocolate Point

With points the color of milk chocolate, this color was not accepted in Britain until the 1950s. It may have been carried recessively: dark Chocolate Points could have passed for Seal Points.

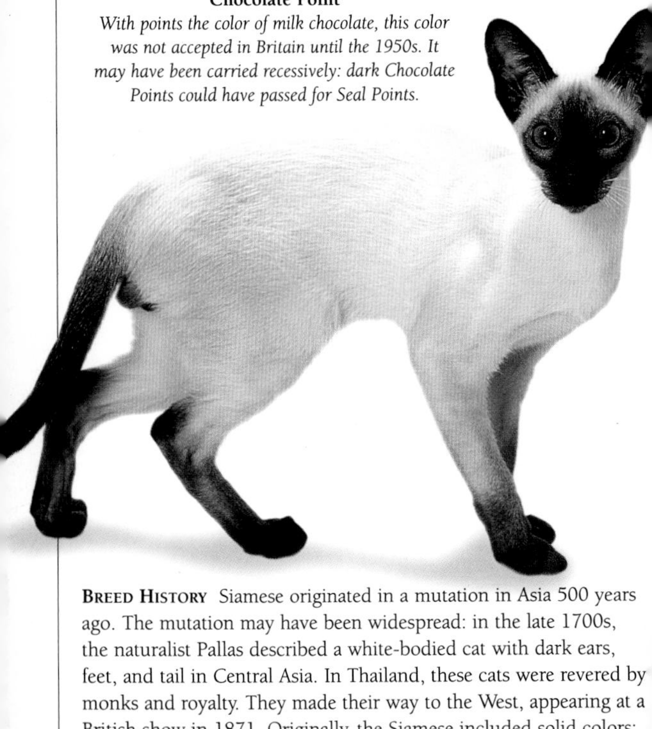

Breed History Siamese originated in a mutation in Asia 500 years ago. The mutation may have been widespread: in the late 1700s, the naturalist Pallas described a white-bodied cat with dark ears, feet, and tail in Central Asia. In Thailand, these cats were revered by monks and royalty. They made their way to the West, appearing at a British show in 1871. Originally, the Siamese included solid colors: these are now known as Oriental Shorthairs (*see page* 292). The popularity of the breed peaked in the 1950s: the decline has been attributed to the more "extreme" look that has developed.

Lilac Point

In 1896, a cat was disqualified from a show for being "not quite blue" – some shows did accept Blue Points. It is possible, but by no means certain, that the cat was an unrecognized Lilac Point. The American standards call for a white body, while the British allows slight shading.

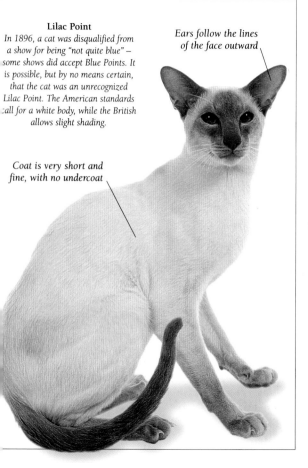

Ears follow the lines of the face outward
Coat is very short and fine, with no undercoat

Siamese head

The long head should have good width between the ears, tapering down to a fine muzzle. In profile, the nose is straight, with only the slightest change in direction at eye level.

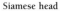

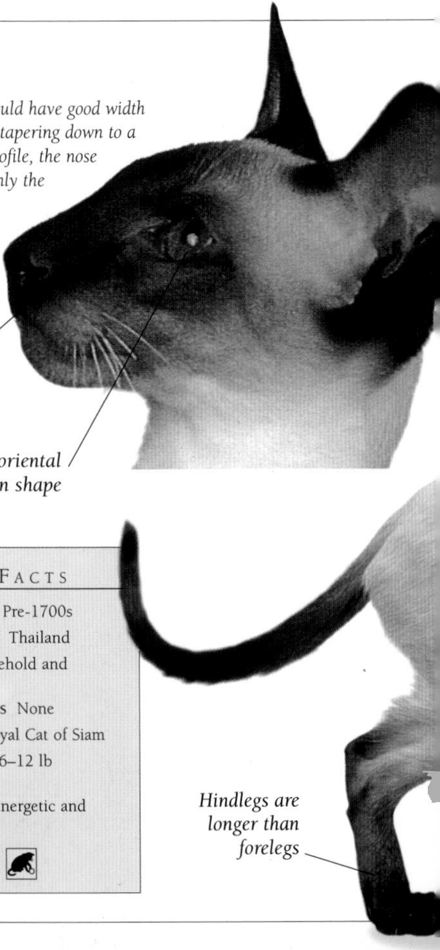
Head is long, narrowing to muzzle in straight lines
Eyes are oriental in shape
Hindlegs are longer than forelegs

Key Facts

Date of origin Pre-1700s

Place of origin Thailand

Ancestry Household and temple cats

Outcross breeds None

Other name Royal Cat of Siam

Weight range 6–12 lb (2.5–5.5 kg)

Temperament Energetic and enterprising

Seal Point

The classic color, this is the Siamese that has appeared in films, advertisements, and cartoons. Genetically, this color is black, translated into a dark seal-brown by the Siamese pointing gene. For a time, this was the only Siamese accepted: other colors existed, but were usually classified as "any other variety," and records are unclear as to what they may have been. For some, this color remains the only "true" Siamese.

Legs are slim, and in proportion to body

NEWER SIAMESE COLORS

New colors and tabby stripes have augmented the original four Siamese colors. These pointed cats live under two names. In Britain and Europe, all colors are classified as Siamese, and pointed Oriental Shorthairs are also registered as Siamese. In North America, TICA takes the same approach, but CFA classifies only the eumelanistic colors as Siamese and calls all others Colorpoint Shorthairs.

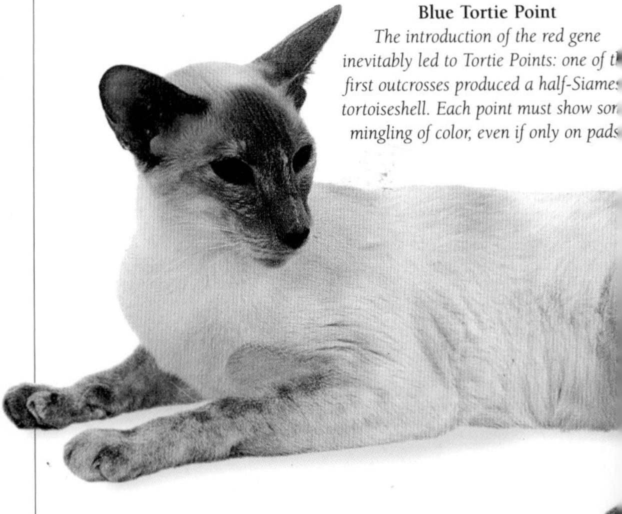

Blue Tortie Point
The introduction of the red gene inevitably led to Tortie Points: one of th first outcrosses produced a half-Siames tortoiseshell. Each point must show som mingling of color, even if only on pads

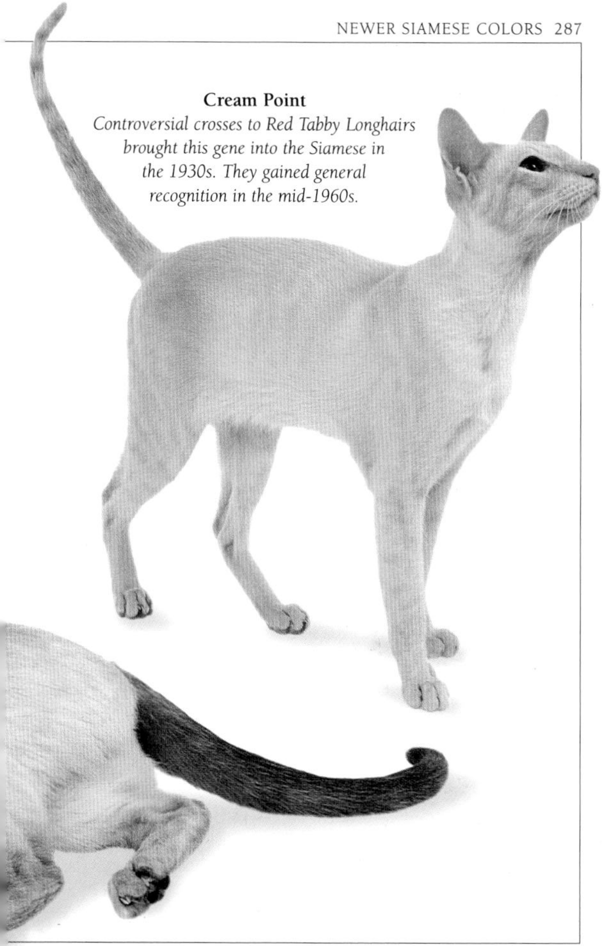

Cream Point

Controversial crosses to Red Tabby Longhairs brought this gene into the Siamese in the 1930s. They gained general recognition in the mid-1960s.

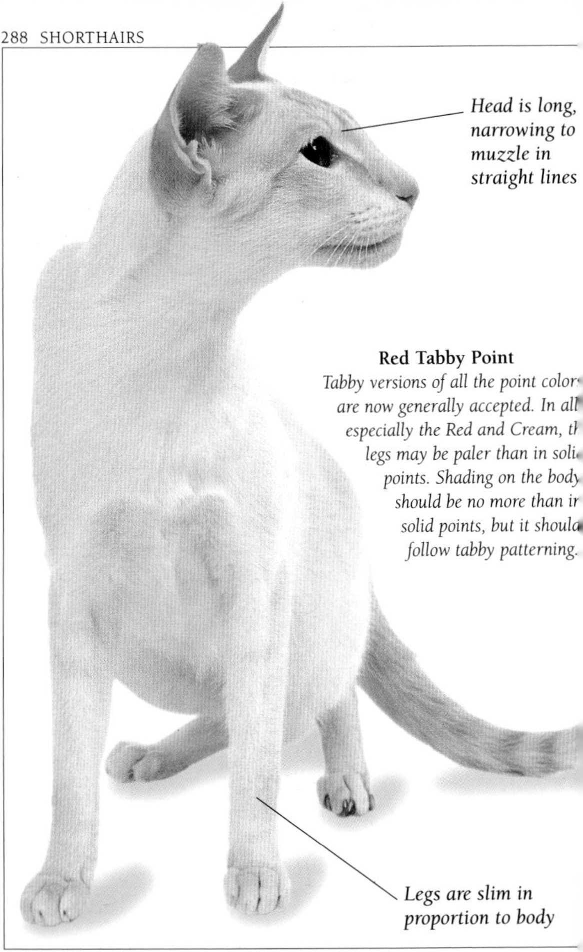

Head is long, narrowing to muzzle in straight lines
Legs are slim in proportion to body

Red Tabby Point

Tabby versions of all the point color are now generally accepted. In all especially the Red and Cream, th legs may be paler than in soli points. Shading on the body should be no more than in solid points, but it should follow tabby patterning.

Cinnamon Point

The Cinnamon Point is one of the newest colors. The body is ivory and the points a warm cinnamon-brown; as in the Chocolate Point and the Caramel Point, the legs may be slightly paler than the other points.

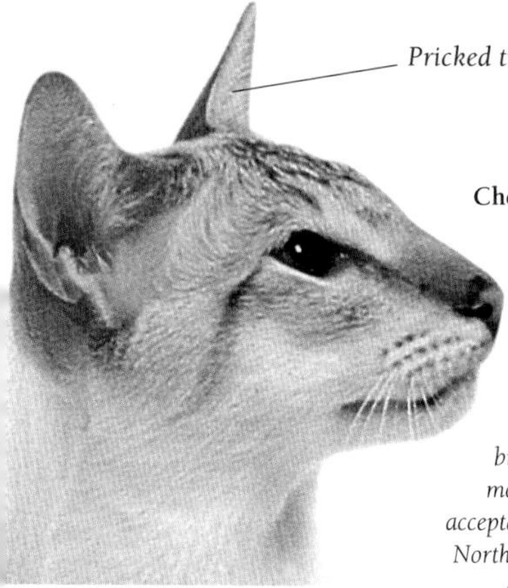

Chocolate Tabby Point

Tabby points have been known since the start of the 20th century, but were generally ignored. A litter of Seal Tabby Points was shown in 1961 in Britain, bringing renewed interest, more active breeding, and acceptance a few years later. In North America, these cats are called Lynx Points.

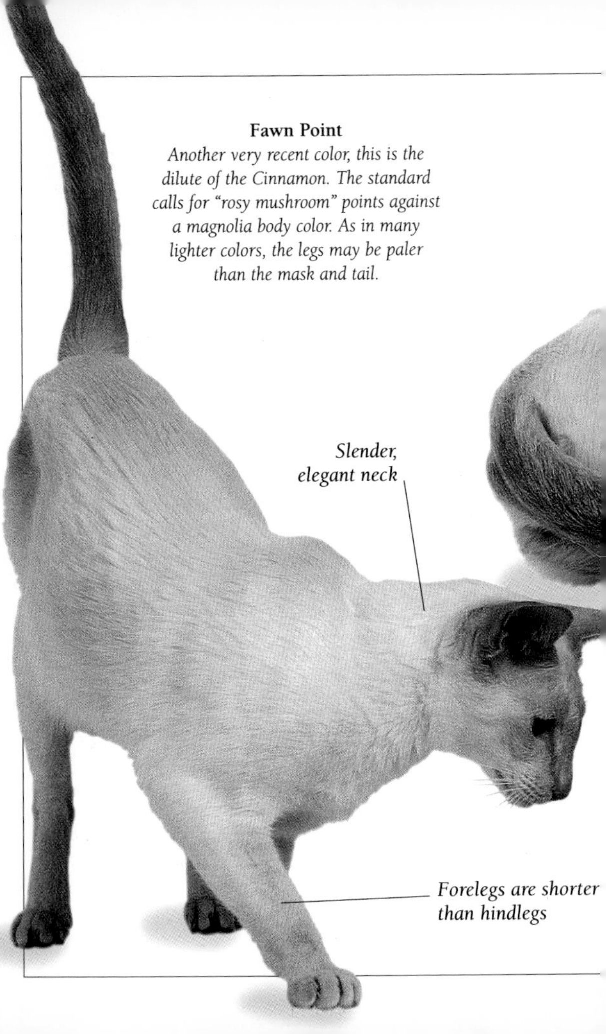
Slender, elegant neck
Forelegs are shorter than hindlegs

Fawn Point

Another very recent color, this is the dilute of the Cinnamon. The standard calls for "rosy mushroom" points against a magnolia body color. As in many lighter colors, the legs may be paler than the mask and tail.

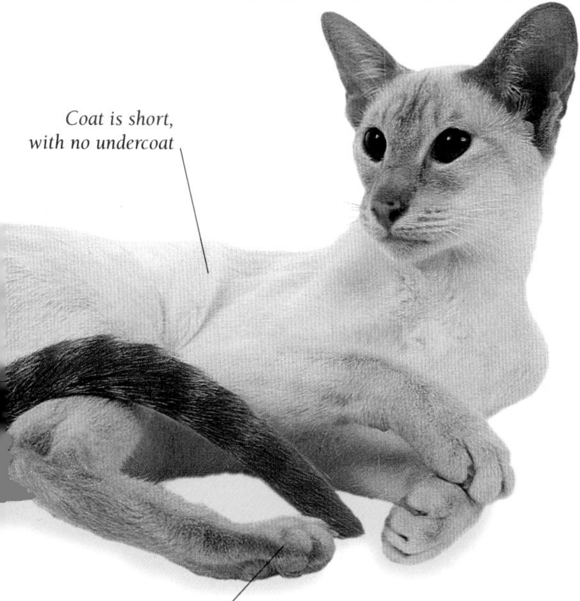
Coat is short,
with no undercoat
Paws are
small and oval

Lilac Tabby Point

The points should all show tabby markings, but these should not extend over the body; in particular, the frown lines on the forehead should not extend over the rest of the head. The Lilac Tabby Point has pinkish-gray markings on a magnolia ground, with faded lilac or pink nose leather and paw pads.

ORIENTAL SHORTHAIR

Every owner can tell you that this breed's favorite place is between you and your book, or newspaper, or keyboard. These active and athletic cats are also outrageously gregarious – breeders call them shameless flirts. In physique and temperament, the Oriental is a Siamese (*see page 280*), but in solid coat colors. There is some dispute over the status of the pointed Orientals that do crop up: most fancies classify them as Siamese, but the CFA in North America does not allow this. Like Siamese, Orientals can suffer from inherited heart problems, but they have impressively long lives, belying their reputation as a delicate breed.

BREED COLORS

TABBIES (ALL PATTERNS)
Colors are as for self and tortie

SMOKE, SHADED, AND TIPPED
Colors are as for self and tortie, excepting White

SILVER SPOTTED TABBY

BLUE AND WHITE

CHOCOLATE TORTIE

RED MACKEREL TABBY

SELF AND TORTIE
Black, Havana, Cinnamon, Red, Blue, Lilac, Fawn, Cream, Caramel, Apricot, Foreign White, Black Tortie, Chocolate Tortie, Cinnamon Tortie, Blue Tortie, Lilac Tortie, Fawn Tortie, Caramel Tortie

SILVER TABBIES (ALL PATTERNS)
Colors are as for standard tabbies

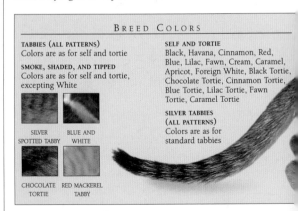

Brown Spotted Tabby kitten

)riental Spotted Tabbies were once alled Maus, but they were confused vith the Egyptian Mau breed in the United States (see page 332). Their spots should be round, clear, and evenly distributed.

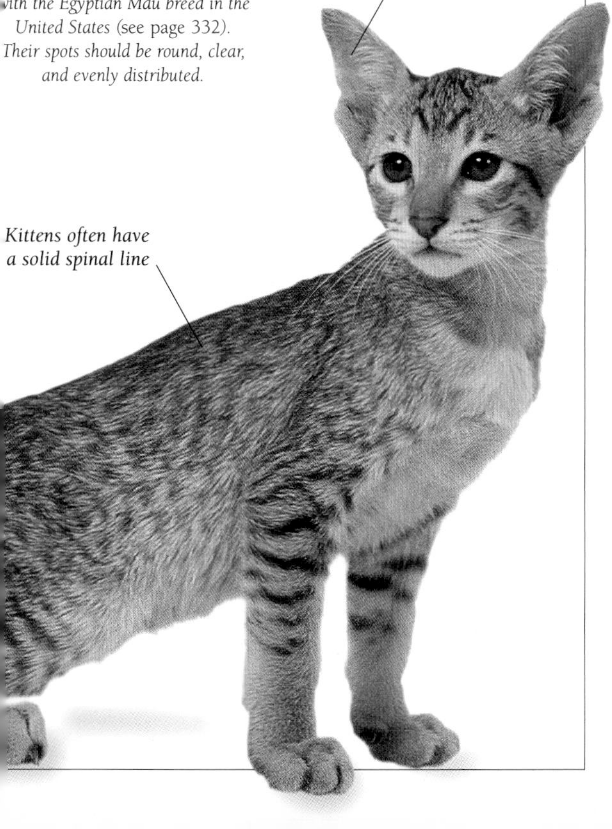

Ears are large, pricked, continuing the lines of the head
Kittens often have a solid spinal line

Oriental Blue

Blue cats were imported from Thailand in the 1800s, but these could also have been Korats (see page 246). There could be no confusing the breeds now: the Oriental Blue has the characteristic elongated build and slanted eyes of the breed.

Lilac or Lavender

The dilute of the Havana, this color was one of the first to be developed in the 1960s. At first it was called Lavender, a term still used in North America. As with all dilute colors, any faint tabby markings are more easily seen, so good color is quite an achievement.

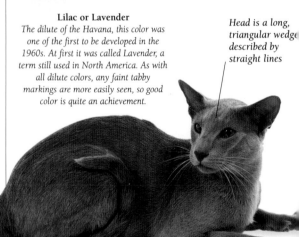

Head is a long, triangular wedge described by straight lines

Foreign White or Oriental White

Internationally, this color is called Oriental White, and in most countries it may have green or blue eyes. In Britain, only blue eyes are allowed, and the designation Foreign" is used to acknowledge this.

KEY FACTS

DATE OF ORIGIN 1950s

PLACE OF ORIGIN Great Britain

ANCESTRY Siamese, Korat, Longhair, Shorthairs

OUTCROSS BREEDS Siamese

OTHER NAME Previously called "Foreigns" in Britain

WEIGHT RANGE 9–14 lb (4–6.5 kg)

TEMPERAMENT Devoted and demanding

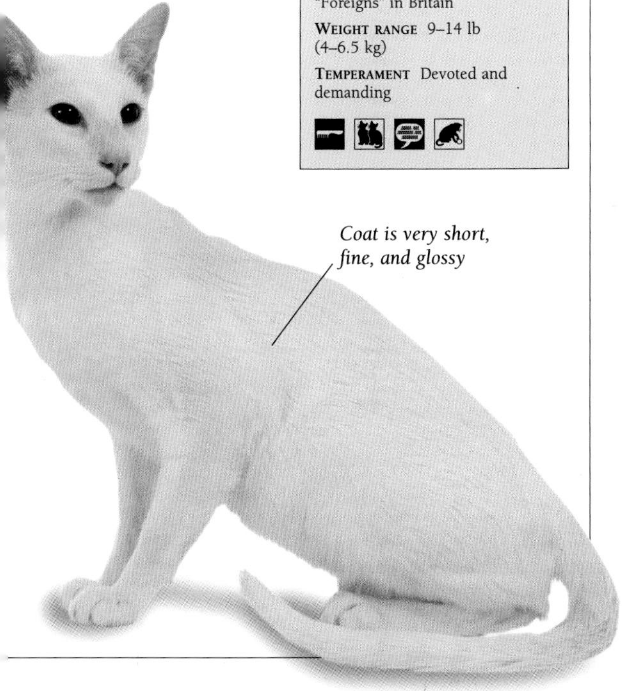
Coat is very short, fine, and glossy

Oriental Black

In sleek, solid black, the Orienta build resembles an Art Nouvea poster come to life. The entire cat must be solid, jet black, fro the tips to the roots of the coat and from the eye rims to the pa pads. Eyes of brilliant green stan out against this background, making a very striking cat.

Body is medium sized and svelte

Havana or Chestnut Brown
This rich, warm-toned brown, genetically a chocolate, was called Havana by early breeders, ut then recognized as the Chestnut Brown Foreign, reverting to its present name in 1970. It is still known as Chestnut Brown in the United States, where the Havana Brown is a separate breed.

REED HISTORY The historical *Cat Book Poems* show Siamese cats n varied colors. Today, over half of their descendants are self or icolor, and fewer than a quarter are pointed. There were self cats mong the first Siamese to be brought to the West, but in the 1920s he Siamese Club of Britain vetoed "any but blue-eyed Siamese," and heir numbers declined, although blacks and blues may have been red in Germany until World War II. Work on a solid chocolate in ritain in the 1950s led to the Chestnut Brown Foreign, recognized n 1957, and the origin of the Havana Brown (*see page 228*). Until ecently, the breed was called "Foreign" in Britain and "Oriental" n America: the British change will remove any confusion.

Newer Oriental Colors

New colors and patterns continue to be developed within the Oriental Shorthair breed. Many of the genes have been present since Our Miss Smith, the breed's Siamese founding mother, gave birth to green-eyed, brown-coated kittens in the 1950s. Since then, other genes have been intentionally added. Today, there are over 50 recognized coat colors, and this number will probably continue to increase.

Bicolors are accepted by North American associations, but not in Britain.

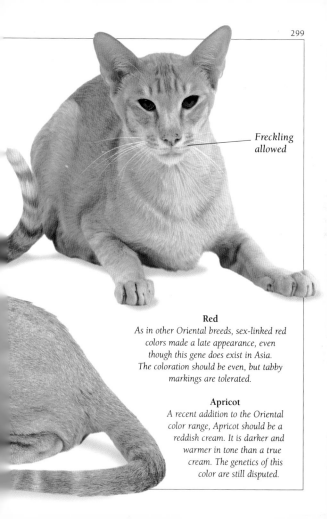

Red

As in other Oriental breeds, sex-linked red colors made a late appearance, even though this gene does exist in Asia. The coloration should be even, but tabby markings are tolerated.

Apricot

A recent addition to the Oriental color range, Apricot should be a reddish cream. It is darker and warmer in tone than a true cream. The genetics of this color are still disputed.

Chocolate Classic Tabby

The earliest Oriental Tabbies were of the spotted pattern, but since then classic, mackerel, and ticked patterns have all been added to the range. Oriental Tabbies often have white lips and chins, but this should not extend over the muzzle or throat.

Orientals usually have green eyes

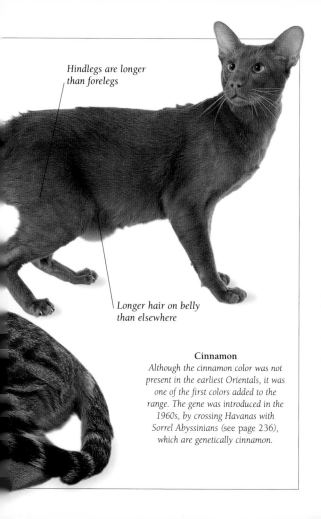

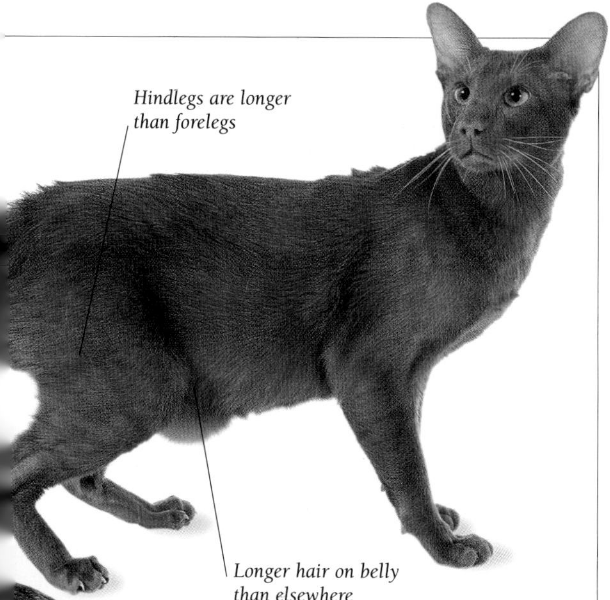
Hindlegs are longer than forelegs
Longer hair on belly than elsewhere

Cinnamon

Although the cinnamon color was not present in the earliest Orientals, it was one of the first colors added to the range. The gene was introduced in the 1960s, by crossing Havanas with Sorrel Abyssinians (see page 236), *which are genetically cinnamon.*

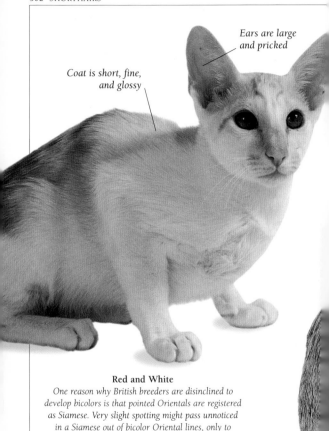

Ears are large and pricked
Coat is short, fine, and glossy

Red and White

One reason why British breeders are disinclined to develop bicolors is that pointed Orientals are registered as Siamese. Very slight spotting might pass unnoticed in a Siamese out of bicolor Oriental lines, only to emerge more strongly in future generations.

Chocolate Silver Tabby

In Silver Tabbies the color is restricted to the tips of the hairs and the undercoat is white. Although the contrast between the markings and the base is quite clear, the color may be so restricted that the pattern cannot be distinguished on the flanks.

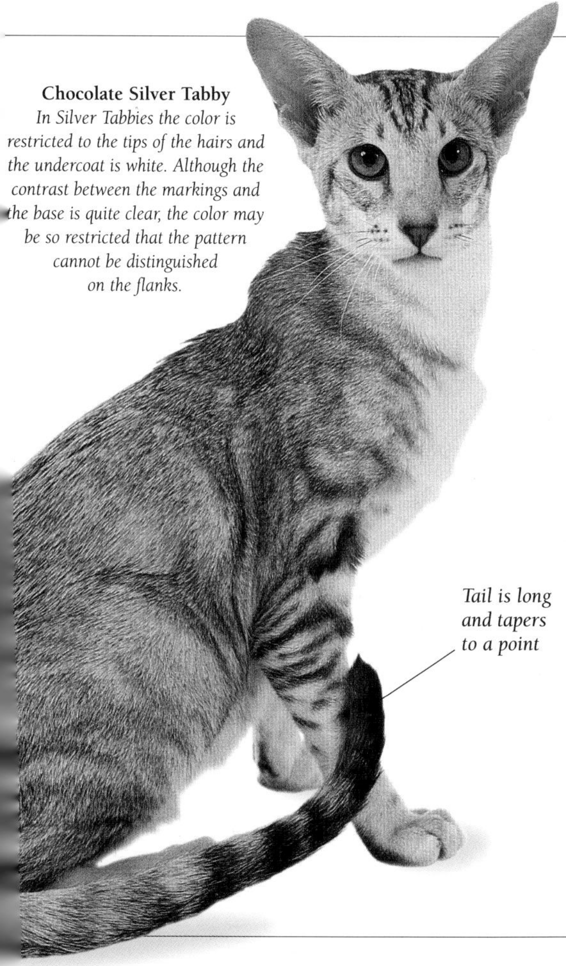
Tail is long and tapers to a point

JAPANESE BOBTAIL

Playful and affectionate, this breed is a distinctly attractive companion. The Japanese Bobtail's ancestors were portrayed in ancient Japanese art, and superstition may have played a role in the perpetuation of its most notable characteristic, its short, 3–4 in (8–10 cm) tail. In ancient Japan, a cat with a bifurcated tail – one with two tips – was considered a demon in disguise. Cats with normal tails may have been persecuted, but those with short tails were left alone, which would have led to more successful breeding among Japan's short-tailed cats. The Bobtail is seen throughout Japan as the famous *Maneki-neko*, or beckoning cat, a popular good-luck symbol.

BREED COLORS

SELF AND TORTIE COLORS
Black, Red, Tortoiseshell, White
All other self and tortie colors, pointed, mink, and sepia

TABBY COLORS (ALL PATTERNS)
All colors

BICOLORS
Black, Red, Tortoiseshell, Red Tabby with White
All other colors and patterns with white

BROWN MACKEREL TABBY

BLACK AND WHITE

Mi-ke
Tortoishell and White Bobtails, known as Mi-ke *in Japan, are the most prized coat color and pattern.* Odd-eyed *Mi-ke cats are even more valued than their blue- or gold-eyed counterparts. The cat should resemble a porcelain figurine, with a pure white coat and minimal splashes of rich color.*

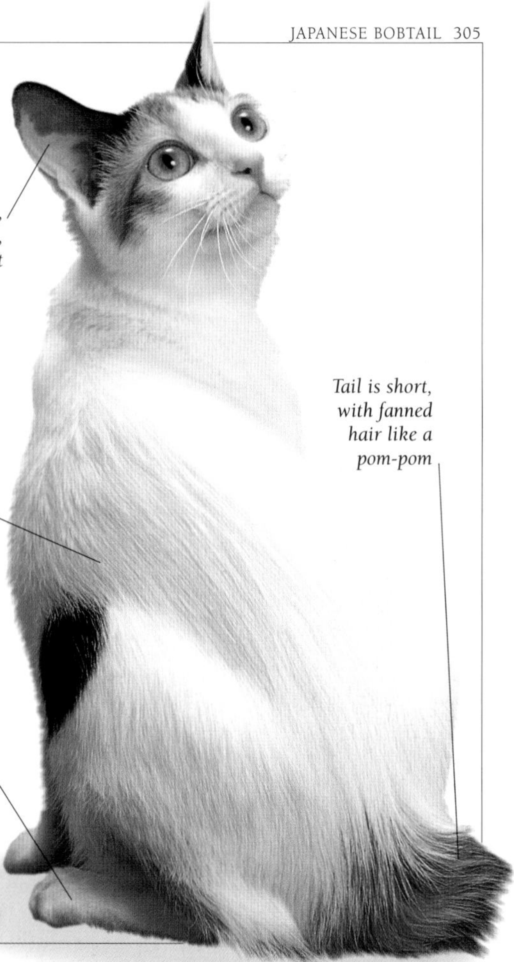
Ears are large,
widely spaced,
and upright
Coat is
medium to
short, with
negligible
undercoat
Legs are
long and
lender, but
not dainty
Tail is short,
with fanned
hair like a
pom-pom

Breed History Legend holds that cats arrived in the Japanese Archipelago from China in AD 999, and that their ownership was restricted to aristocrats for the next five centuries. In reality, cats had arrived hundreds of years earlier, and ownership was more widespread. Among the original feline immigrants from mainland Asia there were individuals with stumpy tails. Within the restricted gene pool of the Japanese islands, the recessive gene for the bobbed tail flourished. In 1968, American breeder Elizabeth Freret established the first breeding program outside Japan. Recognized in North America, the breed is not yet accepted in Britain.

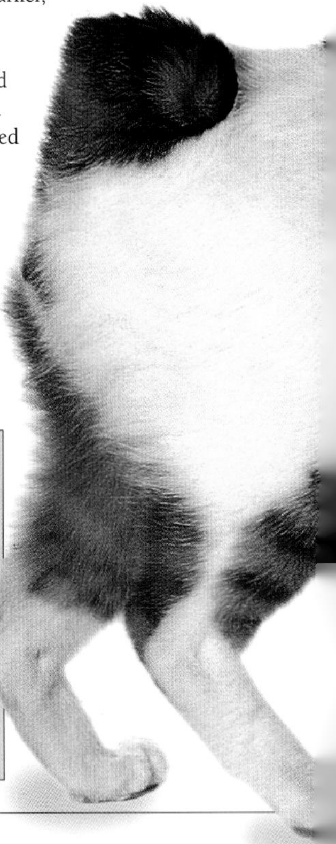

Key Facts

Date of origin Pre-19th century

Place of origin Japan

Ancestry Household cat

Outcross breeds None

Other name None

Weight range 6–9 lb (2.5–4 kg)

Temperament Vibrant and alert

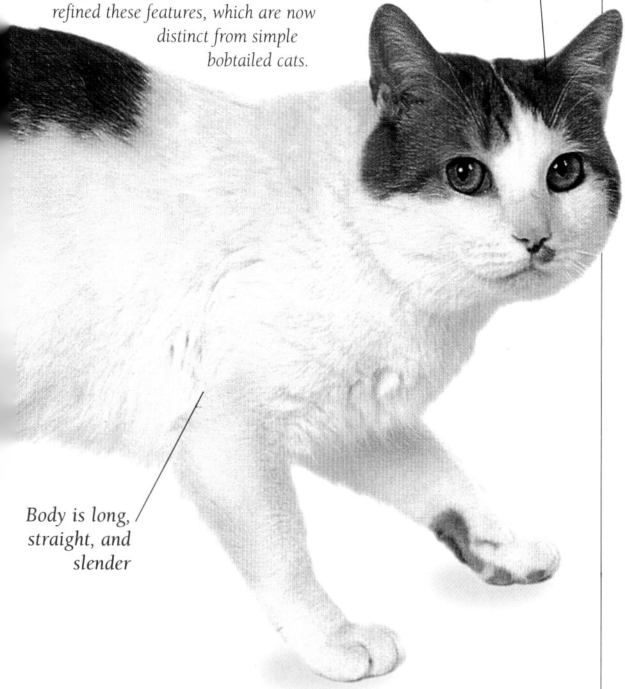
Head is well balanced, triangular-shaped, with curved sides and a long nose
Body is long, straight, and slender

Red Tabby and White

The Bobtail has undergone changes since its arrival in the West. Like this male, the original cats were less delicate in appearance, with broader faces and shorter legs. Breeders have refined these features, which are now distinct from simple bobtailed cats.

LA PERM

For centuries, rex mutations have occurred and then vanished into the random-breeding feline population. The advent of breed registries changed the situation. Since the first major rexed breeds, the Cornish (*see page 312*) and the Devon (*see page 318*) became established, and many more have appeared. The La Perm is undoubtedly the most quirkily named of these, and in some ways the oddest in expression. Cats are born with fur, but at some time in their lives, usually during infancy, they lose it, becoming completely bald. The new coat that grows after this is thick and silky, and often curlier. Unusually for a pedigreed breed, the standard describes them as working cats and "excellent hunters." There is also a longhaired version (*see page 142*); the soft hair of the shorthairs may be more wavy than curly.

BREED COLORS

SOLID COLORS
All colors/patterns, including sepia, pointed, and mink

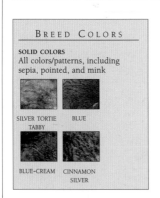

SILVER TORTIE TABBY

BLUE

BLUE-CREAM

CINNAMON SILVER

Brown Tabby kitten

With its softly wedge-shaped head, the La Perm has a foreign look, especially apparent in kittens. Most individuals will go through their bald stage as kittens; straight-coated kittens may become curly after this drastic moult.

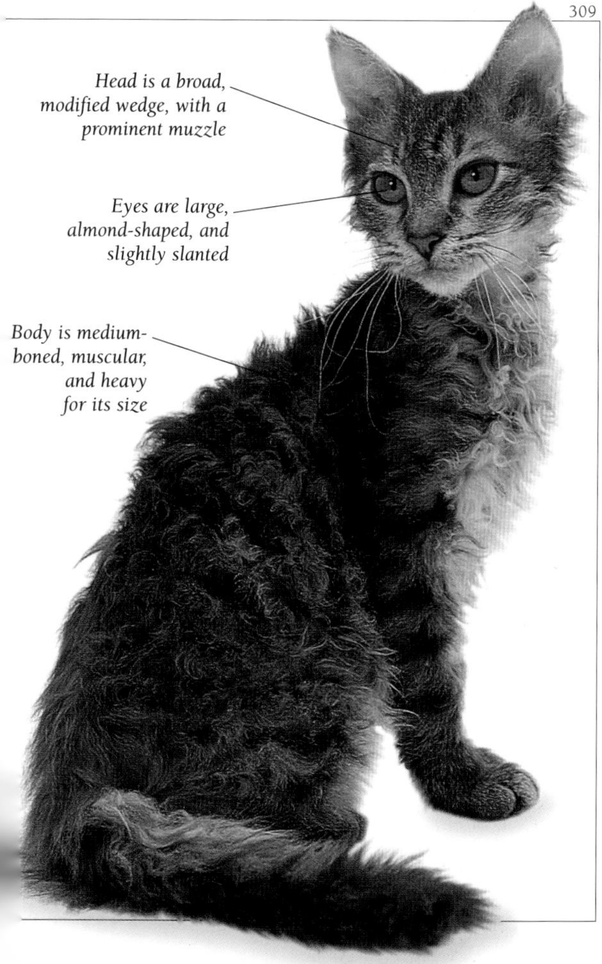
Head is a broad, modified wedge, with a prominent muzzle
Eyes are large, almond-shaped, and slightly slanted
Body is medium-boned, muscular, and heavy for its size

Breed History In 1982, a working farm cat in The Dalles, Oregon, produced a litter of six kittens that included a single bald kitten. In spite of this disadvantage, the kitten survived, and at the age of eight weeks she finally grew a coat. But this coat, unlike that of her littermates, was curly and soft to the touch. Linda Koehl, the owner and founder of the breed, named this kitten Curly. Over the next five years, Koehl produced more curly-coated kittens, which became the basis of the breed. The gene is dominant, so wide outcrossing to increase the gene pool can be done while still producing reasonable numbers of rexed kittens. The breed has been recognized by TICA.

Key Facts

Date of origin 1982

Place of origin United States

Ancestry Farm cats

Outcross breeds Nonpedigreed cats

Other name Also called Dalles La Perm

Weight range 8–12 lb (3.5–5.5 kg)

Temperament Affectionate and inquisitive

Red Tabby

Rexed coats tend to obscure the clarity of tabby markings, and the La Perm is no exception. Frown lines on the forehead and "mascara lines on the temples and cheeks remain clear, as do the rings on the tail and bars on the legs, where the hair is shorter or less curly. Eye and coat color do not need to match.

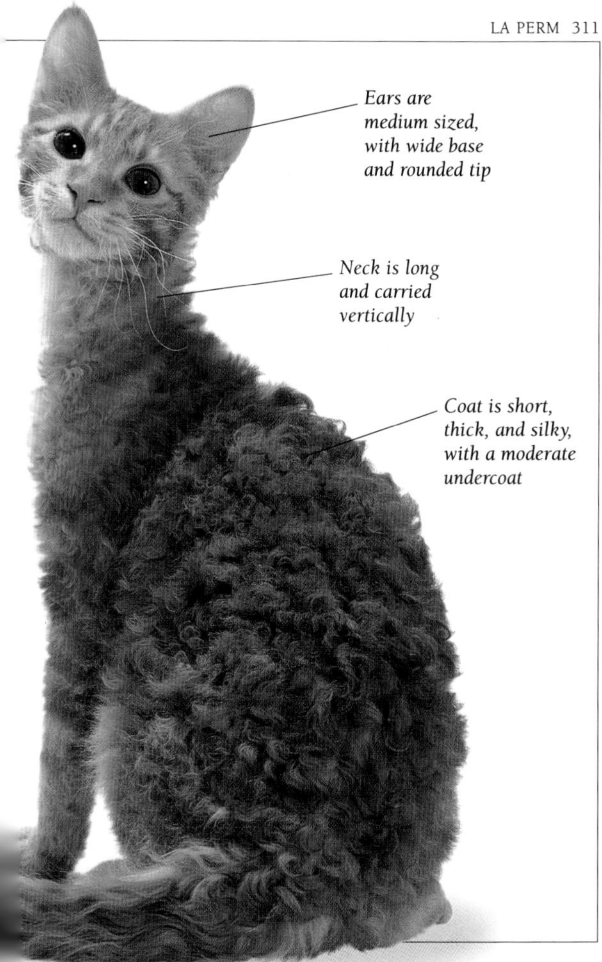
Ears are medium sized, with wide base and rounded tip
Neck is long and carried vertically
Coat is short, thick, and silky, with a moderate undercoat

Cornish Rex

Extrovert and curvaceous, with washboard waves of hair, the Cornish Rex is a show-stopper. The coat lacks guard hairs and is gloriously soft to touch, much like cut velvet. But the breed also has a distinctive physiognomy: dramatic, large ears are set high on a relatively small head, and the arched body is set on fine, lean legs. Although the coat is the same on both sides of the Atlantic, the conformation is slightly different. British cats are less delicate in appearance than their American relations, which have "tucked-up" torsos. This makes them look much like the feline equivalent of a racing hound, an impression in keeping with the breed's lively behavior. This is an Olympic jumper, which thinks nothing of springing from the floor to your shoulder to greet you.

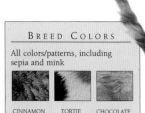

Breed Colors

All colors/patterns, including sepia and mink

CINNAMON SILVER

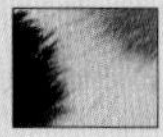

TORTIE WHITE

CHOCOLATE POINT

Red Smoke

Cornish Rexes carry their bodies very high on their legs, with gently arching spines. The waves of the coat are most apparent over the back and rump. The red gene was present in the breed from Kallibunker's own offspring.

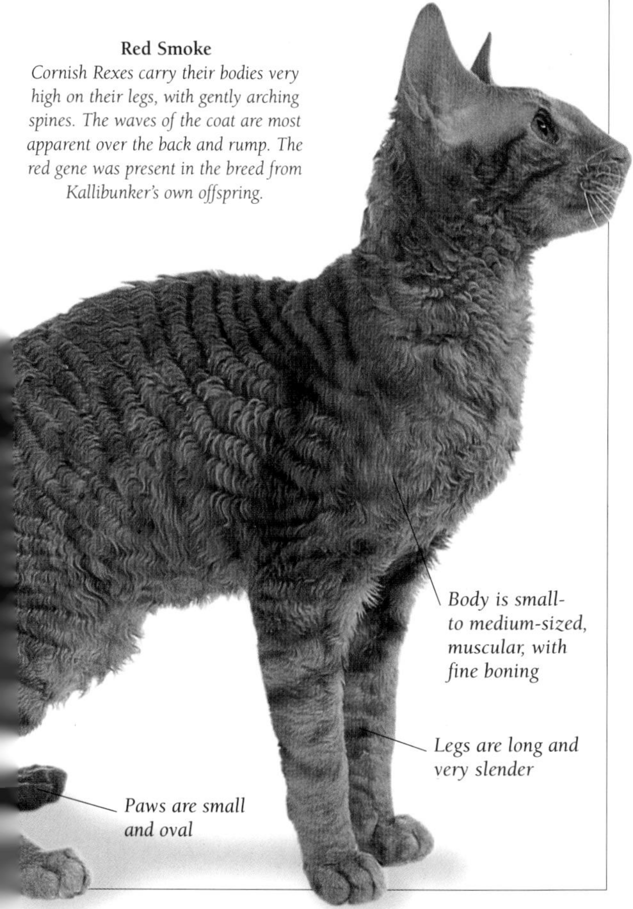
Body is small- to medium-sized, muscular, with fine boning
Legs are long and very slender
Paws are small and oval

White

This male typifies the moderately foreign look of the British type. While the build should be slender, the body is strong and distinctly muscular, and the legs should not be overly long and fine. The original Cornish Rex, Kallibunker, had a distinctly foreign appearance, but the look of the breed was defined by the cats used in the early development of the breed, as well as later breeding choices on each side of the Atlantic.

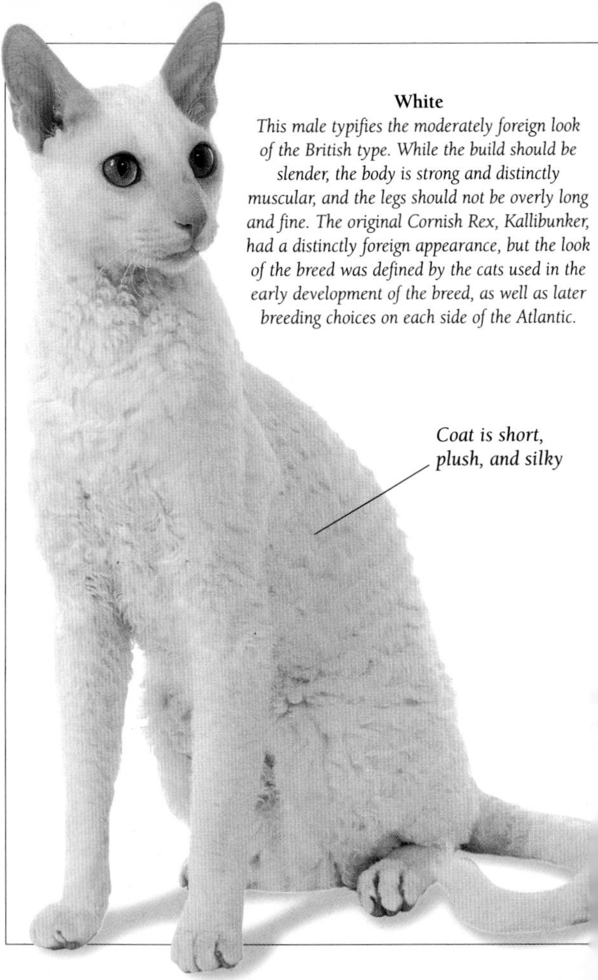
Coat is short, plush, and silky

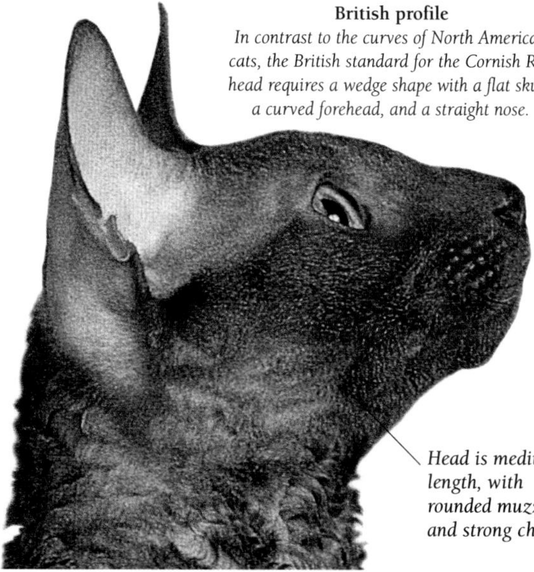
Head is medium length, with rounded muzzle and strong chin

British profile

In contrast to the curves of North American cats, the British standard for the Cornish Rex head requires a wedge shape with a flat skull, a curved forehead, and a straight nose.

Breed History In 1950, a farm cat from Cornwall had a litter with one curly-haired male kitten, Kallibunker. Her owner, Nina Ennismore, recognized this as similar to the "rex" mutation in rabbits. Breeding Kallibunker back to his mother confirmed that the trait was recessive. Descendants were crossed to British Shorthairs and Burmese. In 1957, the Cornish Rex arrived in the United States, where Oriental Shorthair and Siamese lines were introduced. A similar rexed breed was known in Germany, developed from a stray adopted by breeders in 1951.

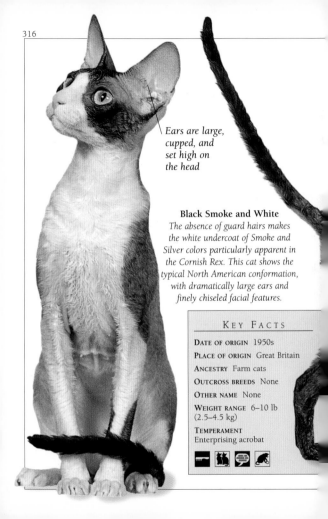

Ears are large, cupped, and set high on the head

Black Smoke and White

The absence of guard hairs makes the white undercoat of Smoke and Silver colors particularly apparent in the Cornish Rex. This cat shows the typical North American conformation, with dramatically large ears and finely chiseled facial features.

KEY FACTS

DATE OF ORIGIN 1950s

PLACE OF ORIGIN Great Britain

ANCESTRY Farm cats

OUTCROSS BREEDS None

OTHER NAME None

WEIGHT RANGE 6–10 lb (2.5–4.5 kg)

TEMPERAMENT Enterprising acrobat

Tortoiseshell

In finely built breeds, such as the Cornish Rex, the breed standards favor female cats. This Tortoiseshell shows the typical Cornish arch of the spine and the upward tuck of the belly required in the North American registries' breed profiles.

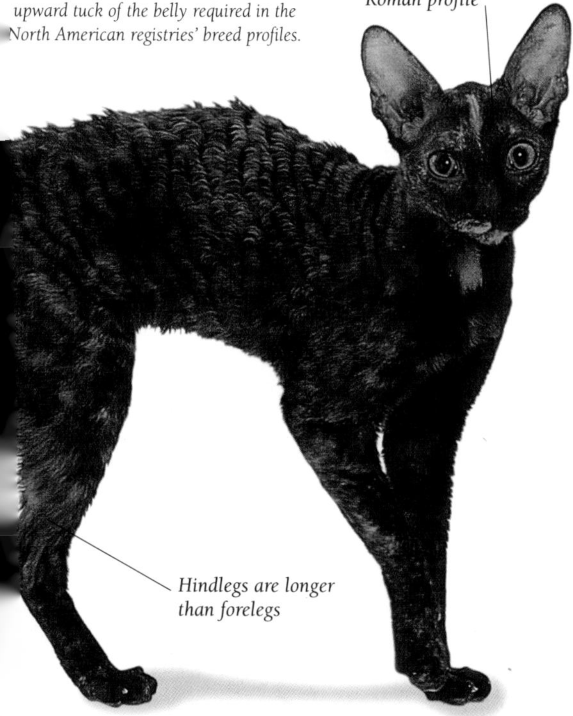
Head is egg-shaped, with curved skull and Roman profile
Hindlegs are longer than forelegs

Devon Rex

Startling, dramatic eyes and strikingly oversized, low-set ears give the Devon Rex the look of an elfin clown. Its coat ripples, unlike the waves of the Cornish Rex (*see page 312*). Good breeding has greatly improved the coat: it now matures in four months rather than a year, and is very rarely patchy. Due to outcrossing with other breeds, including Persians in the 1960s, longhaired cats sometimes occur. The coat has led to claims that the Devon is non-allergenic, but this can never be guaranteed. Breeders are unanimous that Devons never sit around looking bored; they always find life amusing: this has earned them the nickname "poodle cats."

Devon Rex profile
The short, wedge-shaped profile, seen here in a Blue, has a curving forehead, and a well-defined stop to the nose. The whisker pads are prominent.

Ears are lar
and very wi
at the base,
tapering to
rounded tips
Whiskers are
coarse and britt

Breed Colors

All colors and patterns, including pointed patterns

WHITE

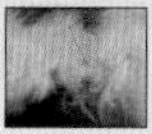

BLACK SMOKE AND WHITE

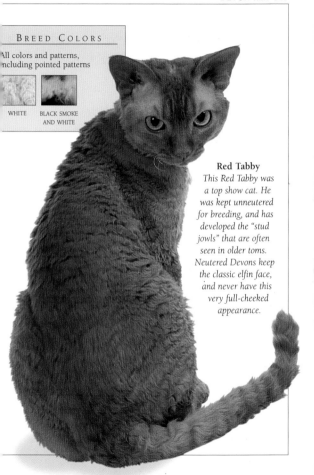

Red Tabby

This Red Tabby was a top show cat. He was kept unneutered for breeding, and has developed the "stud jowls" that are often seen in older toms. Neutered Devons keep the classic elfin face, and never have this very full-cheeked appearance.

Breed History In 1960, Beryl Cox found a curly-coated cat near an old mine in Devon, southwest England. A mating to a local female gave a normal litter with one curly-coated kitten, named Kirlee, showing that the gene was recessive; the parents were almost certainly closely related, and inbreeding was needed to perpetuate the Devon Rex. The Coxes bred Kirlee to some Cornish Rex females, but the offspring had straight hair; the Devon Rex gene is a different mutation, and the breeds have been developed as distinct types. The Devon was soon recognized in Britain; in North America it was distinguished from the Cornish in 1979.

Brown Tabby
The tabby markings a Devon Rex are mo evident on the legs, wh the hair is both short and less curly. All kinds of tabby patterns are allowe

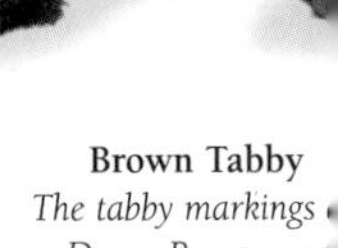

Silver Tortie Tabby

Wide outcrossing in the development of the Devon Rex gave it almost limitless patterns and colors. The curl shows up shaded colors well, and softens the markings.

Coat is very short, soft, and rippled or swirling
Pads of paws can be any color

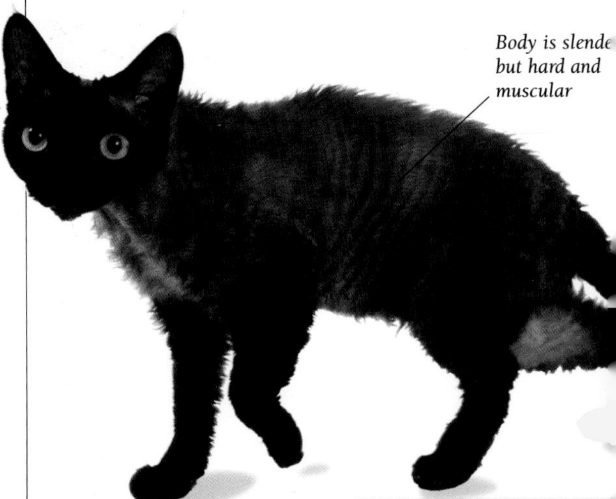

Black Smoke

The first Devon Rex to be bred, Kirlee, was a Black Smoke. Because of its curly coat, the Devon will show the smoke shading better than any straight-coated shorthair, and the darker the color, the more striking will be the contrast with the silvery white undercoat. An Oriental look has been a characteristic of these cats since the early days of the breed, but the elfin appearance of the face can belie the solidity of the body.

KEY FACTS

DATE OF ORIGIN 1960

PLACE OF ORIGIN Great Britain

ANCESTRY Feral and household cats

OUTCROSS BREEDS British and American Shorthairs until 1998

OTHER NAME Nicknamed "poodle cats"

WEIGHT RANGE 6–9 lb (2.5–4 kg)

TEMPERAMENT Appealing clowns

Blue-Cream and White

The broad chest of the Devon Rex can be clearly seen in this cat. Combined with its slender legs, this can give an appearance of bow-leggedness, but the legs do not really curve. There are no skeletal deformities associated with the breed.

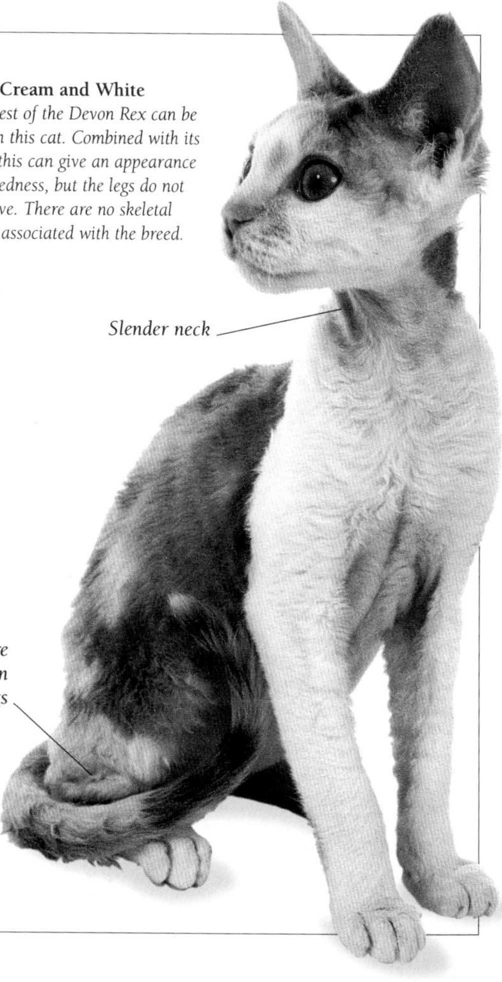
Slender neck
Hindlegs are longer than forelegs

SPHYNX

Hairless cats have appeared worldwide at different times. Not truly hairless, the Sphynx is covered in short, silky, "peach-fuzz" down, with the texture of soft chamois or suede. Without the insulating protection of a coat, Sphynx are vulnerable to both cold and heat and must be housed indoors. Each empty hair follicle has an oil-producing gland. With no hair to absorb the oil, Sphynx need daily rubbing with a chamois. Proponents of the breed feel that its devoted and playful nature is just as unique as its attention-grabbing hairlessness.

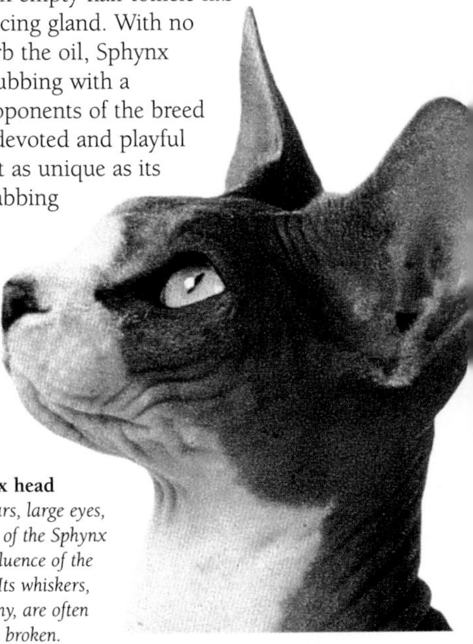

Sphynx head
The jugged ears, large eyes, and elfin face of the Sphynx show the influence of the Devon Rex. Its whiskers, if there are any, are often brittle and broken.

Breed Colors

All colors and patterns, including pointed, sepia, and mink

TORTOISE-SHELL

WHITE

BLACK

Blue-Cream and White

Sphynx show colors on their skin just as other breeds do on their hair; with no tweezing out of stray white hairs possible, these cats show the naked truth. The natural absence of hair apart from "peach-fuzz" down is vital: any evidence of hair removal is strongly penalized in shows.

Breed History The first Sphynx, Prune, was born in 1966, but his line died out. In 1978, a longhaired cat with a hairless kitten were rescued in Toronto. The kitten was neutered, but his mother subsequently had other hairless kittens. Two were exported to Europe, where one was bred to a Devon Rex. Hairless offspring resulted (implying that this recessive gene may have some dominance over the Devon gene). One, nicknamed E.T., was acquired by Vicki and Peter Markstein in New York and bred again to a Devon Rex. Today, the breed is recognized only by TICA: many other associations fear potential health disadvantages. In Britain, GCCF registers Sphynx to ensure that the gene is not carried into Devon Rex lines.

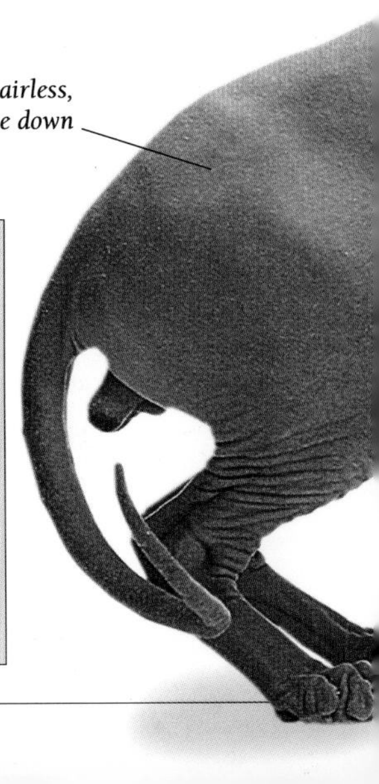

Coat is apparently hairless, but has a fine down

Key Facts

Date of origin 1966

Place of origin North America and Europe

Ancestry Nonpedigreed longhair

Outcross breeds Devon Rex

Other name Once also called Canadian Hairless

Weight range 8–15 lb (3.5–7 kg)

Temperament Mischievous

Blue

:olors in the Sphynx are often vɑrmer than they are in cats ith coats, because the natural :nk of the skin shows through. A Blue like this cat may, in some lights, look closer to a Lilac in other breeds.

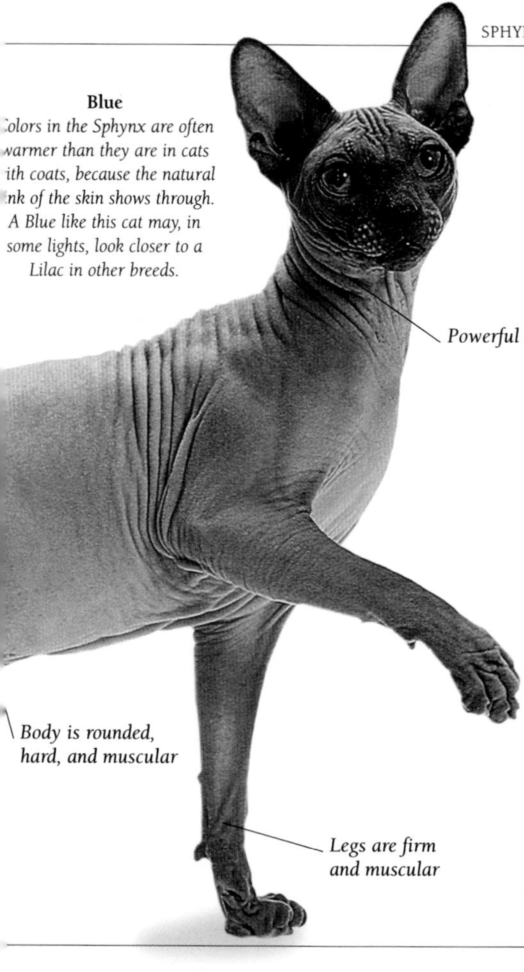
Powerful neck
Body is rounded, hard, and muscular
Legs are firm and muscular

California Spangled

This sociable and active cat is a solid and muscular breed. The body is long and lean, but heavy for its size. The round head is reminiscent of many small wild cats, and the dense, double coat was developed to imitate leopard markings. The wild appearance of the California Spangled indicates that the diversity of coats in the cat family has not been lost in the domestic cat. The breeding program has produced a kitten that was black at birth, except for its face, legs, and underbelly, maturing to show a coat that is similar to that of the rare African king cheetah.

Breed Colors

TABBY (SPOTTED)
Black, Charcoal, Brown, Bronze, Red, Blue, Gold, Silver

SNOW LEOPARD
Colors and pattern are as for standard tabbies

BROWN SILVER GOLD

Gold kitten

All spotted tabby California Spangled kittens are born with their spots. Kittens with the "snow leopard" pattern are born white, and those of the "King Spangled" pattern are born black. Blue eyes will become green or golden.

Ears are upright with rounded tips, set far back on the head

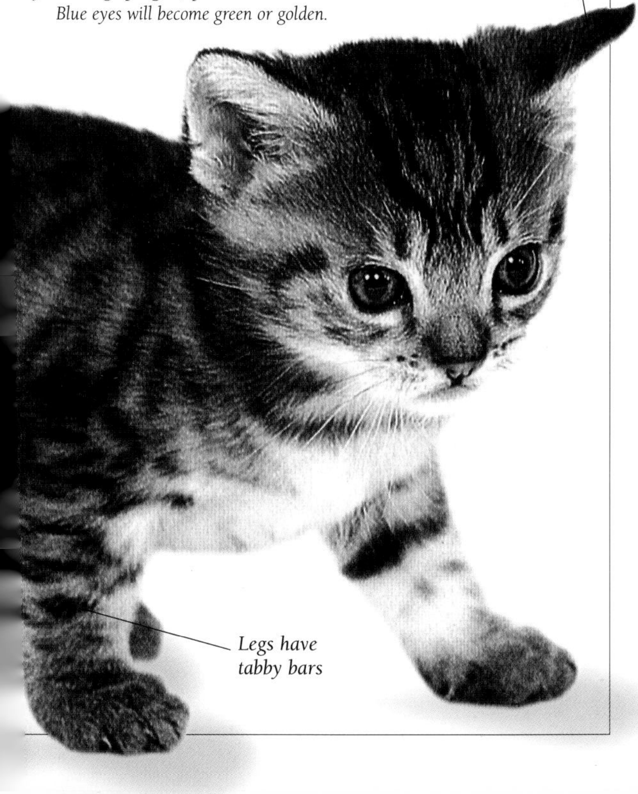

Legs have tabby bars

KEY FACTS

DATE OF ORIGIN 1971

PLACE OF ORIGIN United States

ANCESTRY Abyssinian, Siamese, British and American Shorthairs, Manx, Persians, African and Asian street cats

OUTCROSS BREEDS None

OTHER NAME None

WEIGHT RANGE 9–18 lb (4–8 kg)

TEMPERAMENT Gently sociable

Blue

The spots on a California Spangled vary in shape from round to oval or triangular: the wilder the appearance of the coat, the better. Investigation of patterns and development is still ongoing. The Blue is not as cool as it is in many other breeds: in the paler areas some rufousing may be seen.

BREED HISTORY This breed is the creation of Californian Paul Casey, who set out to create a wild-looking spotted cat without wild-cat bloodlines. Using nonpedigreed cats from Asia and Cairo and a range of pedigreed breeds (including Spotted Manx, Silver Spotted Tabby Persians, Seal Point Siamese, and British and American Shorthairs), he produced the desired cat. It was launched in 1986 in a blaze of publicity through the catalogue of a department store, a move unpopular with other breeders. "Spangled" is an ornithological term for spotted. Rosetted and ringed coats mimic those of the ocelot, margay, and jaguar. The breed has not yet gained wide recognition in North America or elsewhere.

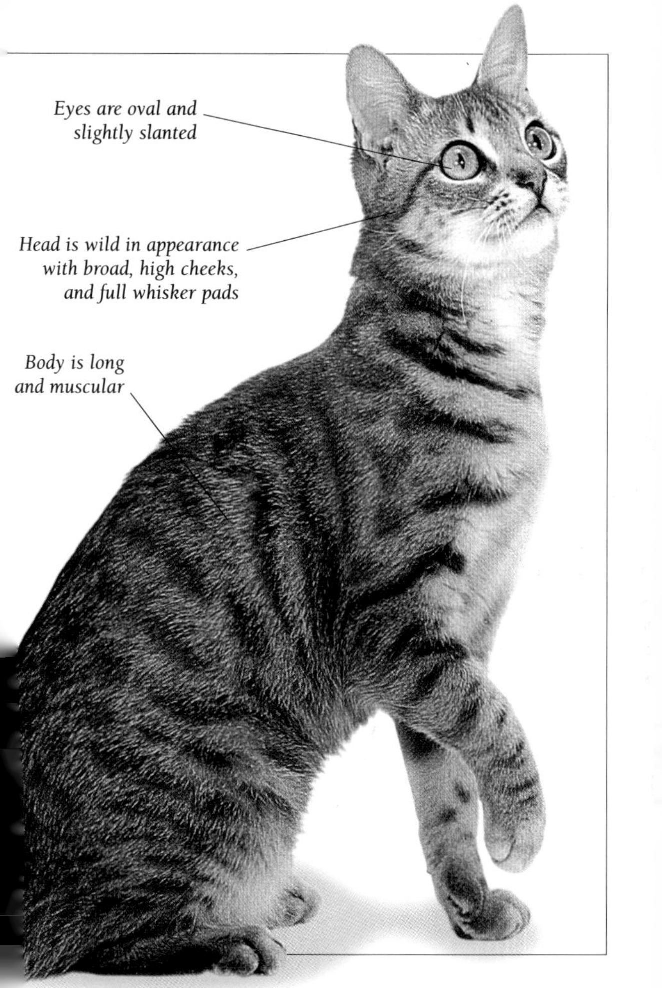
Eyes are oval and slightly slanted
Head is wild in appearance with broad, high cheeks, and full whisker pads
Body is long and muscular

EGYPTIAN MAU

Maus look similar in many ways to the cats featured on ancient wall paintings and scrolls in Egypt, and in fact "Mau" is the Egyptian word for cat. The body and face of the breed are both moderate in form, and the coat has a spotted pattern in shades of the original brown color. Only the eyes do not tally: early portraits have wild-looking eyes, while the modern Mau has wide, round eyes with a decidedly worried look. The helpless expression is deceptive, however: this is an effervescent and gregarious cat with a tendency to "chortle" to itself, and an innate self-reliance carried from its ancestry.

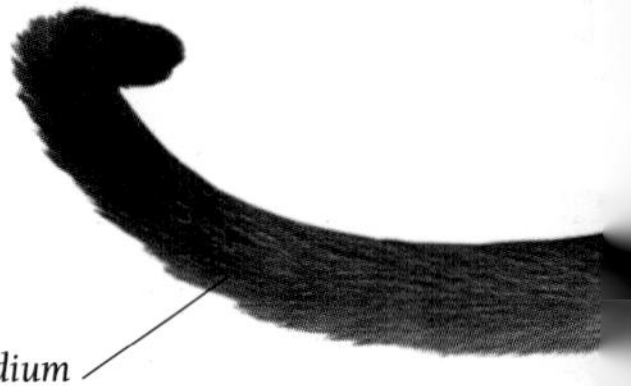

Tail is medium length, tapering from base to tip

BREED COLORS
SELF
Black occurs but is not accepted
SMOKE
Black
TABBY (SPOTTED)
Bronze
SILVER TABBY (SPOTTED)
Silver

Smoke

Mau Smokes differ from smokes of other breeds. Instead of being selfs with no tabby markings, they are distinctly tabbies. Cats of this gene type are usually called shaded, but they are also usually much lighter than Mau Smokes. The white undercoat shows just enough to provide contrast, and no more.

KEY FACTS

DATE OF ORIGIN 1950s

PLACE OF ORIGIN Egypt and Italy

ANCESTRY Egyptian street cats, Italian domestic cats

OUTCROSS BREEDS None

OTHER NAME None

WEIGHT RANGE 5–11 lb (2.25–5 kg)

TEMPERAMENT Friendly and intelligent

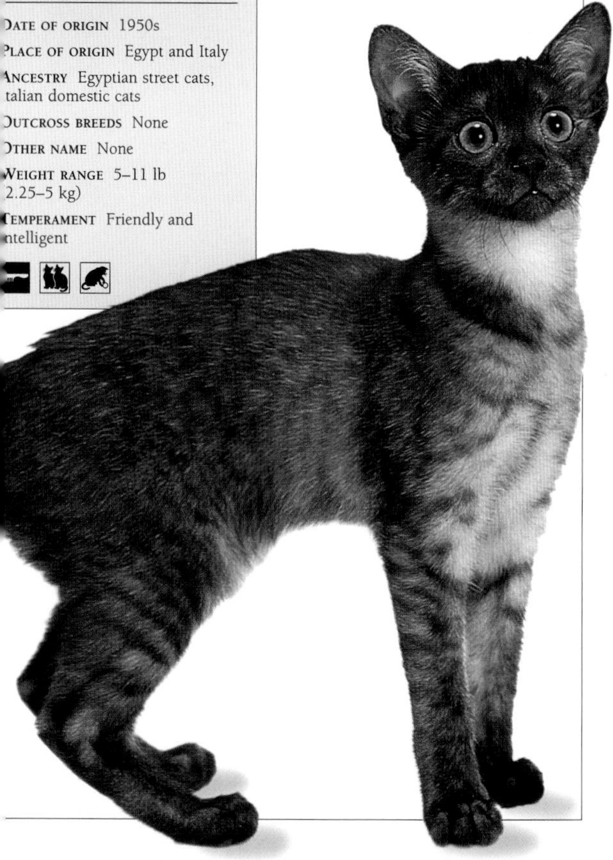

Breed History While all domestic cats can be traced to ancient Egyptian ancestors, the Mau is possibly the breed that resembles them the most. Nathalie Troubetskoy, an exiled Russian, was impressed with the spotted markings of street cats in Cairo, and imported a female to Italy to mate with a local tom. In 1956, she travelled to the United States, where the kittens were registered and shown the following year. The breed received full recognition from CFA by 1977, and is also shown in TICA, but remains almost unknown in Europe. In Britain, it has often been confused with Oriental Spotted Tabbies (*see page 292*).

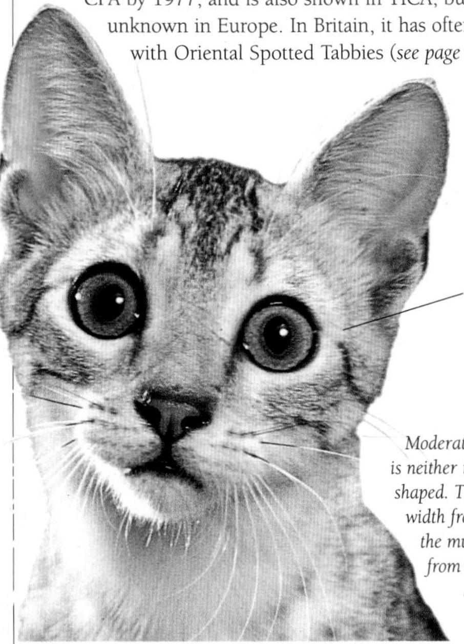

Head is a mediu
sized, rounded v
without flat pla

Mau face

Moderate in shape, the face is neither rounded nor wedge-shaped. The nose is the same width from brow to tip, and the muzzle flows smoothl from the lines of the hea Strong "mascara" lines accentuate the eyes.

Bronze

There are only three color forms of the Egyptian Mau, and the Bronze is the ost ancient in appearance. Markings on the flanks are random, but spots along the spine run in symmetrical lines, ften merging into a dorsal stripe at the start of the tail.

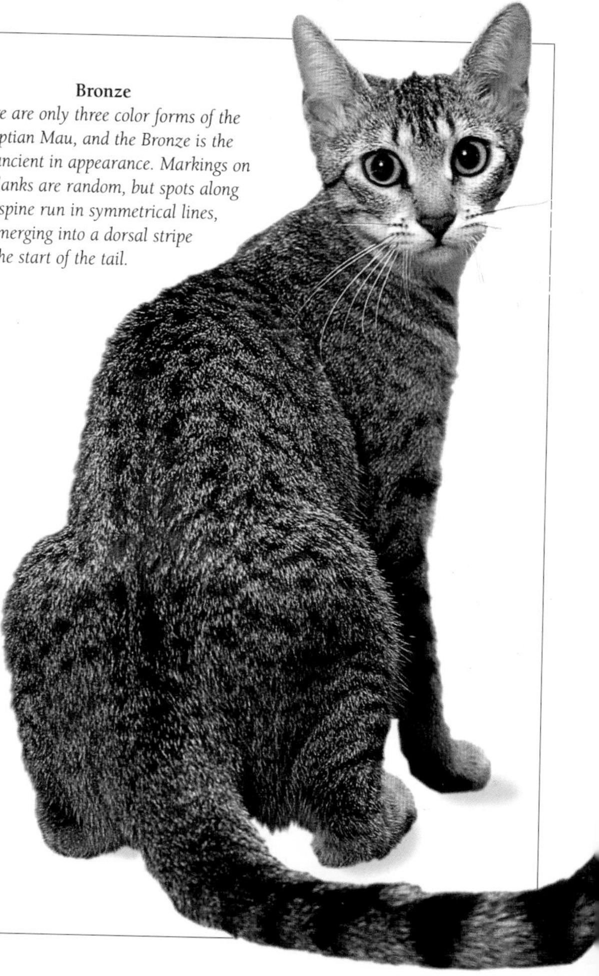

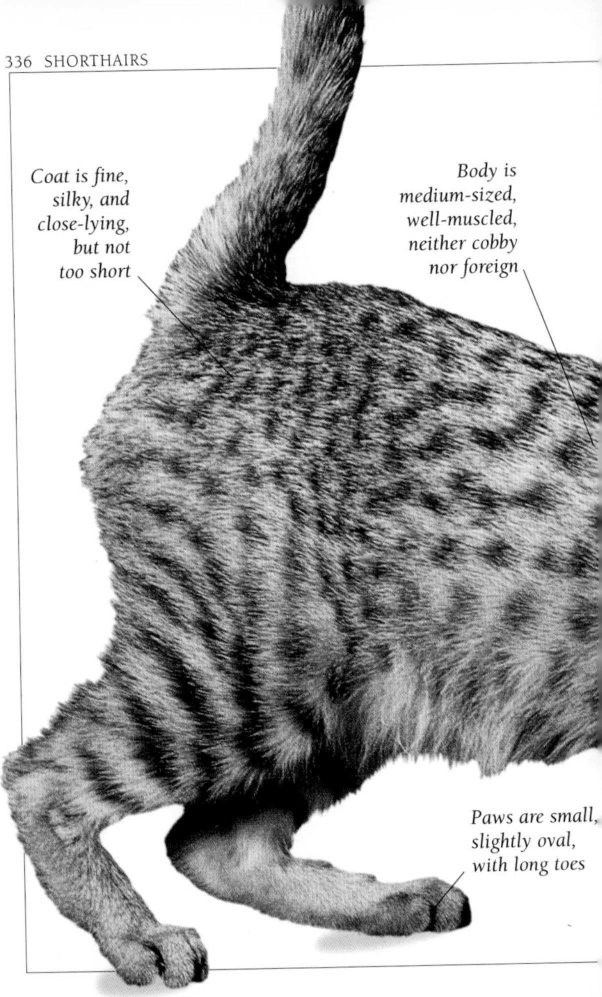
Coat is fine, silky, and close-lying, but not too short
Body is medium-sized, well-muscled, neither cobby nor foreign
Paws are small, slightly oval, with long toes

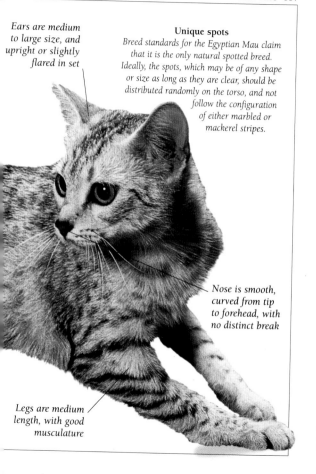

Ears are medium to large size, and upright or slightly flared in set
Nose is smooth, curved from tip to forehead, with no distinct break
Legs are medium length, with good musculature

Unique spots

Breed standards for the Egyptian Mau claim that it is the only natural spotted breed. Ideally, the spots, which may be of any shape or size as long as they are clear, should be distributed randomly on the torso, and not follow the configuration of either marbled or mackerel stripes.

OCICAT

More than just another new breed with unusual spotting, the Ocicat is an excellent blend of the attributes of its Siamese (*see page 280*) and Abyssinian (*see page 232*) blood. Playful and curious, Ocicats enjoy company, respond well to early training, and are not suited to prolonged solitude. They are muscular and surprisingly solid; males are much larger than females. The most distinctiv feature of the breed is its spotting. The distribution should follow the classic tabby pattern, swirling around the center of the flanks. Show-quality Ocicats mus have perfect spots.

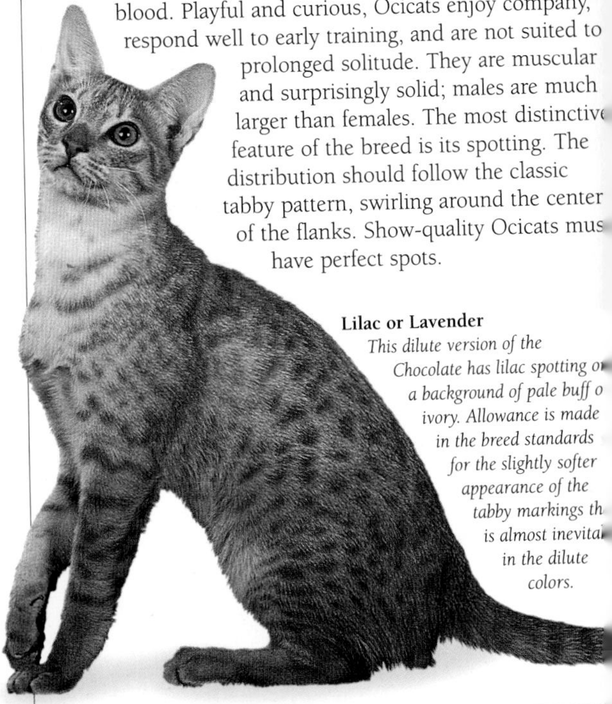

Lilac or Lavender
This dilute version of the Chocolate has lilac spotting o a background of pale buff o ivory. Allowance is made in the breed standards for the slightly softer appearance of the tabby markings th is almost inevita in the dilute colors.

Body is large, solid, and powerful, but graceful
Legs are medium length and well-muscled

Tawny or Brown

Genetically a brown tabby, this color is called Tawny by CFA. has black or dark-brown spotting on a warm, ruddy background, showing the rich rufousing of its Abyssinian ancestors.

BREED COLORS

TABBIES (SPOTTED)
Tawny or Brown, Chocolate, Cinnamon, Blue, Lavender, Fawn
Classic and mackerel patterns

SILVER TABBIES (SPOTTED)
Colors are as for standard tabbies
Classic and mackerel patterns

SELFS
Colors as for tabbies

SMOKES
Colors as for tabbies

SILVER

FAWN

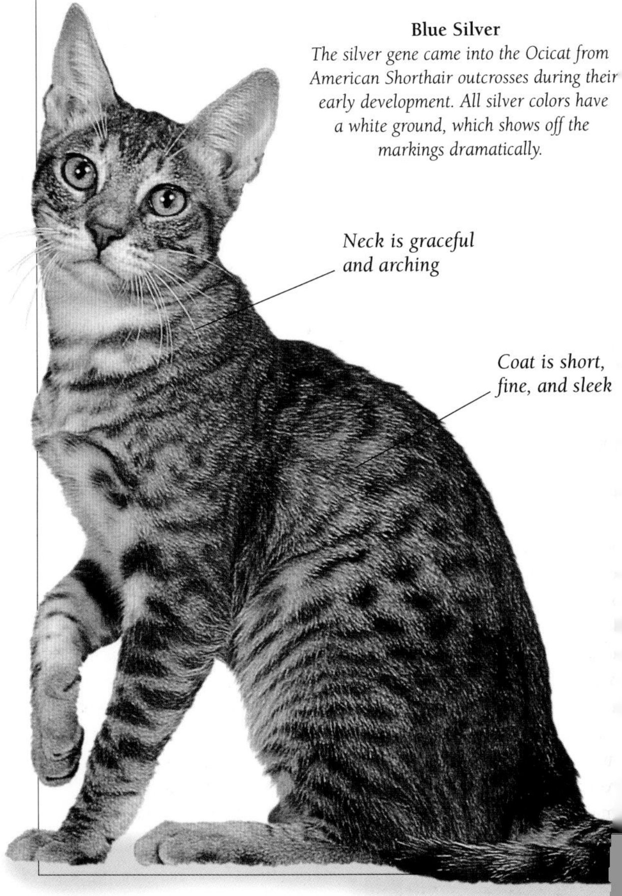
Neck is graceful and arching
Coat is short, fine, and sleek

Blue Silver

The silver gene came into the Ocicat from American Shorthair outcrosses during their early development. All silver colors have a white ground, which shows off the markings dramatically.

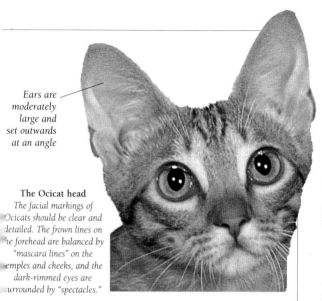

Ears are moderately large and set outwards at an angle

The Ocicat head
The facial markings of Ocicats should be clear and detailed. The frown lines on he forehead are balanced by "mascara lines" on the emples and cheeks, and the dark-rimmed eyes are urrounded by "spectacles."

REED HISTORY The Ocicat is a happy accident. Virginia Daly of erkeley, Michigan, crossed a Siamese with an Abyssinian, aiming) develop an Abyssinian-pointed Siamese. The kittens looked ke Abyssinians, but when one was bred to a Siamese, the litter icluded not only Abyssinian-pointed Siamese but also an odd, ootted kitten. Daly's daughter, noting its resemblance to the ocelot, illed the kitten an "ocicat." This first Ocicat was neutered and sold a pet, but the mating was repeated, producing Dalai Talua, the undation female of this still-rare breed. Another breeder, Tom own, helped to continue the Ocicat's development, introducing merican Shorthairs (*see page 190*), and in 1986 the breed received first official recognition, from TICA.

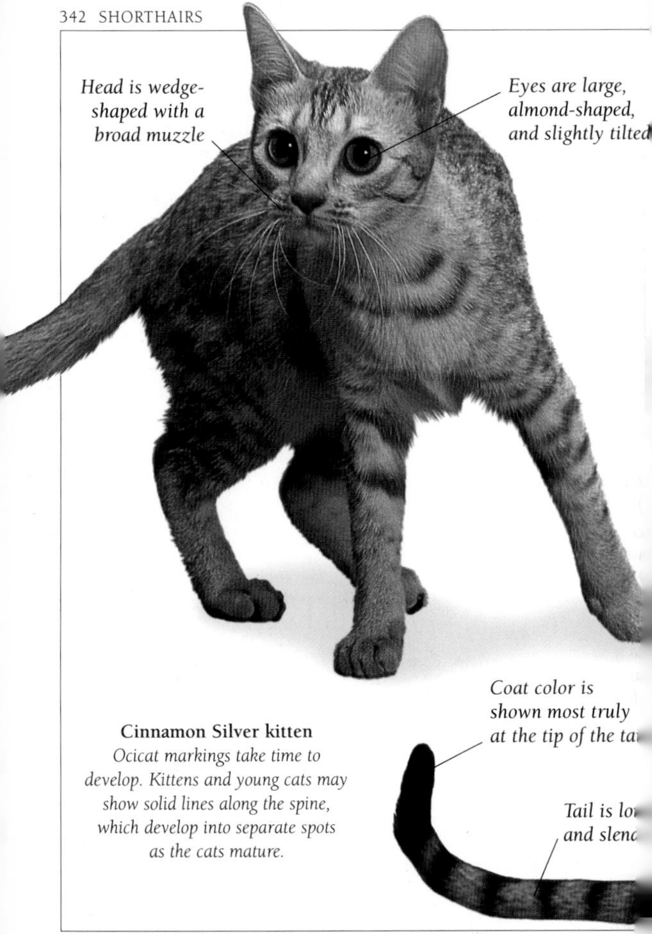

Head is wedge-shaped with a broad muzzle
Eyes are large, almond-shaped, and slightly tilte
Coat color is shown most truly at the tip of the ta
Tail is lo and slen

Cinnamon Silver kitten

Ocicat markings take time to develop. Kittens and young cats may show solid lines along the spine, which develop into separate spots as the cats mature.

Key Facts

Date of origin 1964

Place of origin United States

Ancestry Siamese, Abyssinian, American Shorthair

Outcross breeds Abyssinian until 2005

Other name Oci

Weight range 6–14 lb (2.5–6.5 kg)

Temperament Social and responsive

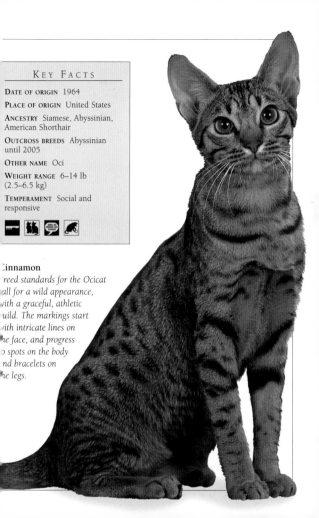

:innamon

'reed standards for the Ocicat all for a wild appearance, ,ith a graceful, athletic uild. The markings start ,ith intricate lines on he face, and progress) spots on the body nd bracelets on he legs.

BENGAL

Still rare worldwide, this breed has a distinctively thick and luxurious coat. The wild cat origins of the breed means a dependable temperament is a vital feature of breeding programs. Curiously, although Bengal numbers are still relatively small, breed clubs abound. In Britain, for example, there are three separate breed clubs, although ther are only a few hundred cats. Early breeding introduced som undesirable genes, for dilution, long hair, and spotting, but also the Siamese coat pattern, which has resulted in the extraordinary "Snow" shades.

Bengal head
Slightly longer than it i wide, the Bengal's face has high cheekbones an a full, broad muzzle. Th chin is strong, and wide set canine teeth help tc produce pronounced whisker pads. Frown lines and broken streak of color cover the head and the "puffed" nose leather is pink outlined black. In profile, there a gentle curve from forehead to nose, rathe than a break.

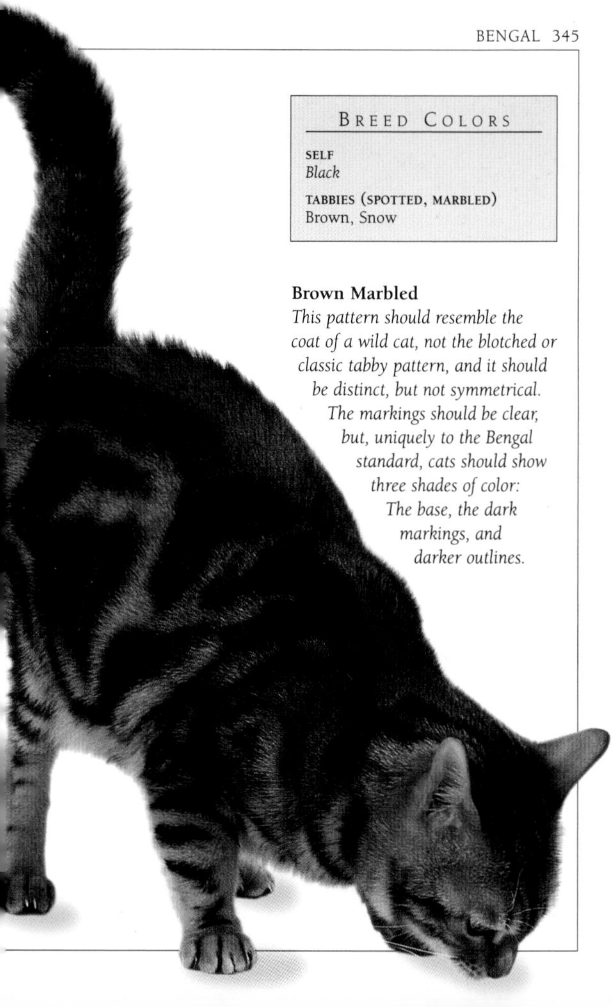

Breed Colors

SELF
Black

TABBIES (SPOTTED, MARBLED)
Brown, Snow

Brown Marbled
This pattern should resemble the coat of a wild cat, not the blotched or classic tabby pattern, and it should be distinct, but not symmetrical. The markings should be clear, but, uniquely to the Bengal standard, cats should show three shades of color: The base, the dark markings, and darker outlines.

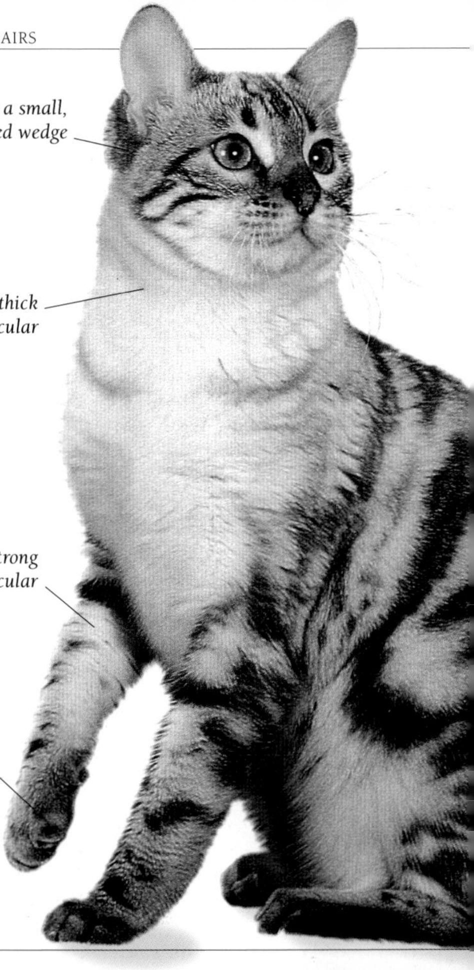
Head is a small, rounded wedge
Neck is thick and muscular
Legs are strong and muscular
Paws are large and rounded

3REED HISTORY When Jean Sugden bought an Asian leopard cat n California in 1963 and bred it with a domestic cat, her concern vas the conservation of the leopard cat. Ten years later, Dr. Villard Centerwall at the University of California continued this ıybridization in order to examine the Asian leopard cat's resistance o feline leukemia virus. From these beginnings the Bengal ippeared. Dr. Centerwall passed eight of his hybrids to Sugden, ıow remarried as Mill. The first Bengal, Millwood Finally Found, vas registered by Jean Mill in 1983. Initially this was a nervous eline family, but continued development has led to a more outgoing preed. Early crosses were to nonpedigrees, but when the leopard-ike coat appeared, individuals were crossed with an Indian street at and Egyptian Maus (*see page* 332).

Coat is dense and soft to touch
Fur is short to medium length

Blue-Eyed Snow Marbled

The Snows come from pointed lines in the nonpedigreed cats used in the Bengal's development. Breed registries are controlled to avoid such unexpected occurrences, but Bengal breeders have used this happy accident to create truly stunning cats. The color restriction should give an impression of "pearl dusting" to the coat; the pattern for these cats is as for their full-colored counterparts.

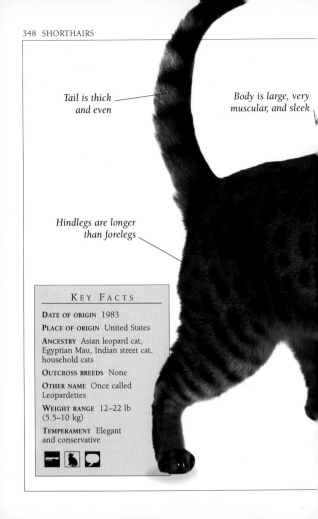

Tail is thick and even
Body is large, very muscular, and sleek
Hindlegs are longer than forelegs

KEY FACTS

DATE OF ORIGIN 1983

PLACE OF ORIGIN United States

ANCESTRY Asian leopard cat, Egyptian Mau, Indian street cat, household cats

OUTCROSS BREEDS None

OTHER NAME Once called Leopardettes

WEIGHT RANGE 12–22 lb (5.5–10 kg)

TEMPERAMENT Elegant and conservative

Ears are short, with a wide base, rounded tips, and no tufts
Eyes are large and oval, with a slightly slanted set
Broad chest

Brown Spotted

The first coat to be stabilized, the Brown Spotted resembles that of the Asian leopard cat, right down to the light-colored "ocelli" on the back of each ear. The base color is buff and the markings are deep brown or black. Facial features are outlined in black, and the spots on the coat should be large, forming rings or rosettes, and randomly distributed. Any resemblance to the vertical stripes of the mackerel pattern, the pattern underlying most spotted tabbies, is avoided.

American Bobtail

There were, until recently, only a couple of bobtailed or tailless breeds. But in the last few years, breeds from the former Soviet Union such as the Kurile Island Bobtail (*see page 146*) have become better known, and new bobtail breeds have been registered in North America. The American Bobtail was the first of these. The genetic background of the breed is uncertain: bobcat parentage is unconfirmed, but both Japanese Bobtail (*see page 304*) and Manx (*see page 176*) genes may be present. Unlike the Manx standard, tailless Bobtails are not showable: They should have a short tail that stops above the hock.

Breed Colors

All colors/patterns, including sepia, pointed, and mink

FAWN AND WHITE

BLUE TABBY

RED TABBY

WHITE

Spotted Tabby shorthair

he American Bobtail breed standard calls for a brawny, hearty, wild-looking cat, with a strong head and a hunting look to the eyes. merican Bobtails are a slow-maturing breed, nd may take as long as three years to reach heir full potential. The shorthair coat is long enough to stand away from the body and appear slightly shaggy.

Body is semi-cobby, with substantial muscling
Legs are heavy, with large, round paws

Breed History This breed can be traced back to a random-bred bobtailed tabby kitten that was adopted from an American Indian reservation in Arizona by John and Brenda Sanders of Iowa. Early work with the breed aimed to produce bobtailed cats with a pattern similar to that of the Snowshoe (*see page 208*), but the cats became inbred and unhealthy. Later work, led by Reaha Evans, reintroduced more colors and patterns, and improved the health of the breed. American Bobtails were recognized by TICA in 1989.

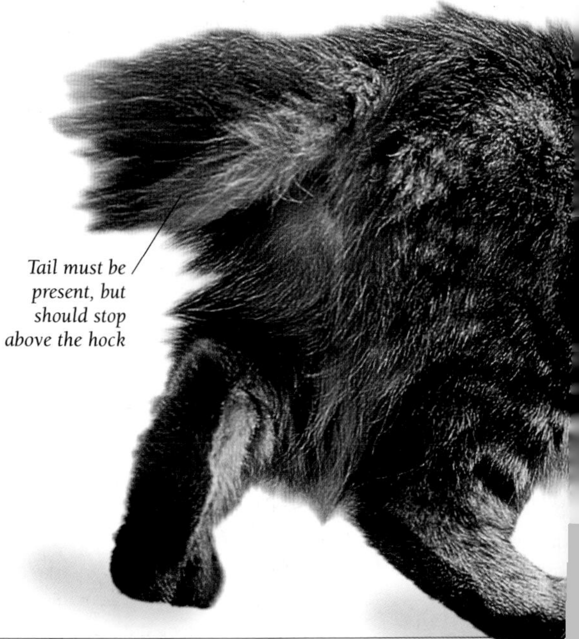
Tail must be present, but should stop above the hock

ars are medium-sized, wide at base, and set high on the head

Classic Tabby longhair kitten

There are both longhaired and shorthaired divisions for the American Bobtail: because the longhair gene is recessive, there are fewer of these. The coat is semi-long, and longer "muttonchops" on the cheeks are desirable. The Bobtail coat does not mat easily, although it appears shaggy.

Head is a broad, modified wedge, with curved contours

Key Facts

Date of origin 1960s

Place of origin United States

Ancestry Uncertain

Outcross breeds Nonpedigreed cats

Other name None

Weight range 7–15 lb (3–7 kg)

Temperament Friendly and inquisitive

PIXIEBOB

Domestic-sized cats with a wild appearance have becom increasingly popular over the last two decades; as a consequence, North American breeders have developed a cat that resembles the native bobcat. Despite their wild loo Pixiebobs are said to have the temperament of faithful dogs breeders recommend that owners consider carefully before acquiring this breed, since it does not readily chan homes, and is often happiest as a single cat. The wild look is described as "essential to the uniqueness of his breed."

BREED COLORS

TABBY COLORS (SPOTTED,ROSETTE)
Brown
Any other tabby pattern, other colors

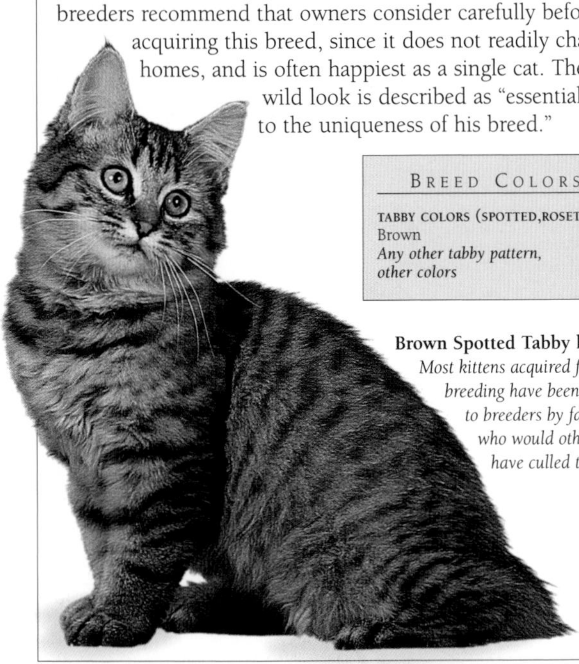

Brown Spotted Tabby kit
Most kittens acquired for breeding have been gi to breeders by farm who would other have culled ther

*Ears are wide at
ıe base, rounded, and set far back on the skull*

'ixiebob head
'he facial markings ıust be strong in ixiebobs, with ıascara" lines on ıe cheeks and light spectacles" around ıe eyes. Lynx tips on ıe ears are desirable, ıt not essential. 'he lips and chin ıould be 'eamy white.

'REED HISTORY The origins of the ixiebob are reputed to be wild obcat-to-domestic cat breedings ı rural areas, although DNA rofiles have not provided ıpporting evidence. Two such ıts were aquired in 1985 by Carol ınn Brewer in Washington State, ho bred them to produce Pixie, e founding cat of the breed. The eed was first allowed by TICA ımost 10 years later, but is not ıown outside North America.

KEY FACTS

DATE OF ORIGIN 1980s

PLACE OF ORIGIN North America

ANCESTRY Domestic cat, possibly bobcat

OUTCROSS BREEDS Brown tabby nonpedigrees

OTHER NAME None

WEIGHT RANGE 9–18 lb (4–8 kg)

TEMPERAMENT Quiet but affectionate

RANDOM-BRED CATS

The random-bred cat has no clubs to promote it and no romantic history or royal connections to beguile the public, yet the "moggie" is still the most popular cat worldwide. Type tends to vary from place to place, with sturdy cats found in cold countries and lighter, more slender cats popular in warmer climates. Oriental colors and pointed patterns remain rare in Western nonpedigrees, although these genes have occasionally filtered from pedigreed breeds into the general population.

Brown Classic Tabby and Whit
In Europe, the classic tabby cam to outnumber the mackerel tabby by the 18th century. It has been suggested that, because it is darker than the mackerel pattern, t classic coat provided better camouflage in the urban environment.

Red Classic Tabby and White
· white spotting gene 's dominant, making bicolors common in domestic cats.

Cream Tabby
In the first pedigreed cats, creams were often regarded as poor reds. Over the decades, breeders have bred out the red tones to produce paler, cooler coats in pedigreed Creams.

Blue and White
Blue is a common color in many rts of Europe, and the Chartreux : page 218) *was developed from h stock. Many random-bred cats are a darker blue than pedigree breeds, and lack the intense and varied eye colors achieved by dedicated selective breeding.*

FELINE DESIGN

The cat is an almost perfectly designed predator. Its superb balance and flexibility enable it to catch small prey and escape from larger predators. Its brain, nerves, and hormones harmonize to avoid wasting energy, while st being capable of explosions of activity. The domestic cat's anatomy is almost identical to that of its close wild relation most medical problems are caused by injury or illness rath than poor design. Its internal organs and body functions have adapted for survival; its digestive and excretory systems allow it to cope without food for longer than other domesticated animals; and its unique reproductive system is adapted to ensure successful matings each year.

Kitten at bay
Cats fold back their ears as a sign of fear.

Although the cat is a solitary hunter, content to live on its own in the absence of other cats or people, it is now in the process of evolving from total independence to a more willing dependence. Its behavior toward other cats and people reflects this evolutionary change. Human intervention in the environment of the domestic cat has modified its natural behavior. Humans have encouraged the kitten in cats, making adult cats more dependent on people and more sociable in the process. However, despite these crucial developments, the cat's inherent need to hun, as well as its way of conceiving and mothering kittens, are unlikely to change.

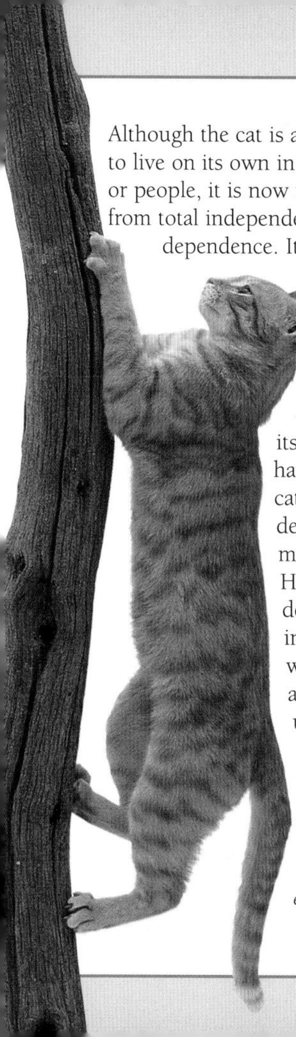

Vertical climbing
Powerful leg muscles, flexible joints, extendable claws, and a sophisticated sense of balance allow the cat to adapt to a vertical environment.

FELINE GENETICS

Although the details of genetics are complex, the basis of these inherited characteristics are quite simple. All the information needed for life is carried in the genes contained in each body cell. Genetics follows simple, mathematical laws. Every cell in a cat's body contains a nucleus at some stage in its development. Each nucleus contains 38 chromosomes, arranged in 19 pairs, which are just large enough to be seen with a powerful optical microscope. Each chromosome is formed from a tightly wound double helix of deoxyribonucleic acid (DNA), which in turn is made up of thousands of units called genes, strung together like beads. Each gene is made from four different proteins – A, T, C, and G – which combined, provide the information for all aspects of a cat's life.

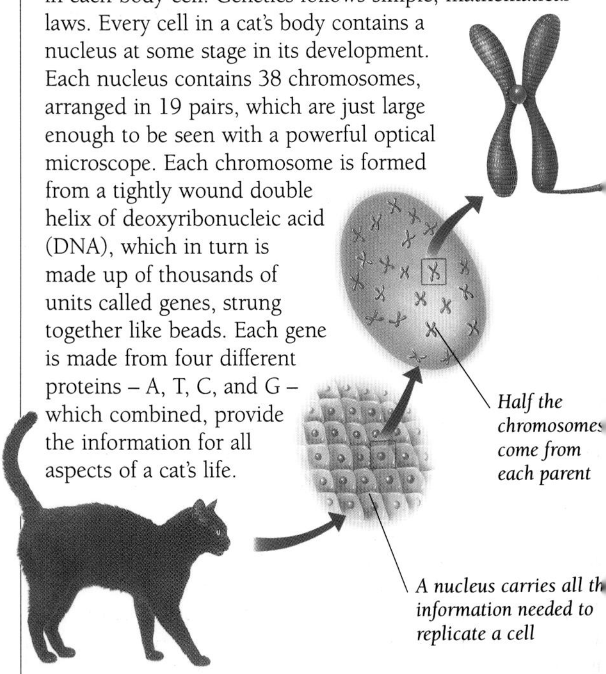

Half the chromosomes come from each parent

A nucleus carries all the information needed to replicate a cell

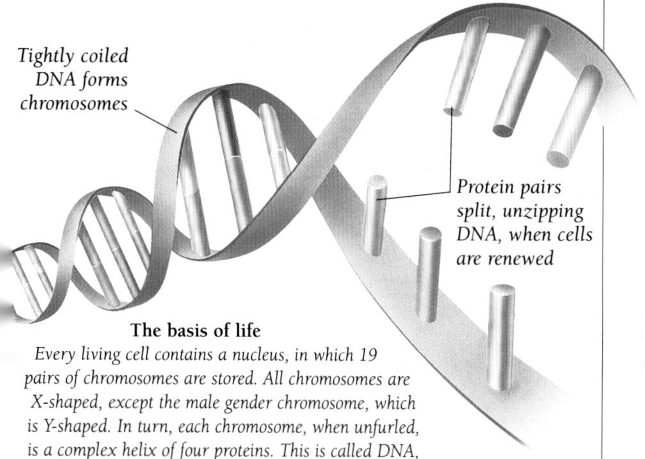
Tightly coiled DNA forms chromosomes
Protein pairs split, unzipping DNA, when cells are renewed

The basis of life

Every living cell contains a nucleus, in which 19 pairs of chromosomes are stored. All chromosomes are X-shaped, except the male gender chromosome, which is Y-shaped. In turn, each chromosome, when unfurled, is a complex helix of four proteins. This is called DNA, and it forms the basis of all inherited characteristics.

COPYING AND MUTATIONS

Each time a cell, such as a skin cell, is replaced, its chromosomes are copied. Ribonucleic acid (RNA) is generated to match each half-strand, and then used as a template on which new DNA forms from proteins. The copying process is so accurate that there may be only one mistake, or mutation, in one gene, for every million copies. Information is passed down the generations in a different way. Egg and sperm cells contain only 19 chromosomes, each one half of a pair. At conception, the 19 chromosomes in the egg unite with the 19 in the sperm, creating a new set of 19 pairs. Each kitten inherits half of its genetic material from each parent. When chromosomes pair up, the genes for each characteristic also pair up. Mutations sometimes occur in egg or sperm cells, creating new traits.

ALLELES

Specific information about a trait is always carried at the same site on each chromosome: In a pair of chromosomes, this pair of sites is called an allele. The information may vary in an allele. If the information is the same at both sites, the instructions are homozygous; if it is different, the instructions are heterozygous.

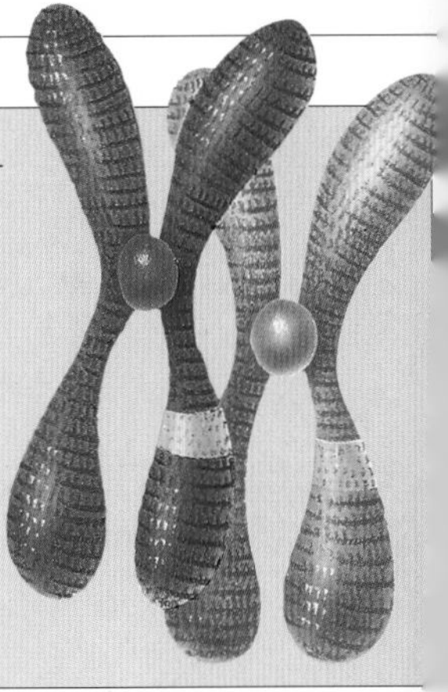

Matching pair
A genetic trait is determined by the genes from both parents, located at matching sites on the paired chromosomes.

DOMINANT AND RECESSIVE TRAITS

Genetic variations in characteristics, such as coat length, are called dominant if one copy of them is needed to show its effect, and recessive if two copies, one on each chromosome in a pair, are needed. Original traits tend to be dominant, and new mutations recessive: cats originally had short coats, and the gene for it is notated *L*, but a mutation occurred long ago, producing a recessive gene for long hair, which is notated *l*.

A cat showing a dominant trait may be heterozygous, carrying the recessive alternative "masked" beneath the dominant one: A cat with a recessive trait must be homozygous for it, carrying no alternatives. Two heterozygous shorthaired cats – both *Ll*, carrying the recessive gene for long hair – produce, if mated, an average of two *Ll* kittens, one *LL* kitten, and one longhaired *ll* kitten. Appearance gives no clue as to which of the three kittens carry the *l* gene that enables them to produce longhaired kittens.

MEDELIAN INHERITANCE PATTERNS

Several major traits in feline appearance have been identified. Dominant traits are notated in capitals, recessive traits in lower case. A shorthaired cat is notated *L*; unless test matings show it to be *LL*, because *L* needs to appear only once in an allele to show an effect; the nature of the second gene in the pair usually remains unknown.

A	agouti, or tabby
a	non-agouti, or self
B	black
b	brown, or chocolate
b^l	light brown, or cinnamon
C	full color, or solid
c^b	Burmese pattern, or sepia
c^s	Siamese pattern, or pointed
D	dense, dark color
d	dilute, light color
I	inhibitor, or silvering
i	pigmentation sound to roots
L	short hair
l	long hair
O	orange, or sex-linked red
o	melanistic, non-red color
S	white spotting, or bi-color
s	solid color over whole body
T	striped, or mackerel, tabby
T^a	Abyssinian, or ticked, tabby
t^b	blotched, or classic, tabby
W	white, masking all other colors
w	normal color

Inheritance patterns

This diagram shows how long- and short-haired traits are passed on, giving the average results over many matings.

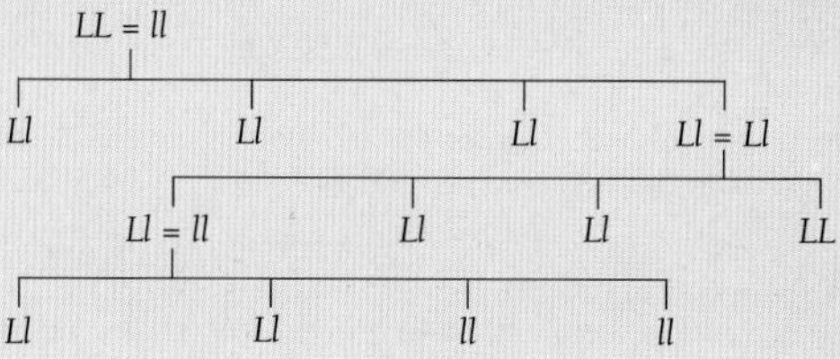

The Founder Effect

For hundreds of millennia, the African ancestors of today's domestic cats were almost uniformly shorthaired, striped tabbies. Yet after only a few millennia of migration out of Africa, hundreds of coat colors, patterns, and lengths have emerged. In the large cat population of North Africa, any random gene mutation had little chance of spreading widely unless it offered a substantial advantage to the cat. Most genetic mutations simply vanished within a few generations. In an isolated feline population, mutations have more chance of surviving. The orange-and-white cats of Scandinavia or the polydactyls of Boston, Massachusetts, and Halifax, Canada, are both mutations from the genetic "norm," when these cats were taken to regions with few or no cats, they represented a large percentage of a small gene pool.

The long-term genetic influence of early members of a cat population is called the "founder effect." The founders have a potent influence on a new population: this is why certain patterns or colors are prevalent in some countries. So what makes a breed? From a purely genetic perspective, there is no such thing, because the potential genetic differences within a breed outweigh the average genetic differences between two different breeds. For example, the DNA profiles of two Siamese can differ far more than those of a Siamese and a Persian. The definition of a breed is decided on a few obvious effects, such as coat color or length and body type.

Breeds and Genetic Diseases

Breeders use the laws of genetics to select for specific features such as color or body type. Unfortunately, they may also unwittingly select other hidden, dangerous genes. This is how genetic diseases gain ground. For example: Pesians suffer from polycystic kidney disease, while the Devon Rex carries a muscular disorder.

With the survival of the fittest, such dangerous genes are removed from the gene pool or persist at a very low level: Selective breeding has allowed them to survive and be passed on. This is the greatest genetic problem facing cats. Scientists are learning more about cats' genetics. The National Cancer Institute in the United States has a gene-mapping project investigating feline genetics. In England, Alex Jeffreys developed "genetic fingerprinting," which can identify an individual from a sample of DNA. This can be used to investigate paternity. However, because pedigreed cats often have similar DNA, especially in the rarer breeds, genetic profiling can only exclude a sire, not identify one. In reality, the vast majority of cat matings remain random, and natural selection remains the most powerful influence on the genetic future of the domestic cat.

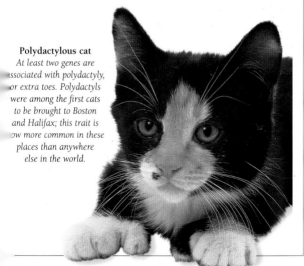

Polydactylous cat
At least two genes are associated with polydactyly, or extra toes. Polydactyls were among the first cats to be brought to Boston and Halifax; this trait is now more common in these places than anywhere else in the world.

COAT COLORS

The cat's original coat was of color-banded agouti hair, designed for camouflage in the natural environment. The first mutation away from hair with bands of color to a single color was probably to black; this mutation is often seen in other cats, such as the "black leopard" or "black panther." Other mutations occurred for red, white, and dilution of the solid colors. These few genetic variations created the framework for the many kinds of coat colors that exist today.

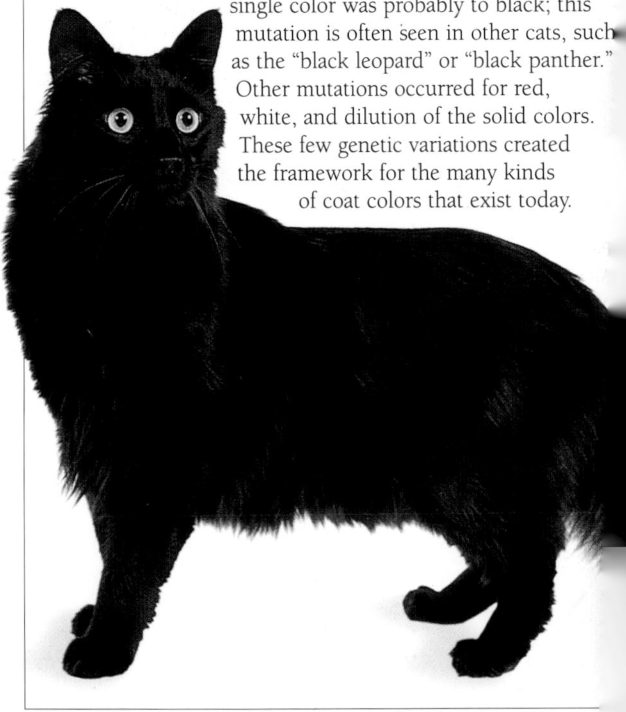

Natural distinction

Dilute self colors always breed true; they have become a defining characteristic of several naturally developed breeds, including the Russian Blue.

PIGMENTATION

All colored hairs contain varying amounts of the two components of melanin, eumelanin and phaeomelanin. Eumelanin produces black and brown, while phaeomelanin produces red and yellow. All colors are based on the absence or presence of these pigment granules in the shafts of each hair. Pigment is made in skin cells called melanocytes, and the distribution of these cells is genetically determined. Cats with single-colored "non-agouti" hair are called self or solid. Self coats are recessive: the cat must carry two copies of the non-agouti gene (*see pages 362–363*) in order to conceal its "true" original tabby pattern (*see pages 374–377*).

Under wraps

Black is the most dominant eumelanistic color. It is masked by white or red, but itself masks the genetic potential for other coat colors.

Density of Color

Some cats have vibrant, full-strength self coats. These come in the colors black, chocolate, cinnamon, and sex-linked red. Cats with these coats have at least one copy of the "dense" gene (*D*), which is dominant and ensures that each hair is packed tightly with numerous pigment globules to give the richest color. Other cats have lighter, "dilute" coats in blue, lilac, fawn, and sex-linked cream. These cats have two copies of the dilute gene (*d*), which is recessive and results in fewer globules of pigment in each hair: The effect is to create a paler shade of the dense colors. Some breeders think that there is a "dilute modifier" gene, called D^m, which is dominant over the dilute gene *d*, but located at a different site on the chromosome and so able to "interact" with *d*. If a cat carries both the *dd* dilute trait and the D^m gene, it will have a "modified" color: Blue.

Cat Colors

DENSE	DILUTE	DILUTE MODIFIER
Black *B– D–*	Blue *B–dd*	Caramel $B\text{–}\ d^md^m$
Chocolate *bb D–*	Lilac or Lavender *bb dd*	Caramel $bb\ d^md^m$
Cinnamon b^lb^l *D–*	Fawn b^lb^l *dd*	Undefined brown $b^lb^l\ d^md^m$
Red *D–O/O(O)*	Cream *dd O–/O(O)*	Apricot d^md^m *O–/O(O)*
Chocolate tortie *bb D– Oo*	Lilac tortie or Lilac-Cream *bb dd Oo*	Caramel tortie $bb\ d^md^m$ *Oo*
Cinnamon tortie b^lb^l *D– Oo*	Fawn tortie b^lb^l *dd Oo*	Undefined tortie $b^lb^l\ d^md^m$ *Oo*
Tortoiseshell *B– D– Oo*	Blue tortie or Blue-Cream *B–dd Oo*	Caramel tortie $B\text{–}\ d^md^m$ *Oo*

Red Burmese

Although sex-linked red existed in East Asia, the first Burmese in the West were brown. Red was re-created, and it is still not widely recognized.

x-Linked Red

ere is firm evidence that the gene red or orange colors in cats is located at a specific site on the sex- ermining X chromosome. In its dominant form (*O*), it makes the red; in its recessive form (*o*), it lets whatever other color the cat carrying show through. A male cat, with an XY chromosome nbination, can only ever have one copy of the gene: If he carries e *O* he is red, and if he has one *o* he will be any other color. The nale cat, because she has an XX combination, can carry two copies. e will be red if she carries two copies of *O*, or another color if she ries two copies of *o*. This combination makes her tortoiseshell. s mosaicking combination interacts with all of the other color- trolling genes, producing torties in all the solid and dilute colors.

Eastern and Western Colors

The traditional Western cat coat colors are black and its dilute blue and red and its dilute cream, together with their bicolor versions and solid white. Western breeds, such as British, American, and European Shorthairs (*see pages 164, 190, and 212*), Maine Coons (*see page 46*), and Norwegian Forest Cats (*see page 58*), began with these colors. Scme breeders have even more exclusive colors, such as the Turkish Van (see page 86), which appears in red and cream bicolors only. (However, other colors are now being bred, and have been accepted by FIFé.)

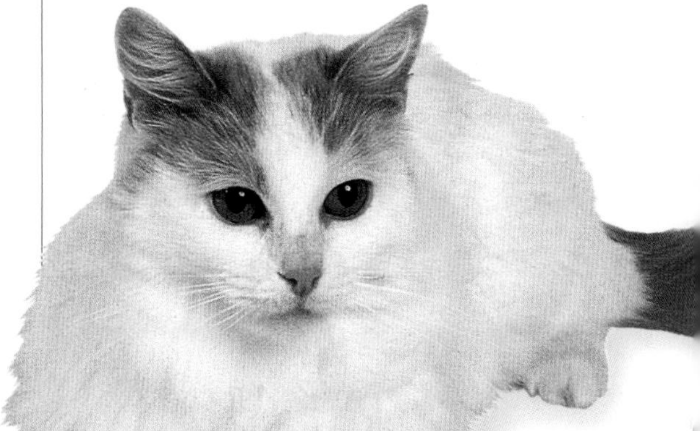

Van pattern
Found naturally in cat populations in the Mediterranean areas c Europe, this pattern is n widespread in carefully b pedigree cats.

The traditional Eastern colors are chocolate and its dilute lilac, and cinnamon and its dilute fawn. Cat coat colors have now been "transposed" from one group of breeds to another. In Britain, British Shorthairs are accepted in Eastern colors and, similarly, Burmese (*see page 262*) are now often bred in "Western" reds and creams.

WHITES AND BICOLORS

White is dominant over all other color genes, whether as all-over white (*W*), or as the white spotting gene (*S*) that gives us the bicolors. White hair, unlike all other hairs, does not contain any color-producing pigment. Behind its snow-white exterior, the white cat is genetically colored, and it passes on this color potential to its offspring. White cats carry the dominant *W* gene, which masks the xpression of all other color genes. Often, a hint of a cat's underlying olor breaks through in a "kitten cap" in the hair on the heads of ewborn kittens. As the kitten grows, the cap disappears to leave pure white hair. Deafness is sometimes associated with the *W* and *S* genes, although it is more common in white cats with blue eyes than in those with yellow or orange eyes. These white cats are different from albino white cats that have no pigment in their pink eyes: albino white is extremely rare.

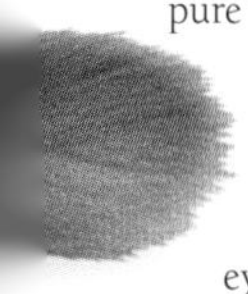

Bicolored cats are white-coated with patches of color – tortie-ıd-whites are variously classified as bicolor or tricolor – and ›me in two types. The standard bicolor is defined as being one-ird to -half white, with the white concentrated on the legs ıd underparts. The Van pattern, originally associated solely with e Turkish Van, but now also seen in other cats, consists of edominant white with solid or tortoiseshell patches restricted to e head and tail. One theory is that these cats carry two copies of e white spotting gene *S*, giving them a superabundance of white.

Standards for Colors

Although there are only a few genes responsible for solid colors, breed associations complicate matters by giving the same genetic color different names, depending on the cat. This tendency is most prevalent in patterned coats but also happens with self colors. Lilac is called lavender in some North American associations, black Oriental Shorthairs (*see page 292*) are called Ebony, genetically chocolate Oriental Shorthairs are called Havana in Britain and Chestnut in North America, and chocolate Havana Brown (*see page 228*) looks closer to cinnamon and is called Chestnut. Reds are often specified to be Red Selfs, because the distinction between red selfs and red tabbies is a subtle one, and in the Turkish Van

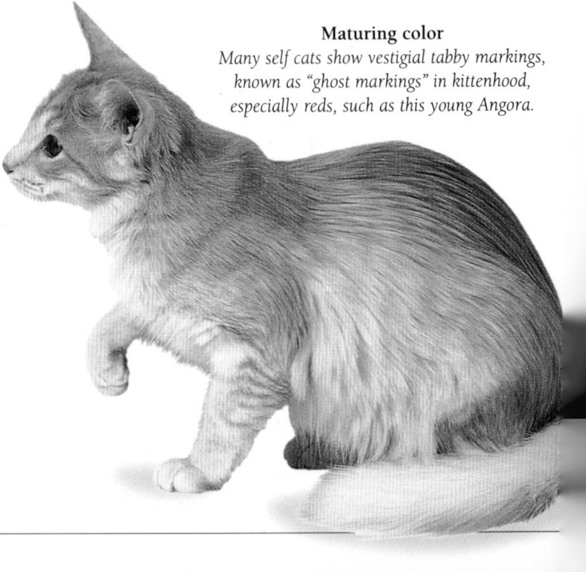

Maturing color

Many self cats show vestigial tabby markings, known as "ghost markings" in kittenhood, especially reds, such as this young Angora.

Mosaic color
The spotting gene S seems to have a predictable effect on tortoiseshell mosaicking. Solid tortoiseshells may have subtly mixed colors, but tortie-and-whites almost always show large, crisply distinct patches of black and red.

l-and-white is called Auburn-and-White. Tortie-and-white
s are called Calicos by CFA, because of a perceived resemblance to
nted calico cloth. According to breed standards, the color of the
se, lips, and paw pads (the leather) should be in harmony with the
t color: Pink in white cats, black in black cats, blue in blue cats,
k to brick-red in reds. This can vary: in some cases, the color of
leather depends on the particular breed, or even the association.

Coat Patterns

Beneath the extravagant variety of shades and coat patterns, all cats remain tabbies in disguise. Just as the most cossetted of pet cats retains the abilities of its predatory ancestors, the hidden tabby pattern is a reminder of the cat's roots (under the sophisticated exterior), an origin to which it can return at any time.

Through selective breeding, spotted, tipped, and pointed patterns are nurtured, or even created, by breeders. These are made possible by mutations in the genetics of feline coat patterns, mutations that would have reduced natural camouflage in the wild, but were no longer dangerous once the cat lived in the human environment.

Cat in disguise
All selfs are tabbies in disguise: if a self cat is bred to a tabby, at least some of the kittens will be tabbies.

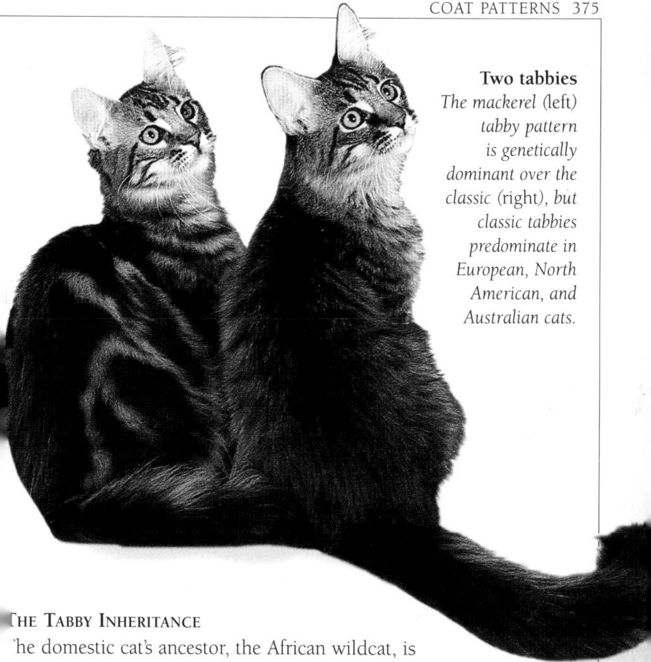

Two tabbies
The mackerel (left) *tabby pattern is genetically dominant over the classic* (right), *but classic tabbies predominate in European, North American, and Australian cats.*

ˈHE TABBY INHERITANCE

ˈhe domestic cat's ancestor, the African wildcat, is striped tabby, camouflaged for hiding and hunting in the wild. The original, genetically dominant tabby pattern is inherited by all domestic cats. The hair between the tabby stripes or spots contains bands of color, almost always light at the base and dark the tip, which act as a camouflage. This pattern is found in other ıimals, including squirrels, mice, and agoutis, the rodents after ˈhich the pattern is named. The bands of color give a "salt-and-epper" appearance, which combines with tabby stripes to help cat blend into a variety of environments.

Dominant Pattern

All cats inherit some form of the tabby gene, even those with solid, or "self" coats. Geneticists call the dominant agouti gene *A*. Any cat that inherits *A* from at least one parent will have a patterned coat, and is notated as *A*–. Solid colors exist because there is a genetically recessive alternative to agouti, called non-agouti or *a*.

In cats that inherit this from both parents, which are notated *aa*, the coat appears to be a single, even color, but careful examination may reveal disguised tabby markings. This "ghosting" is most apparent in young kittens, often disappearing with age. There are four basic types of tabby markings in felines: mackerel or striped; classic or blotched; ticked or Abyssinian; and spotted. Although these four patterns look distinctively different, they are in fact all mutated variations of the same naturally dominant tabby gene.

Pattern on pattern
Tabby markings over tortoiseshell mosaicking creates the most complex of all coat patterns.

New spots
The patterns of new breeds, such as the Ocicat, have often been created to emulate those of wild feline species. The genetics behind these newer spotted patterns are undefined.

COLORING

Mackerel tabby stripes are narrow, parallel, and run from the spine down the flanks to the belly. This pattern was predominant in Europe until a few centuries ago. It was superseded by the classic abby pattern. Classic abbies have wide stripes hat form "oyster" swirls on the flanks, centred on blotch. The distribution of this pattern in North American and ustralian cats shows that it was a popular, if accidental, export om 18th- and 19th-century Britain.

Ticked tabbies are more subtle: clear markings are restricted to ne head, legs, tail, and body. Ticked coats appear to have spread astwards into Asia, rather than northwards into Europe. Ticked ats are found in Sri Lanka, Malaysia, and Singapore.

Spotted tabbies have spotted bodies. Spotted patterns are formed hen tabby stripes are broken up. The spots of many European and merican breeds follow mackerel tabby lines, but there are other atterns. Spots of the Ocicat (*see page 338*) fall in a blotched pattern, hile those of the Egyptian Mau (*see page 332*) appear random.

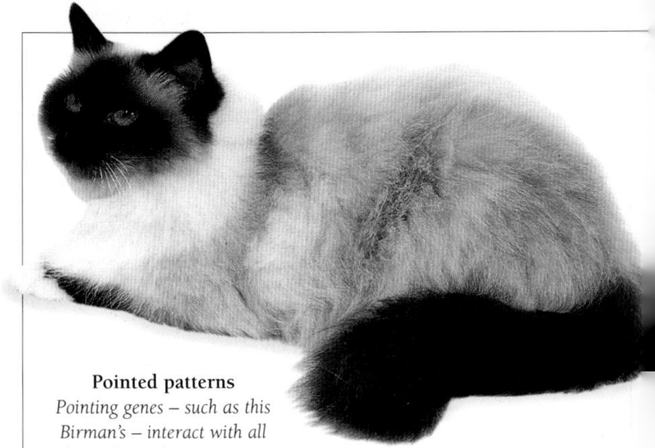

Pointed patterns
Pointing genes – such as this Birman's – interact with all other color and pattern genes.

COLORPOINT PATTERNS

The *I* gene is not the only gene to restrict color. Color restricted to the extremities is called pointing. Pointed cats are light on their bodies and darker on their "points," namely their ears, feet, tail, and nose. In male cats, hair is also darker on the scrotum. A heat-sensitive enzyme in the pigmenting cells in the cat's skin controls this pattern. Normal body temperature inhibits pigment production over most of a cat's body, but the enzyme is activated and hair pigmented at the points where skin temperature is lower.

Pointing can occur in any color or pattern. Because hair is temperature-sensitive, kittens are born white, cats in cool countries have darker coats than those in warm parts of the world, and all cat bodies darken markedly with age. The clearest form is the Siamese pattern (*see page 280*): an almost-white body and dark points. The Burmese pattern (*see page 262*), shows so little difference between body and points that some do not regard it as pointed.

Coat Patterns

SELF (*aa*, non-agouti) **TABBY** (*A*–, agouti)	All cats carry a tabby pattern, either striped (*T*–), ticked (T^a–), blotched (t^bt^b), or some other, as yet undefined pattern. The *aa* allele masks tabby markings: melanic pigment fills the entire hair and cats appear self or tortie. The *A*– allele shows the tabby markings. Whether a cat is *aa* or *A*– has no effect on sex-linked red colors. The difference between selfs and tabbies in these colors is one of subtle polygenetic effects that determine whether the markings are faint or strong.
SMOKE (*aa I*–, shaded non-agouti) **SILVER TABBY, SHADED, TIPPED** (*A*– *I*–, shaded agouti)	The inhibitor gene *I* blocks color production. In non-agouti cats only the roots are white, while in agouti cats, more of the hair shaft is affected. The difference between shaded selfs and silver tabbies is polygenetic, depending on the strength of the tabby markings. Polygenetic effects also divide shaded from tipped coats, although some claim there is a "wide-band" inhibitor gene. In the sex-linked red colors, the differences between the smoke, shaded, silver tabby, and tipped cats are all polygenetic.
SIAMESE (c^sc^s, pointed) **BURMESE** (c^bc^b, sepia) **TONKINESE** (c^bc^s, mink)	Technically, all of these patterns are pointed. All are heat-sensitive, with virtually all the color (in the Siamese) or the deepest color (in the Burmese) concentrated in the cooler extremities, or points of the body. Color is also slightly degraded or lightened; for example, black becomes Seal in the Siamese and Sable in the Burmese. The Tonkinese does not have its own gene: it is a softly pointed hybrid of pointed and sepia genes. It will always produce variants in these patterns, as well as its own mink pattern.

FACE SHAPE AND BODY FORM

Most cat breeds are not defined by coat color or pattern: many breeds share these attributes with each other. Breeds are more often differentiated by the characteristic shapes of their bodies and faces, and sometimes by distinctive physical characteristics such as a lack of a tail or folded ears. Cat breeds show personality differences that are consistent to a considerable extent with these different body shapes: Lean, long breeds are generally more lively and demonstrative than more compact, densely muscled breeds. These differences in breed type, from compact and cobby to sleek and sinuous, follow a geographical West-to-East path.

Old-fashioned face
The Chinchilla is the one Longhair coat color that has avoided the breed's radical facial shortening; in South Africa, it even has its own standard within the breed, allowing it to have a longer nose

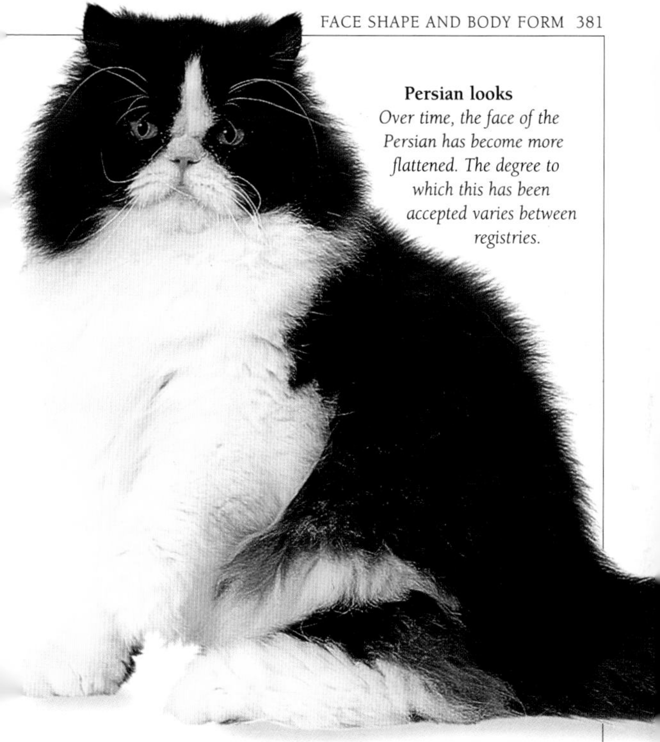

Persian looks

Over time, the face of the Persian has become more flattened. The degree to which this has been accepted varies between registries.

REED DIFFERENCES

ne breed differences that we see today have been developed from tural variations found in free-breeding cat populations. To a eat extent, these original variations in type were molded by the vironments in which they evolved, and a breed's type is often a od indication of its geographical origin.

Unique departure
The Scottish Fold, like many recently developed breeds, is distinguished by a single unique, striking characteristic. Registries are strict about breed identity being unmistakable, so this trend is likely to increase.

Cold-Weather Cats

The heaviest and most compact of domestic cats evolved through natural selection in cold climates. Many of these "natural breeds" have large, rounded heads, moderately short, broad muzzles, solid bodies with broad chests, sturdy legs and round paws, and short- to medium-length, thick tails. Essentially, they are built to retain as much body heat as possible.

Shorthair examples of these cobby cats are the British Shorthair (*see page 164*) and American Shorthair (*see page 190*), as well as the chunky-looking Chartreux (*see page 218*). Other breeds that derive from these may differ at first in just a single aspect of their body type. The Scottish Fold (*see page 186*) was developed through the us of British Shorthairs, and is distinguished primarily by its abnormal ears. American Shorthairs were used to breed the American Wirehai (*see page 196*), although this breed has now changed in its looks, becoming increasingly "Oriental" or "foreign" in appearance. The development of the Manx (*see page 176*) was parallel to that of the British Shorthair, rather than as an offshoot; it now looks even heavier than its close relation.

The original longhaired cats, the Persians, or Longhairs (*see page 16*), were also thickset and muscular, physical features that enabled them to withstand the harsh winters in the high mountains of Turkey, Iran, and the Caucasus. The breed still retains its original powerful body; other distinguishing features, such as the flattened face, have been introduced and exaggerated through decades of selective breeding. Other solid and robustly built longhaired cats developed naturally in northern climes. Norwegian Forests (*see page 58*), Siberians (*see page 64*), and Maine Coons (*see page 46*) evolved in cold climates from farm cats that lived partly outdoors.

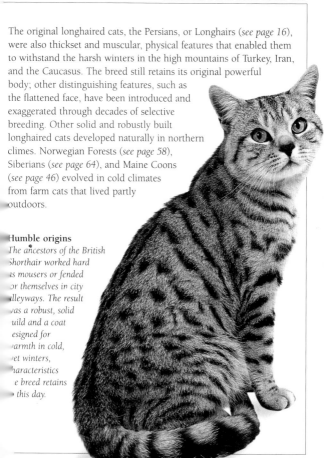

Humble origins
The ancestors of the British Shorthair worked hard as mousers or fended for themselves in city alleyways. The result was a robust, solid build and a coat designed for warmth in cold, wet winters, characteristics the breed retains to this day.

Oriental Breeds

The most dramatically slender cats are the Oriental breeds. Most evolved in warm climates where losing excess body heat was much more important than retaining it. With their large-eared, wedge-shaped heads, fine legs, slender bodies, and long, thin tails, these cats have developed maximum body surface area for their size, in order to rid themselves of excess heat. This conformation traditionally has oval, slanted eyes, and its most classic example is the Siamese (*see page 280*). Some claim, with good evidence, that Siamese did not always have their current appearance, and that stereotyped, Western notions about Oriental delicacy has created their shape. For example: the Japanese Bobtail (*see pages 150 and 304*), which is distinctly chunkier in Japan than in North America, is being bred to look

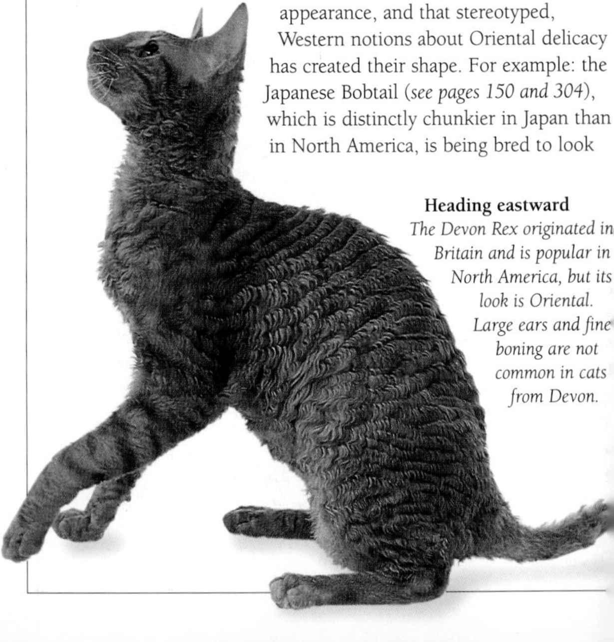

Heading eastward
The Devon Rex originated in Britain and is popular in North America, but its look is Oriental. Large ears and fine boning are not common in cats from Devon.

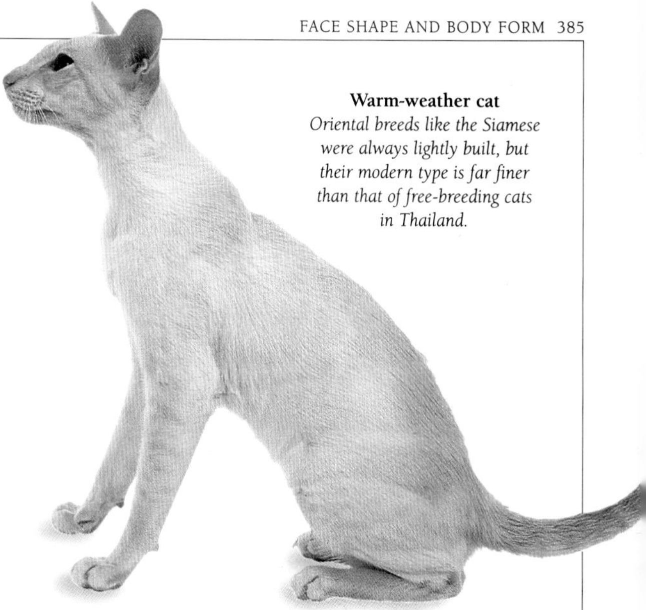

Warm-weather cat
Oriental breeds like the Siamese were always lightly built, but their modern type is far finer than that of free-breeding cats in Thailand.

ore typically "Oriental" and delicate. Newer breeds have been eated in the West to mimic Oriental style. The Oriental Shorthair *e page 292*) was created in the West, after non-pointed shorthaired s from Southeast Asia died out from among the original Siamese ports. Other distinctly Western breeds like the Cornish Rex *e page 312*) and Devon Rex (*see page 318*) have been bred to look e Eastern breeds. Among the Oriental breeds, the Siamese remains most popular, but less so than it was in the past. This may be cause some people are now repelled by the extreme look. By ntrast, the Siamese–Burmese hybrid, the moderate-looking nkinese (*see page 274*), is very popular.

Transatlantic contrasts
In contrast to their American cousins, the European descendants of the Burmese have developed a typically angular look.

SEMI-FOREIGN BREEDS

Another group of cats has physical characteristics that are somewher between the muscular cats of northern Europe and the more sinuou cats from warmer climates of Africa and Asia. These lean but muscular cats are often called "semi-foreign." Breeds like the Turkis Angora (*see page 100*), Russian Blue (*see page 224*), and Abyssinian (*see page 232*) have slightly oval, slanted eyes set in moderately wedge-shaped heads, slender but muscular legs, oval paws, and long, gently tapering tails.

A number of new breeds have been derived from the natural semi-foreigns. Some are simply new colors or coat lengths of their parent breeds, including the Nebelung (*see page 96*), and the more controversial Russian Blacks and Russian Whites (*see page 224*). Fashion seems to favour the semi-foreign look: the Somali (*see page 106*) is a very popular cat in North American advertising, where it is perceived as elegant and striking without being extreme

New Departures in Build

The possibility of breeding bigger or smaller cats intrigues many breeders. When this has been successful, the cats tend to revert back to normal domestic-cat size in the next generation. Unlike dogs, the domestic cat seems to have a genetically pre-determined size range. Only outcrossing to another species, which is a controversial move, is likely to change this. A few breeds are classified according to a single anatomical feature, often arguably a malformation. For example, the Manx lack of a tail is linked with lethal medical conditions. The domestic cat evolved to virtual perfection through many years of natural development. Intervention by breeders that threatens such inherent flawlessness seems arrogant and unwarranted.

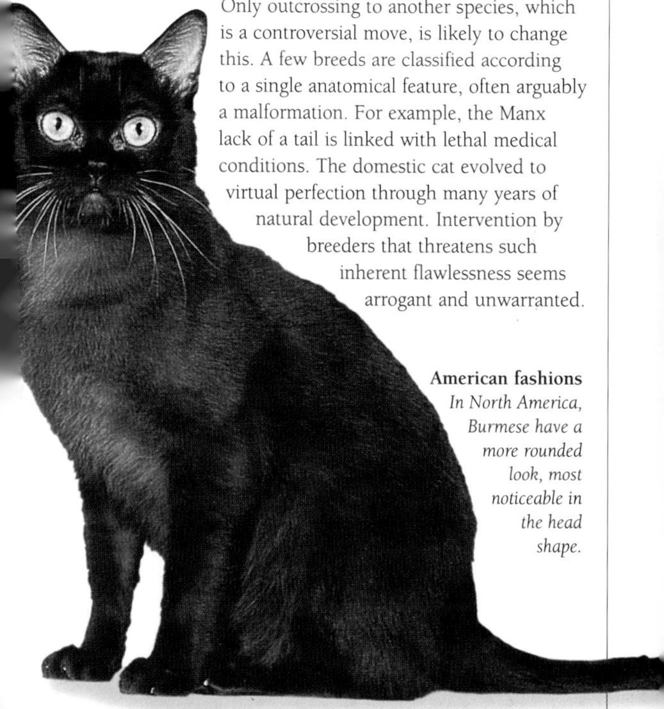

American fashions
In North America, Burmese have a more rounded look, most noticeable in the head shape.

Eye Shape and Color

Cats have unusually large eyes for the size of their heads. This relationship between eye size to head size mirrors the proportions seen in most animals, including humans, during infancy: it is without doubt one of the subliminal factors that triggers our willingness to care for young animals, and cats benefit from this.

Many breeders take great pains to breed for specific eye colors, creating a range of intense shades. Kittens are born with blue eyes, but their eyes change color as they mature. Adult cats have eyes of coppery brown, orange, yellow, or green; a few remain blue due to coat-color genes. Some cats are shown only during their early years when the color is most vivid, while others may not begin to show their best eye color for a few years.

COPPER

GOLD

Yellow-toned eyes

These eye colors are closest to those of wildcats. Many green eyes go through an early brown or yellow stage before they mature to their adult color. Copper eyes may "fade" with age, while yellow-gold eyes can vary greatly in appearance, depending on the ambient light.

E SHAPE

ldcats' eyes are oval and slightly slanted. Breeds considered close the "natural" cat, such as the Maine Coon (*see page 46*), have these ild" eyes. Natural shape has been altered in two ways: Eyes may be ınder, or more slanted. Broadly, old Western breeds, such as the artreux (*see page 218*), have round, prominent eyes. Some Eastern s, such as the Burmese (*see page 262*), also have rounded eyes, but almond-shaped eyes are most common in Oriental breeds. Extremes of shape can cause problems. Prominent eyes in flat faces are prone to tear overflow and infection, while extremely slanted eyes tend to retain mucus.

n

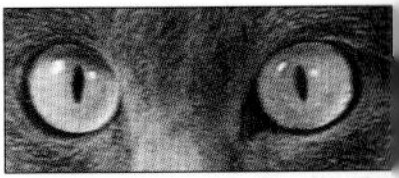

PURE GREEN

SEA-GREEN

Green-toned eyes

Green eyes have become common in random-bred cats, and pure greens of varying shades define several breeds.

Eye Colors

Wildcats have hazel or copper eyes, sometimes tending towards yellow or green. Breeding has produced a range of colors in domestic cats from sparkling blue to orange. Most eye colors in cats are not governed by coat color, although some breed standards do link the two: Silver tabbies, for example, are often required to have green eyes, but genetically they can have copper or gold-colored eyes.

The only eye color that is linked to coat color is blue. Blue eyes are caused by forms of albinism that lead to a lack of pigmentation in both the coat and the iris; this condition can occur in cats with a high degree of white in their coats. Blue-eyed cats with white coats are often deaf, because the gene causing the lack of pigment unfortunately causes fluid to dry up in the organ of Corti, the receptor for hearing in the cochlea, leading to deafness.

Siamese (*see page 280*) blue eyes – found by the 19th-century naturalist Peter Pallas in the Caucasus – have a different source. They are not linked to deafness, but may be associated with poor vision. Early Siamese often squinted to compensate; breeding has removed the squint, with no apparent loss of visual acuity. There is at least one other rare blue-eyed gene in cats, appearing in any coat color. It was noted in Britain in the 1960s, in New Zealand in the 1970s, and in the United States during the 1980s. The genetics of these rare cats, now called Ojos Azules, are still under investigation.

Blue eyes

The lack of pigment in blue eyes allows higher absorption of sunlight, used by the body to produce vitamin D. Consequently, blue eyes are usually found in light-starved regions; the Siamese mutation may have occurred in northern Asia and spread south with human help. Blue eyes vary considerably in depth.

Birman blue

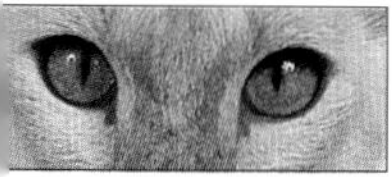

SIAMESE BLUE

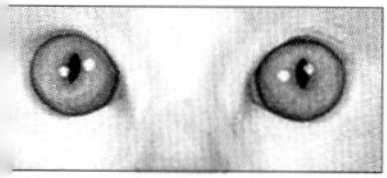

BABY BLUE

INDEX

ACKNOWLEDGMENTS

We are indebted to the many owners who gave up their time to allow us to photograph their cats. Without their assistance, this book would not have been possible.

The cats used in the profiles are credited here page by page: page numbers are given in bold, and (where necessary) positions on the page in terms of top (t), bottom (b), left (l), center (c), and right (r). Each cat's name is followed by that of its breeder and (in brackets) owner. Any awards the cat holds are given, such as champion (Ch), Grand Champion (GrCh), Premier (Pr), Grand Premier (GrPr), Supreme Grand Champion (SupGrCh), Supreme Grand Premier (SupGrPr), European Champion (EurCh), or International Champion (IntCh). Many of the younger cats that were photographed have gone on to win further awards, but the details remain as they were at the time of photography.

All Dorling Kindersley photographs were taken by Tracy Morgan and Marc Henrie. We regret that it is beyond the scope of these credits to give the same depth of information for the photographs provided by Chanan and Tetsu Yamazaki, which were not commissioned by Dorling Kindersley.

6, 17, 18 all Yamazaki; **19** *Mowbray anamera* D Cleford (D Cleford); **21** hanan; **22** *Cashel Golden Yuppie* A urley (A Curley); **23** GrPr *Bellrai aberge* B & B Raine (B & B Raine); **4** *Honeymist Roxana* M Howes (M owes); **25** *Bellrai Creme Chanel* B & Raine (B & B Raine); **26** *Adirtsa oc Ice* D Tynan (C & K Smith); **27** *lhuilo Meadowlands Alias* P Hurrell Josling); **28** *Amocasa Beau Brummel* lliott (I Elliott); **30** *Impeza okolotti* C Rowark (E Baldwin); **31** *neby Sunset* A Bailey (A Bailey); **–33** *Watlove Mollie Mophead* H tson (H Watson); **34** cl *Lizzara Rumbypumby Redted* G Black (G Black); bl *Chanterelle Velvet Cushion* L Lavis (G Black); **35** Ch&GrPr *Panjandrum April Surprice* A Madden (A Madden); **36** *Schwenthe Kiska* FE Brigliadori (FE Brigliadori & K Robson); **37** *Panjandrum Swansong* A Madden (S Tallboys); **38** *Saybrianna Tomorrow's Cream* A Carritt (A Carritt); **39** *Aesthetical Toty Temptress* G Sharpe (H Hewitt); **40** *Chehem Agassi* (Christine Powell); **41** *Chehem BryteSkye* (Christine Powell); **42–43** *Pandapaws Mr Biggs* S Ward-Smith (J Varley & J Dicks); **44–45** *Rags n Riches Vito Maracana* Robin Pickering

(Mrs J Moore); **46, 47, 48, 50, 51, 52** Chanan; **53** Ch *Keoka Ford Prefect*; **54** GrCh *Adinnlo Meddybemps*; **55** *Keoka Max Quordlepleen* D Brinicombe (D Brinicombe); **56** *Keoka Aldebaran* D Brinicombe
(D Brinicombe); **57** Ch *Keka Ursine Edward* D Brinicombe
(D Brinicombe); **59** *Lizzara Bardolph* (Ginny Black); **60** *Skogens SF Eddan Romeo* AS Watt (S Garrett); **61** *Tarakatt Tia* (D Smith); **62** *Sigurd Oski* (D Smith); **63** *Skogens Magni* AS Watt (S Garrett); **64, 65, 66** all Yamazaki; **68** *Olocha* A Danveef (H von Groneberg); **69, 71** Yamazaki; **73** Chanan; **74, 75, 76–77** Yamazaki; **78** Chanan; **79** Yamazaki; **82, 83** Yamazaki; **85** Chanan; **86** *Bruvankedi Kabugu* B Cooper (B Cooper); **87** *Cheratons Simply Red* Mr & Mrs Hassell (Mr & Mrs Hassell); **88** Ch *Lady Lubna Leanne Chatkantarra* T Boumeister (J Van der Werff); **89** *Champion Cheratons Red Aurora* Mr & Mrs Hassell (Mr & Mrs Hassell); **90–91** *Bruvankedi Mavi Bayas* (Mr R Cooper); **92, 94–95** Chanan; **97, 98–99** Yamazaki; **100** *Shanna's Yacinta Sajida* M Harms (M Harms); **101** Chanan; **102** *Shanna's Tombis Hanta Yo* M Harms-Moeskops (G Rebel van Kemenade); **103, 104–105** Chanan; **106** *Bealltaine Bezique* T Stracstone (T Stracstone); **107** unnamed kitten; **108–109** *Dolente Angelica* L Brisley (L Brisley); **110–111** *Beaumaris Cherubina*, A & B Gregory (A & B Gregory); **113, 115** G & T Oraas; **117** *Favagella Brown Whispa* J Bryson (J Bryson); **118** *Kennbury Dulcienea* C Lovell (K Harmon); **120–121** *Palvjia Pennyfromheaven* J Burroughs (T Tidey); **122** GrPr *Nighteyes Cinderfella* J Pell (J Pell); **122–123** *Blancsanglier Rosensoleil* A Bird (A Bird); **123** Ch *Apricat Silvercascade* R Smyth (E & J Robinson); **124** Pr *Blancsanglier Beau Brummel* A Bird (A Bird); **125** Pr *Pandai Feargal* E Corps (BV Rickwood); **126–127** *Jeuphi Golden Girl* J Phillips (L Cory); **128** GrPr *Nighteyes Cinderfella* J Pell (J Pell); **129** t Ch *Apricat Silvercascade* R Smyth (E & J Robinson), b *Ronsline Whistfull Spirit* R Farthing (R Farthing); **130** *Dasilva Tasha* J St John (C Russel & P Scrivener); **131** *Mossgems Sheik Simizu* M Mosscrop (H Grenney); **132–133** *Chantonel Snowball Express* R Elliott (R Elliott); **134** *Palantir Waza Tayriphyng* J May (J May); **135** *Lipema Shimazaki* P Brown (G Dean); **136–137** *Quinkent Honey's Mi-Lei-Fo* IA van der Reckweg (IA van der Reckweg); **139, 141** all Chanan; **143, 145** Yamazaki; **146–147, 148–149** all K Leonov; **151** Chanan; **152–153** Yamazaki; **154** *Maggie* (Bethlehem Cat Sanctuary); **155** *Dumpling* (Bethlehem Cat Sanctuary); **158** Chanan; **159** Yamazaki; **160** *Pennydown Penny Black* SW McEwen (SW McEwen); **161** t Yamazaki, b Chanan; **162–163** Yamazaki; **164** GrCh *Starfrost Dominic* E Conlin (C

Greenal); **165** Ch *Sargenta Silver Dan* U Graves (U Graves); **166** GrCh *Maruja Samson* M Moorhead (M Moorhead); **167** *Susian Just Judy* S Kempster (M Way); **168** *Miletree Black Rod* R Towse (R Towse); **169** Ch & SupGrPr *Welquest Snowman* A Welsh (A Welsh); **170** *Miletree Magpie* R Towse (M le Mounier); **172** Ch *Bartania Pomme Frits* B Beck (B Beck); **173** t *Kavida Kadberry* L Berry (L Berry), c GrCh *Westways Purrfect Amee* A West (GB Ellins); **174** *Cordelia Cassandra* J Codling (C Excell); **175** *Kavida Misty Daydream* L Berry (L Berry); **177** Yamazaki; **178** *Minty* L Williams (H Walker & K Bullin); **179** *Adrish Alenka* L Price (L Williams); **180** Chanan; **181, 182** Yamazaki; **185** Chanan; **186, 187, 189, 190** Yamazaki; **192, 193, 194, 195, 197, 198–199, 201** Chanan; **203, 204–205, 206, 207** Yamazaki; **209, 210, 211** Chanan; **213** *Aurora de Cantanoe* L Kenter (L Kenter); **214** *Eldoria's Yossarian* O van Beck & A Quast (O van Beck & A Quast); **215** GrCh *Orions Guru Lomaers* (Mulder-Topma); **216** *Eldorias Goldfinger*, **217** *Eldoria's Crazy Girl*, **219** Ch *Comte Davidof de Lasalle*, **220** *Donna Eurydice de Lasalle*, **221, 222–223** GrCh *Amaranthoe Lasalle*, all K ten Broek (K ten Broek); **224** *Astahazy Effirelli* (M von Kirchberg); **227** Yamazaki; **228–229, 230** Chanan; **231** Yamazaki; **232–233** *Karthwine Elven Moonstock* R Clayton (M Crane); **234** t and bl Ch *Anera Ula* C Macaulay (C Symonds), bc *Braeside Marimba* H Hewitt (H Hewitt); **235** GrCh *Emarelle Milos* MR Lyall (R Hopkins); **236** *Satusai Fawn Amy* I Reid (I Reid); **237** *Lionelle Rupert Bear* C Bailey (C Tencor); **239, 240–241** T Straede; **243** *Silvaner Pollyanna*, **244–245** *Silvaner Kuan*, all C Thompson (C Thompson); **249** *Phoebe* (F Kerr); **247, 248** GrCh *Aerostar Spectre* JED Mackie (S Callen & I Hotten); **250, 251** Chanan; **252–253** Yamazaki; **254** *Ballego Betty Boo* J Gillies (J Gillies); **255** *Kartuch Benifer* C & T Clark (C & T Clark); **256** *Vatan Mimi* D Beech & J Chalmers (J Moore); **257** *Lasiesta Blackberry Girl* GW Dyson (GW Dyson); **258** *Boronga Blaktortie Dollyvee* P Impson (J Quiddington); **259** *Boronga Black Othello* P Impson (J Thurman); **260** *Vervain Goldberry* N Johnson (N Johnson); **261** *Vervain Ered Luin* N Johnson (N Johnson); **262, 264, 265, 266, 267** Chanan; **268** GrCh *Bambino Alice Bugown* B Boizard Neal (B Boizard Neal); **269** Ch *Bambino Seawitch* B Boizard Neal (B Boizard Neal); **270** *Impromptu Crystal* M Garrod (M Garrod); **271** *Braeside Red Sensation* H Hewitt (H Hewitt); **272** Ch *Hobberdy Hokey Cokey* A Virtue (A Virtue); **273** Ch *Bambino Dreamy* B Boizard Neal (B Boizard Neal); **275** *Romantica Marcus Macoy* (Mrs

Davison); **276** *Grimspound Majesticlady* Miss Hodgkinson (Miss Hodgkinson); **277** *Tonkitu's Adinnsh Xin Wun* D Burke (D Burke); **278** *Tonkitu Mingchen* D Burke (D Burke); **279** *Episcopus Leonidas* (Mrs Murray-Langley); **281** Ch *Pannaduloa Phaedra* J Hansson (J Hansson); **282** Yamazaki; **283** Ch *Willowbreeze Goinsolo* Mr & Mrs Robinson (TK Hull-Williams); **284, 285** Yamazaki; **286** GrCh *Dawnus Primadonna* A Douglas (A Douglas); **287** GrCh *Pannaduloa Yentantethra* J Hansson (J Hansson); **288** Ch *Darling Copper Kingdom* I George (S Mauchline); **289** tr *Mewzishun Bel Canto* A Greatorex (D Aubyn), bl *Indalo Knights Templar* P Bridham (P Bridham); **290** *Merescuff Allart* (E Mackenzie-Wood); **291** Ch *Sisar Brie* L Pummell (L Pummell); **293** *Jasrobinka Annamonique* P & J Choppen (P & J Choppen); **294** tl *Tenaj Blue Max* J Tonkinson (K Iremonger), r *Simonski Sylvester Sneakly* S Cosgrove (S Cosgrove), b ChPr *Adixish Minos Mercury* A Concanon (A Concanon); **295** GrCh *Sukinfer Samari* J O'Boyle (J O'Boyle); **296** *Simonski Sylvester Sneakly* S Cosgrove (S Cosgrove); **297** GrPr *Jasrobinka Jeronimo* P & J Choppen (P & J Choppen); **298** *Saxongate Paler Shades* (D Buxcey); **299** *Adhuish Tuwhit Tuwhoo* N Williams (N Williams); **300** *Parthia Angelica* MA Skelton (MA Skelton); **301** *Sunjade Brandy Snap* E Wildon (E Tomlinson); **302** *Scilouette Angzhi* C & T Clark (C & T Clark); **303** *Scintilla Silver Whirligig* P Turner (D Walker); **305** Yamazaki; **306–307** *Ngkomo Ota* A Scruggs (L Marcel); **309, 311** Yamazaki; **313** *Myowal Rudolph* J Cornish (J Compton); **314** Pr *Adkrish Samson* PK Weissman (PK Weissman); **315** *Leshocha Azure My Friend* E Himmerston (E Himmerston); **316, 317** Chanan; **318** *Adhuish Grainne* N Jarrett (J Burton); **319** UKGrCh *Nobilero Loric Vilesilenca* AE & RE Hobson (M Reed); **320** Pr *Bobire Justin Tyme* IE Longhurst (A Charlton); **321** GrCh *Ikari Donna* S Davey (J Plumb); **322** GrPr *Bevilleon Dandy Lion* B Lyon (M Chitty); **323** *Myowal Susie Sioux* G Cornish (J & B Archer); **324** *Reaha Anda Bebare* S Scanlin (A Rushbrook & J Plumb); **325, 326–327** Yamazaki; **329, 331** Chanan; **333, 334, 335, 336–337** Yamazaki; **338** Chanan; **339** Yamazaki; **340, 341** Chanan; **342** Yamazaki; **343** Chanan; **344** *Gaylee Diablo* M Nicholson (M Nicholson); **345** *Gaylee Diablo* M Nicholson (M Nicholson); **346** Chanan; **348–349** *Gaylee Diablo* M Nicholson (M Nicholson); **351, 352–353, 354, 355** Yamazaki; **356** *Friskie* (Bethlehem Cat Sanctuary); **357** t name unknown, c name unknown Jane Burton, b *Sinbad Sailor Blue* (V Lew).